BLACK
ON BLACK

BLACK
ON
BLACK

TWENTIETH-CENTURY
AFRICAN AMERICAN WRITING
ABOUT AFRICA

JOHN CULLEN GRUESSER

THE UNIVERSITY PRESS OF KENTUCKY

Publication of this volume was made possible in part by a grant
from the National Endowment for the Humanities.

Scholarly publisher for the Commonwealth,
serving Bellarmine College, Berea College, Centre
College of Kentucky, Eastern Kentucky University,
The Filson Club Historical Society, Georgetown College,
Kentucky Historical Society, Kentucky State University,
Morehead State University, Murray State University,
Northern Kentucky University, Transylvania University,
University of Kentucky, University of Louisville,
and Western Kentucky University.

Editorial and Sales Offices: The University Press of Kentucky
663 South Limestone Street, Lexington, Kentucky 40508-4008

04 03 02 01 00   5 4 3 2 1

Library of Congress Cataloging-in-Publication Data

Gruesser, John Cullen, 1959-
　 Black on Black : twentieth-century African American writing about Africa / John
　 Cullen Gruesser
　　　 p. cm.
　　 Includes bibliographical references and index.
　　 ISBN 0-8131-2163-9 (cloth : alk. paper)
　　 1. American literature—Afro-American authors—History and criticism. 2. Africa—
In literature. 3. Africa—Foreign public opinion, American—History—20th century.
4. Literature and history—United States—History—20th century. 5. American
literature—20th century—History and criticism. 6. Public opinion—United States—
History—20th century. 7. Afro-Americans—Attitudes—History—20th century. 8.
American literature—African influences. I. Title.

PS159.A35 G78 2000
810.9'326'08996073—dc21   99-047796

This book is printed on acid-free recycled paper meeting
the requirements of the American National Standard
for Permanence of Paper for Printed Library Materials.

Manufactured in the United States of America

This book, written by Jack number three,
is dedicated to the First Jack,
John Adam Gruesser (1887–1983),
the Fourth Jack, John Ryan Gruesser (1990–),
and especially the Second Jack,
John Anthony Gruesser (1928–).

Everyone has such high hopes for what can be done in Africa. Over the pulpit there is a saying: *Ethiopia Shall Stretch Forth Her Hands to God.* Think what it means that Ethiopia is Africa!

ALICE WALKER, *THE COLOR PURPLE*

Contents

Preface

*Ach, Harry, wir müssen durch so viel Dreck und Unsinn tappen, um
nach hause zu kommen! Und wir haben niemand der uns führt,
unser einziger Führer ist das Heimweh.*

HERMAN HESSE, DER STEPPENWOLF

All you got is your friends. . . .

WALTER MOSLEY, DEVIL IN A BLUE DRESS

From the earliest slave narratives and Phillis Wheatley's poetry to contemporary works such as Alice Walker's *The Color Purple* and Charles Johnson's *The Middle Passage,* Africa has been a prevalent theme for black American authors. In "The Negro in American Culture" (1929), Alain Locke describes "the conscious and deliberate threading back of the historic sense of group tradition to the cultural backgrounds of Africa" as "the most sophisticated of all race motives" and claims that Africa is "naturally romantic" for the African American writer. Because of important recent developments in a variety of scholarly disciplines, the time is right for an extended analysis of a largely unexplored but rich and vital topic: the depiction of Africa in twentieth-century African American writing. In the last two and a half decades, the field of African American Studies has undergone a remarkable transformation. A truly impressive number of lost or unknown primary texts has become available, and groundbreaking studies of slave narratives, the Harlem Renaissance, Black Nationalism, Pan-Africanism, the relationship between African and black American art, African American missionary work in Africa, and African American attitudes towards Africa, as well as important works of African American literary theory and intellectual history, have been published. Moreover, scholarship in the fields of cultural and literary criticism and African Studies has delineated both the distortions and the powerful influence of Africanist writing, that is, texts written about Africa by Western authors. This scholarship is highly significant because African American depictions of the continent have not only been influenced by but also responded directly or indirectly to white writing about Africa. Although scholars have recently devoted attention to various aspects of the African American relationship with Africa, surprisingly little work has been done on black American literature written about the continent. Only one book that I am aware of, Marion Berghahn's *The Image of Africa in Black American Literature* (1977), has been published on this subject. This present study, *Black on Black: Twentieth-Century African American Writing about Africa,* addresses this fascinating topic in light of recent scholarly developments and rediscoveries.

During the more than a dozen years that this book has been in the making, taking several twists and turns along the way, I have become indebted to many people and organizations without whose help this project would not have been completed. No doubt I am forgetting the assistance of several persons in following paragraphs, and for this I apologize. To all of you, I express my heartfelt thanks.

The National Endowment for the Humanities (NEH) generously awarded me a fellowship for the 1992–1993 academic year to work on *Black on Black,* making that most precious of commodities available to me, time. In addition, NEH Summer Seminars under the direction of Eric Sundquist at the University of California, Berkeley in 1990 and Earl Miner at Princeton University in 1994 enabled me to make significant progress on this book by providing me with thoughtful mentors, stimulating intellectual communities, and access to superior research facilities.

Because many of the texts I analyze and refer to can be found only in the unpublished papers of specific writers, obscure black periodicals, special collections, and rare book rooms, I have greatly profited from the knowledge, suggestions, and, in some cases, legwork of librarians and curators at several institutions. These include the Atlanta, Kean, Princeton, Rutgers, and Seton Hall University Libraries; the Boston, New Bedford, and San Francisco Public Libraries; the DuSable Museum of African American History; the Hatch-Billops Archives; the Library of Congress; the Libraries of the University of California, Berkeley; the Moorland-Spingarn Library at Howard University; Yale University's Beinecke Rare Book Room; and the Performing Arts Library and the Schomburg Center for Research in Black Culture of the New York Public Library. Moreover, I am grateful to Jim Hatch and Camille Billops, the New York Public Library, and Northeastern University Press for permission to print the illustrations of dramatic performances, writers, and the map of George Schuyler's Black Empire that appear in this book.

The opportunity to present my work and receive comments on it from colleagues at professional meetings, scholarly conferences, and institutions of higher learning has been invaluable to me. Provisional versions of sections of *Black on Black* were read at the British Commonwealth and Post-colonial Studies Conference, the International Conference for the Fantastic in the Arts, the Modern Language Association Convention, the MELUS Conference, the New Jersey College English Association Conference, the Society of Research on African Cultures Conference, the Twentieth-Century Literature Conference, and Cornell University. Furthermore, portions of this book have appeared in somewhat different form in *African American Review* (formerly *Black American Literature Forum*), *American Drama,* the *Journal of African Travel Writing,* and *Modes of the Fantastic* (an essay collection edited by Robert Collins and Robert Latham and published by Greenwood Press). I am grateful to the editors of these publications for permission to reprint this material here.

Certainly I cannot fail to mention the advice and encouragement offered to me by the following teachers, scholars, authors, colleagues, friends, and editors: Nellie McKay, Malin Walther Pereira, Kelly Anspaugh, Eli Goldblatt, Aldon Nielsen, Eric Sundquist, Styrk Fjose, Stephen Soitos, Kathy Perkins, John Burger, Lamont Thomas, Lois Lamphere Brown, Jennie Kassanoff, Christine Gray, Dean Casale, Richard Katz, Bert Wailoo, Rita Disroe, Theresa Sears, Ann Lowry, Arnold Rampersad, Jim Hatch, Hanna Wallinger, Wilson Moses, David Chioni Moore, John A. Williams, Frank Mullin, Joe Murphy, Tim Ungs, Mike Herrmann, Phil Johnson, and especially Craig Werner and Carole Doreski.

Lastly, the support and inspiration of my parents, my sister, my wife Susan, our son Jack, and our daughter Sarah have been indispensable.

1

Historical and Theoretical Introduction to African American Writing about Africa

Africa is at once the most romantic and the most tragic of continents. . . . [I]n the literature it is the seat of the Sphinx and the lotus eaters, the home of the dwarfs, gnomes, and pixies, and the refuge of the gods.

W.E.B. Du Bois, *The Negro*

Africa? A book one thumbs
Listlessly, till slumber comes.

Countee Cullen, "Heritage"

African American literary depictions of Africa published between 1902 and 1982 either invoke or react against one or more aspects of Ethiopianism, the teleological and uniquely African American view of history inspired by the Psalms verse "Princes shall come out of Egypt, Ethiopia shall soon stretch forth her hands unto God" (68:31). Dating back to the eighteenth century, Ethiopianism figured prominently in sermons, pamphlets, speeches, and articles by black Americans throughout the nineteenth century.[1] Because classical authors and the King James Bible used "Ethiopia" as the term for Africa south of Egypt, Ethiopianism refers to the whole continent rather than simply the East African nation also known as Abyssinia. In fact, except for the 1930s, when a series of events focused African American attention on the country of Ethiopia, black American texts about Africa—when specific at all—have tended to focus on West Africa, particularly Liberia (founded by freed Americans slaves in the 1820s) and, later, Ghana. Ethiopianism undergirded white and black efforts to Christianize and civilize Africa (which intensified in the latter half of the nineteenth century), spawned religious and political movements in West and Southern Africa in the 1890s and early 1900s, and greatly influenced early twentieth-century Pan-Africanism. Ethiopianism pervaded the Garvey Movement in the late

1910s and 1920s, became refocused during the Italian invasion and occupation of Ethiopia (1935–1941), and, although its popularity steeply declined after the Second World War, indirectly influenced a wide variety of religious, cultural, and intellectual movements, including the Nation of Islam, the Black Arts Movement, and Afrocentrism.

Unlike Mary Lefkowitz's *Not Out of Africa: How Afrocentrism Became an Excuse to Teach Myth as History* (1996), this study's aims are literary historical rather than polemical. Although I agree with Lefkowitz that in its most extreme forms Afrocentrism poses a danger to the integrity of American higher education, her decision simply to rebut rather than attempt to historicize the major assertions of the Afrocentrists deprives her project of significant long-term value. Several of the nineteenth- and early twentieth-century black American figures discussed below subscribe to a version of what Lefkowitz refers to as the myth of the Stolen Legacy—in its narrowest form the totally unsubstantiated contention that the Greeks plagiarized their philosophical works from the Egyptians, which Lefkowitz devotes much of her book to refuting, but more generally the claim that Greek (and by extension European) achievements in the arts and sciences derive from Egypt (and hence Africa).[2] Although she criticizes scholars who address subjects outside of their area of expertise, Lefkowitz proves to be guilty of this herself when she shifts her focus from the classical world to African American history. It is inaccurate and perhaps even irresponsible on Lefkowitz's part to trace the myth of the Stolen Legacy only as far back as Marcus Garvey and never to situate this myth within the much larger context of Ethiopianism.[3]

St. Clair Drake's short book *The Redemption of Africa and Black Religion* (1970) remains the most comprehensive discussion of Ethiopianism, the scope and significance of which it describes as follows: "Black people under slavery turned to the Bible to 'prove' that a black people, Ethiopians, were powerful and respected when white men in Europe were barbarians. Ethiopia came to symbolize all of Africa; and, throughout the 19th century, the 'redemption of Africa' became one important focus of meaningful activity for leaders among New World Negroes. 'Ethiopianism' became an energizing myth both in the New World and in Africa itself. . . . Its force is now almost spent, but 'Ethiopianism' left an enduring legacy on the people who fight for Black Power in the Twentieth Century" (11). For over twenty years, Wilson Moses has investigated the literary implications of Ethiopianism in several works, including *The Golden Age of Black Nationalism, 1850–1925* (1978), *The Wings of Ethiopia* (1990), and *Afrotopia: The Roots of African American Popular History* (1998).[4] Similarly, Eric Sundquist discusses the impact of turn-of-the-century American and African Ethiopianist movements on W.E.B. Du Bois's literary productions in *To Wake the Nations: Race in the Making of American Literature* (1993).[5] Going beyond Drake, Moses, and Sundquist, I contend that black American literary depictions of Africa cannot be fully understood without being read in the context of Ethiopianism.

With the exception of Martin Delany's *Blake; or, The Huts of America* (1859–1860), which includes a very brief description of the continent, there are, to my knowledge, no depictions of Africa in nineteenth-century African American fiction. Invoking Ethiopianism triumphantly and uncritically, black American literary texts about the continent began to appear with some frequency in the first decade of the twentieth century. New Negro–era writers reacted against these early texts, but their own portrayals of Africa frequently retain some vestiges of Ethiopianism. In Langston Hughes, Melvin Tolson, and George S. Schuyler's literary texts inspired by the Italo-Ethiopian War, Ethiopianism was briefly reenergized and reoriented. Tolson's long poem *Libretto for the Republic of Liberia* (1953) stands at the intersection of the overwhelmingly Ethiopianist literature that preceded it and the predominantly non-Ethiopianist literature that followed. The final rejection of Ethiopianism was initiated a year later by Richard Wright's *Black Power* (1954) and continued in a wide variety of texts, including Lorraine Hansberry's *Les Blancs* (1973) and Alice Walker's *The Color Purple* (1982).

Along with its major contention that Ethiopianism has profoundly influenced black American literary depictions of Africa, this book makes three ancillary arguments. First, African American literature about Africa often signifies on earlier portrayals of black characters with varying degrees of success. Second, the relationship between black American depictions of the continent and Africanist discourse, Christopher Miller's term for white texts about Africa, is fraught with ambiguity and irony. Lastly, those texts about the continent by African American writers that revise the dominant discourse most successfully have frequently been those conceived as generic hybrids, several of which were serialized in black periodicals rather than published in book form.

The Origins, Evolution, and Influence of Ethiopianism

History informs us that we sprung from one of the most learned nations of the whole earth; from the seat, if not the parent of science; yes, poor, despised Africa was once the resort of sages and legislators of other nations, was esteemed the school of learning, and the most illustrious men in Greece flocked thither for instruction. But it was our gross sins and abominations that provoked the Almighty to frown thus heavily upon us, and give our glory to others. Sin and prodigality have caused the downfall of nations, kings, and emper-

ors; and were it not that God in wrath remembers mercy, we might indeed despair; but a promise is left us; "Ethiopia shall again stretch forth her hands unto God."

MARIA W. STEWART,
"AN ADDRESS DELIVERED AT THE
AFRICAN MASONIC HALL BOSTON,
FEBRUARY 27, 1833"

Why ever since I was three years old, . . . I knew that somebody somewhere was doing something to hurt black and brown peoples. Little as I was I remember the newsreels of the Ethiopian war and the feeling of outrage in our Negro community. Fighters with spears and our people in passion over it, my mother attacking the Pope blessing the Italian troops going off to slay Ethiopians. When the Pope died that was the thought of him that came to my mind. I didn't know a thing about Spain but I certainly did know about Ethiopia. . . . But we just expected that things would change. We had been saying for a long time: "Ethiopia will stretch forth her hands!" This always meant that they were going to pay for all this one day.

LORRAINE HANSBERRY, 1960

The preceding statements made over 125 years apart by Maria Stewart and Lorraine Hansberry not only indicate Ethiopianism's longevity but explicitly state some of its basic tenets, although these have by no means been as rigidly fixed as this overview may seem to suggest. The excerpt from Stewart's 1833 "Address" provides a vivid illustration of four key Ethiopianist elements. First, it asserts a common heritage shared by African Americans and Africans: "We sprung from one of the most learned nations of the whole earth." Second, the passage adopts the biblical notion of a Supreme Being who raises and punishes nations, leading to a belief in a cyclical view of history in which the fortunes of peoples rise and fall: "But it was our gross sins and abominations that provoked the Almighty to frown thus heavily upon us, and give our glory to others. Sin and prodigality have caused the downfall of nations, kings, and emperors." Third, it predicts a bright future for peoples of African descent: "a promise is left us; 'Ethiopia shall again stretch forth her hands unto God.'" Fourth, Stewart's statement exhibits monumentalism, which Wilson Moses defines, in an essay entitled "More Stately Mansions," as "an expression of the desire to associate black Americans with symbols of wealth, intelligence, stability, and power" such as those of ancient Egypt and Ethiopia (42): "Africa was once the resort of sages and legislators of other nations, was esteemed the school of learning,

and the most illustrious men in Greece flocked thither for instruction."
Although he does not discuss monumentalism in detail, Moses' term is a
useful one, particularly in clarifying the difference between an earlier
Ethiopianism that is fixated on the African past—like Stewart's—and a later
Ethiopianism, such as the one Hansberry describes, which is oriented to-
ward contemporary Africa.[6]

In Hansberry's statement the link (contemporary as well as ancestral)
between black Americans and Africans is clear and the biblically inspired
teleology found in Stewart also remains intact. Moreover, in its assertion
that "*they* were going to pay for all this," the Hansberry passage augments
Ethiopianism's cyclical view of history to include the prophecy that the
redemption of Africa (and the diaspora) will be accompanied by the decline
of the West. In some versions of the Ethiopianist myth, materialism and
godlessness would be the downfall of white, Western society while people
of African descent were destined to rise again because of their moral and
spiritual purity. Ethiopianism thus propounds "the idea," as Moses puts it,
"that the ascendency of the white race was only temporary, and that the
divine providence of history was working to elevate the African peoples"
(*The Golden Age*, 24). In other versions, it would become the responsibility
of black Americans and other oppressed peoples to return America and the
West generally to the true path of Christianity. As Albert Raboteau explains,
"America had been displaced in God's plan of salvation and it would be the
mission of 'the darker races of the world' to finally put into practice the
gospel, which Europeans and Americans had only managed to preach. The
darker races would develop a classless, raceless, and weaponless Christianity that would welcome the return of the Universal Christ" (13).

The Stewart and Hansberry passages illustrate not only the movement away from monumentalism but also another important change that
occurred within Ethiopianist thought between the early nineteenth century and the middle of the twentieth. Whereas Stewart's "Address" looks at
the relationship between peoples of African descent and the West primarily
in religious terms, Hansberry's statement, although likewise imbued with
Ethiopianism, is more openly political, alluding not only to the Italian invasion of Ethiopia in 1935 but also the Spanish Civil War. In general, African American literary depictions of Africa reflect a similar shift from an
ignorance of or indifference toward—and even in some cases support for—
European colonialism in Africa to an unequivocal condemnation of it.

In addition to the assertion of a common heritage linking black Americans and Africans, a cyclical view of history, the prediction of a bright future for Africa, and monumentalism, a fifth component of Ethiopianism,
assumed but not always overtly stated, is what Paul Gilroy in *The Black*

Atlantic: Modernity and Double Consciousness (1993) refers to (and decries) as an African American exceptionalism—the belief that because of their experiences in the West and adoption of Christianity black Americans were the people best qualified to lead Africans and members of the diaspora to the bright future foretold for them. As James Wesley Johnson explains, "As an idea, Ethiopianism provided African Americans with a messianic tradition that was uniquely African American in origin. This tradition was not centered exclusively on Jesus, nor was it limited to the story of the Jewish exodus. Ethiopianism became a kind of messianic ancestralism derived primarily from the uniqueness of African American experience and expressed as an important tradition in African American religion in general and Christianity in particular. It defined the fundamental mission of African Americans as a divine mission in its own right" (543). Frequently this exception- alism resulted in an arrogance and even a condescension toward contemporary Africans on the part of black Americans that greatly complicated cooperative efforts between the two peoples.

Although the first people of African descent arrived in what became the United States before the Pilgrim landing at Plymouth, the slave system did not become well established until the end of the seventeenth century, and most slaves were not Christianized until the last quarter of the eighteenth century. In his study of Christianity in America, *Awash in the Sea of Faith,* Jon Butler asserts that between 1680 and 1760 "an African spiritual holocaust" occurred, depriving slaves of their traditional African belief systems and thus rendering them highly receptive to conversion to Christianity (130). According to Butler, "No other religious event of the entire colonial period, including the evolution of Puritanism or the emergence of American evangelicalism, so shaped a people's experience of religion in America" (157). At the start of the eighteenth century, the Church of England endeavored to convert slaves to Christianity; however, these efforts met with only limited success, in part because Anglicans attempted to work within rather than against the slave system. Using more accessible methods than the Episcopalians and initially opposed to slavery, evangelical preachers enjoyed great success in converting slaves after 1770. Although these Methodists and Baptists later abandoned their demands for an end to the slave system for fear of alienating slaveholders, their willingness to sanction black preachers had profound consequences. According to Raboteau, "it would be difficult to overestimate the importance of these early black preachers for the development of an African American Christianity. In effect, they mediated between Christianity and the experience of the slaves (and free blacks), interpreting the stories, symbols, and events of the Bible to fit the day-to-day lives of those held in bondage" (24). Foremost among these powerfully evocative scriptural materials, along with the story of Exodus, was Psalms 68:31.

At the end of the eighteenth century and throughout the nineteenth, the notion of Providential Design or the Fortunate Fall doctrine was used to explain and in some cases justify the slave trade that had brought Africans to the New World. Quakers and others opposed to slavery expounded the idea that God, working in mysterious ways, had temporarily countenanced slavery so that Africans could be Christianized and civilized in the New World and then return to their ancestral homeland to convert Africans. Some of Phillis Wheatley's letters and poems, most notably "On Being Brought from Africa to Africa," reflect this view. Onto the concept of Providential Design, black preachers and political activists grafted an Ethiopianist vision of the past and the future. Although belief in the fortunate fall of slavery was never accepted by some New World blacks and declined during the 1800s, African Methodist Episcopal (AME) Bishop Henry McNeal Turner's "The American Negro and the Fatherland," the address he sent to the 1895 Congress on Africa, an event sponsored by the Stewart Missionary Foundation for Africa of Gammon Theological Seminary in Atlanta, adhered to an Ethiopianist version of this doctrine, asserting that because of their experiences in the New World black Americans were the people most qualified to redeem Africa religiously and politically.

Ethiopianism also influenced efforts to repatriate black Americans in Africa, which began in the late eighteenth century and continued with limited success into the twentieth. The impetus behind these back-to-Africa movements was both religious and political, with both proslavery and antislavery whites offering their support. Slaveholders saw emigration as a means of ridding the country of free blacks, thus removing their complicating presence from the debate over slavery. As early as 1787, the British shipped a group of free blacks to Sierra Leone, and in 1816 the American Colonization Society (ACS) was founded by white people who were both for and against slavery. The ACS established the colony of Liberia in 1822, ran it until the Liberians declared their independence in 1847, and continued to send people there into the 1900s. Although the total number of emigrants was relatively small—by 1893 the society had transported 16,413 people across the Atlantic (Jacobs, "Pan-African Consciousness," 70)—the issue of emigration greatly divided African Americans. As early as 1773, slaves wrote petitions for their freedom so that they could return to Africa, and in 1816 Paul Cuffe, the most affluent black American of the day, transported thirty-eight free blacks to Sierra Leone in his own ship. Other key nineteenth-century black figures such as Alexander Crummell and Martin Delany advocated emigration, invoking Ethiopianism in speeches and writings in favor of it. However, such schemes were roundly condemned by another set of prominent race leaders, including AME founder and bishop Richard Allen; Sam Cornish and John Russwurm, who together founded *Freedom's Journal* as an anti-emigrationist newspaper in New York City in 1827; and Frederick Douglass—all of whom regarded themselves first and foremost as Americans and with some justification attributed racist motives to the ACS.

Although the first black American missionary was sent to Africa in 1787 and noted black ministers such as Daniel Coker and Lott Cary left for what would become Liberia before 1822, significant African American participation in the missionary movement in Africa did not begin until after the Civil War.[7] It was during the period prior to the war, however, that Ethiopianism was developed and widely disseminated. African American religious leaders expended considerable energy and creativity in explicating not only the sixty-eighth Psalm but other biblical references to Ethiopia. Meanwhile, politically charged documents, such as Robert Alexander Young's mystical "Ethiopian Manifesto" (1829), David Walker's sensational *Appeal to the Coloured Citizens of the World* (1829), and Stewart's "Address" either explicitly or implicitly invoked Ethiopianism. By the latter portion of the nineteenth century, when black American missionary activity in Africa was on the rise, Ethiopianism's basic tenets, among them African American exceptionalism, had long been fully elaborated.

The tradition of Ethiopianist biblical exegesis and political propagandizing was continued and taken to a new level after 1850 by Edward Wilmot Blyden, a West Indian by birth who, after a brief sojourn in America, was transported by the ACS to Liberia, where he spent most of the rest of his life. Drake, Hollis Lynch, and V.Y. Mudimbe credit Blyden with being perhaps the most influential black intellectual of the second half of the nineteenth century, responsible for changing African American perceptions of Africa and founding the idea of the African Personality, which significantly influenced prominent turn-of-the-century West Africans as well as such key independence figures as Ghana's Kwame Nkrumah, Kenya's Jomo Kenyatta, and Senegal's Leopold Senghor. Blyden's early essay "The Call of Providence to Descendants of Africa in America" (1862), for example, not only invokes Ethiopianist Providential Design but, in inviting black Americans to come to Liberia and create a great "African power" there, elaborates a doctrine of manifest destiny for African Americans in Africa: "We call it, then, a providential interposition, that while the owners of the soil have been abroad, passing through the fearful ordeal of a most grinding oppression, the land, though entirely unprotected, has lain uninvaded. We regard it as a providential call to Africans every where, to 'go up and possess the land'; so that in a sense that is not merely constructive and figurative, but truly literal, God says to the black men of this country, with reference to Africa: 'Behold, I set the land before you, go up and possess it'" (193). Although he continued to believe in and work for a brighter future for Africa, later in his career Blyden moved away from exceptionalism and even away from Christianity, writing favorably about Islam because of its tendency to preserve indigenous culture.

Drake's assertion that after the turn of the century the "political myth" of Pan-Africanism gradually came to replace religiously oriented Ethiopianism (74) has some value as a general rule; however, it simplifies the evolution of and minimizes the variations within each movement. On the one hand, because of its African American exceptionalism and its emphasis on the need to Christianize and civilize Africa, Ethiopianism in America during the nineteenth century and the first decade of the twentieth was certainly more religiously than politically oriented. Bishop Turner and the early Blyden had little trouble incorporating European colonial rule in Africa into their belief in Ethiopianist Providential Design, seeing colonialism as merely hastening the process of Africa's regeneration. In contrast to the 1895 Congress on Africa, moreover, the Pan-African Conference in London five years later was indeed primarily a political event.[8] On the other hand, very little of the proceedings of the 1900 Conference, at which Ethiopianism played a considerable but largely unrecognized role, could be accurately characterized as anticolonial. Furthermore, when African American Ethiopianism was transplanted into Africa in the 1890s, it acquired an unmistakably anticolonial dimension. In West Africa, Ethiopianism became identified with two of Blyden's disciples, the Yoruba Baptist minister Majola Agbebi and the Gold Coast journalist and activist J.E. Casely Hayford. Both asserted that Africans were the ones who must redeem Africa. Convinced that Africans needed a Christianity that was African in its design, teachings, and administration, Agbebi rejected missionary efforts to convert Africans and founded the Independent Native Baptist Union of West Africa. Casely Hayford took aim at colonialism in his writings, most notably his polemical novel *Ethiopia Unbound* (1911), arguing that Africans could only fulfill their destiny by running their own affairs (S.K.B. Asante, 12–14). In Southern Africa, as George Shepperson has amply documented, African American missionaries, particularly those affiliated with Turner's AME church, directly inspired an Ethiopianist movement that was both religious and political in character. On an 1898 visit to South Africa, Turner formalized the relationship between the Ethiopian church founded by Mangena Mokone in 1892 and his own. Three years later, AME leaders sent the first resident African American bishop, L.J. Coppin, to South Africa, and the Cape government quickly came to view the church, which within fifteen years had eighteen thousand full members, as a hotbed of subversion and initiated a policy of harassment against it (Chirenje, 62, 89, 164–65).

Events in East Africa transpired at roughly the same period that would eventually help to create a new but short-lived reorientation of Ethiopianism in America. Claiming descent from the Queen of Sheba, reputed to have been the kingdom of the legendary Christian ruler Prester John, and associated by name with the Psalms verse that inspired the belief that Africa and the people of the diaspora would once again assume a leading role in world affairs, the nation of Ethiopia came to figure more prominently in the black American imagination as a result of its defeat of the Italians at Adowa in 1896. The antiquity, independence, and Christianity of the country of Ethiopia made it a source of pride for African Americans. The timing of Menelik II's victory was particularly significant because it not only derailed Italy's colonial ambitions, thereby putting a stop to the all-but-complete European Scramble for Africa, which had begun in earnest with the 1884–1885 Berlin Conference, but also occurred during the worst postbellum period for African Americans, an era characterized by disenfranchisement campaigns, lynching, and legally sanctioned segregation. Identification with Ethiopia's victory over Italy introduced a specifically anticolonial dimension into African American Ethiopianism, although this political stance would not become dominant for another generation.[9]

In their efforts to overturn stereotyped notions about people of African descent, white and black abolitionists who sought to restore to Africans the history that had long been ignored, distorted, or dismissed by the West, such as Lydia Maria Child in *An Appeal in Favor of That Class of Americans Called Africans* (1833), E.H. Sears in "The African Race" (1846), and William Wells Brown in *The Black Man, His Antecedents, His Genius, and His Achievements* (1863), had promoted evidence of Africa's erstwhile glory to be found in the works of classical authors and eighteenth- and nineteenth-century explorers and travelers. With the intensification of racist rhetoric after 1876, African American scholars and writers continued this historiographic project. Led by George Washington Williams, whose two volume *History of the Negro Race in America* (1883) begins with an account of ancient Africa, early African American historians attempted to provide black Americans with a past of which they could be proud. According to Dickson Bruce, the story of Africa's former glory enabled the early African American historians "to claim equality and an American identity, but in ways that maintained pride in a distinctive black heritage of achievement" (699).

As African American writers increasingly turned from autobiography and biography to fiction in the 1890s and early 1900s, a period in which the foundation stones of black citizenship erected during Reconstruction were being systematically dismantled, Ethiopianism provided a powerful counterdiscourse to the pervasive anti-Negro propaganda of the day. Specifically, with its monumentalist invocation of past African greatness and its promise of a glorious future for black people, Ethiopianism offered African American writers a means of looking beyond the present, as literary texts by Sutton E. Griggs, Pauline E. Hopkins, John E. Bruce, and the early W.E.B. Du Bois attest. A key monumentalist work of art was Meta Warrick Fuller's *The Awakening of Ethiopia* (1907–1910). Edmund Barry Gaither asserts that this sculpture "reiterates the popular image of Africa as a sleeping giant, one that would once again come into its own and recover its ancient Egyptian/Nubian glory. Fuller depicted Ethiopia in allegorical terms—sighing deeply and beginning to stir with renewed self-awareness—a work of such African consciousness that it is an all-encompassing declaration of heritage. [*The Awakening of Ethiopia*] stands at the head of a direction in Afro-American art which was to become increasingly important: the reclamation of African themes and styles in the remaking of black American identity" (19).

Monumentalism was perpetuated after 1920 by such figures as race historian J.A. Rogers, artists Lois Mailou Jones (who painted the magnificent *Ascent of Ethiopia* [1932]) and Aaron Douglas (painter of the famous *More Stately Mansions* [1944] depicting Egyptians with markedly black African features constructing the pyramids), and Marcus Garvey. As Tony Martin's books on the Universal Negro Improvement Association (UNIA) document, Ethiopianism, particularly the monumentalist variety, pervaded Garvey's rhetoric and the pageantry of his organization, which adopted Arnold J. Ford's "Universal Ethiopian Anthem" as its official song and whose officers bore aristocratic African titles. Moreover, echoing Bishop Turner's 1896 contention that "God is a Negro" and emulating distinctively African Christian churches, Garvey established the African Orthodox Church. The UNIA's religious arm not only featured the Black Madonna and the Black Christ, it also propagated an Ethiopianist catechism that was solidly anticolonial:

Q. What prediction made in the 68th Psalm and the 31st verse is now fulfilled?

A. Princes shall come out of Egypt, Ethiopia shall soon stretch out her hands to God.

Q. What does this verse prove?

A. That Black Men will set up their own government in Africa with rulers of their own race. (Quoted in Martin, *Race First,* 77)[10]

In contrast to Garvey, those writers most closely associated with the New Negro Movement—Alain Locke, Langston Hughes, Countee Cullen, and Claude McKay—sought but did not always manage to distance themselves from the previous generation of African American writing and its monumentalist and exceptionalist approach to Africa. Locke advocated direct contact and a reciprocal relationship between Africans and black Americans, and several African American writers did indeed travel to the continent to experience it firsthand. Among the second generation of twentieth-century black American authors, the iconoclastic George S. Schuyler was the most vehement opponent of the monumental approach to Africa, writing several texts denouncing race chauvinism, particularly that associated with Garveyism.

Although Garvey's imprisonment in 1924 and deportation in 1927 resulted in his movement's quick decline, Ethiopianism continued to have great appeal, as the widespread feelings of racial pride evoked by the coronation of Haile Salassie as the Ethiopian Emperor in 1930 revealed. The combination of a new focus on the world's oldest independent black nation and the ignominies recently suffered by two other independent black nations, Haiti and Liberia,[11] elevated Ethiopia to the chief symbol of black dignity and autonomy for many African Americans during the Depression era. When Mussolini invaded Ethiopia in 1935 to avenge the Italian defeat forty years previously, pride turned to outrage, and in some Eastern American cities this outrage led to violence. African American newspapers such as the *Pittsburgh Courier* extensively covered the war and the emperor's unsuccessful efforts to get help from the League of Nations, fueling black American hatred for Italy in particular and colonialism generally. Similar protests against the Italian attack and occupation were occurring throughout the black world; however, London rather than New York served as the base of pro-Ethiopian operations, and Africans and West Indians such as Kenyatta, George Padmore, and C.L.R. James rather than African Americans acted as the leaders for this and later Pan-African efforts, including the founding of the International African Service Bureau and the Pan-African Federation, which would organize the Fifth Pan-African Congress in 1945 (Legum, 30; Hill, Introduction, 37).

The aforementioned Pan-African Conference of 1900 and Fifth Pan-African Congress of 1945, in fact, mark significant moments in the history of the relationship between black Americans and Africa. The London Pan-African Conference, the first event of its kind, reflected the recognition of a common heritage and shared political interests among people of African descent throughout the world. Although there were some Africans in attendance, black Americans and West Indians organized and dominated the meeting, which was well attended and received fairly extensive press coverage. Projected follow-up conferences in Boston in 1902 and Haiti in 1904 never took place, however. W.E.B. Du Bois, who had participated in the London meeting, was elected vice president of the Pan-African Association's branch office in the United States, and thus was presumably among those charged with planning the ill-fated Boston conference, revived the concept in 1919, organizing the First Pan-African Congress that year in Paris and additional Congresses in 1921, 1923, and 1927, each of which featured a better balance of New World and African participants than the 1900 event. In 1945, after another extended hiatus, the Fifth Pan-African Congress met in Manchester. Although Du Bois attended, he was the only African American to do so and functioned largely as a figurehead. In contrast to previous Pan-African meetings, the 1945 version was organized and run mainly by Africans, including Nkrumah and Kenyatta, who would afterward play indispensable roles in liberating and governing their countries.[12] In general, a gradual shift away from African American exceptionalism to a reassessment of relations with Africa can be found in black American literary treatments of the continent appearing between the start and the middle of the twentieth century, leading toward an acknowledgment of the leadership role of Africans in the fight for black freedom that can be seen in many African American texts about Africa published since 1950.

Over time the combination of active resistance to white oppression by Africans and a clearer understanding of the people of Africa, colonialism, and their own situation by African Americans enabled black Americans to see the illegitimacy and/or superfluity of African American exceptionalism. Like Blyden, who had moved away from exceptionalism before his death in 1912, Du Bois ultimately came to change his opinion about who was most qualified to lead Africans and people of the diaspora to a brighter future. Although closely identified with Pan-Africanism, much of Du Bois's writing between 1895 and 1925, as Sundquist has shown, can accurately be characterized as Ethiopianist. A firm believer in African American exceptionalism early in his career, referring to black Americans as "the advance guard of the Negro people" in "The Conservation of Races" (1897), Du Bois significantly shifted his position later in his life. By 1936, the year Ethiopia fell to the Italians, he had moved away from exceptionalism, asserting the interconnectedness of black American and African freedom in the *Pittsburgh Courier*: "I do not believe that it is possible to settle the Negro problem in America until the color problems of the world are well on the way toward settlement. I do not believe that the descendants of Africans are going to be received as American citizens so long as the people of Africa are kept by white civilization in semi-slavery, serfdom, and economic exploitation" (quoted in Fredrickson, 151). Although Du Bois's primary concern here appears to be the status of blacks in America, the implication is that equal citizenship in the United States will coincide with or follow rather than precede African independence, a position he would state explicitly in "American Negroes and Africa's Rise to Freedom" (1961), written with the benefit of hindsight in the midst of the civil rights struggle in the United States: "American Negroes of former generations had always calculated that when Africa was ready for freedom, American Negroes would be ready to lead them. But the event was quite the opposite. The African leaders proved to be Africans, some indeed educated in the United States, but most of them trained in Europe and in Africa itself. American Negroes for the most part showed neither the education nor the aptitude for the magnificent opportunity which was suddenly offered. Indeed, it now seems that Africans may have to show American Negroes the way to freedom" (337). By then in his nineties, Du Bois himself had been one of the leading "American Negroes of former generations" who had subscribed to African American exceptionalism. Acting upon his conviction in his later years that it would be Africans who would lead black Americans to a better future, Du Bois shortly thereafter formally renounced his American citizenship and settled in Nkrumah's newly independent Ghana.

It is highly appropriate, therefore, that Du Bois, whose definition of double-consciousness serves as the starting point of this study, becomes a character in Alice Walker's *The Color Purple,* the final literary text discussed in this book. As a result of her decision to make African American missionaries who journey to Africa major characters in her novel, Walker grapples with and roundly condemns Ethiopianism and by extension black American literature about Africa informed by it. She perceptively recognizes that to engage comprehensively the relationship between black Americans and Africa, as she attempts to do in *The Color Purple,* she must confront Ethiopianism. In doing so, Walker fittingly chooses to reckon with the twentieth century's most important early proponent of Ethiopianism, W.E.B. Du Bois himself.

Discourse and Genre Tensions in African American Depictions of Africa

Black American writers who have portrayed Africa in literary texts have had to decide how to respond to not only the longstanding African American Ethiopianist tradition but also the well-established white discourse about Africa and people of African descent. Whereas Drake refers to Ethiopianism as a "countermyth" and Gilroy reads it as part of a much larger black Atlantic "counternarrative" to modernity, I regard Ethiopianism and the black American literature about Africa that employs it as an understandable but only intermittently successful counterdiscourse to white (and in some cases black) portrayals of people of African descent. As black American writers gradually came to realize, Ethiopianism's mysticism, ahistoricism, monumentalism, and African American exceptionalism have frequently complicated attempts to produce revisionary depictions of Africa. Moreover, the difficult question of audience, particularly what genre or genres to use in portraying the continent, has posed serious challenges for black American writers.

Ethiopianist texts serve as counterdiscursive responses to the "discourse of the black," Henry Louis Gates Jr.'s term for texts by white and black authors that portray black characters. Gates's literary criticism, especially *The Signifying Monkey: A Theory of Afro-American Literary Criticism* (1988), has had a profound impact on the study of African American literature. In an effort to map out a tradition that is distinctively black but avoids the essentialism of Negritude, the Black Arts movement, and Afrocentrism, Gates argues that black American writing does not simply repudiate assertions of black inferiority by either imitating white literature or refuting its assumptions, nor does it reflect a distinctive black essence; instead, it employs a rhetorical strategy associated with the African American trickster figure of the Signifying Monkey, which derives from the Yoruba trickster and messenger of the gods, Esu-Elegbara. Acknowledging that "all texts Signify upon other texts" and suggesting that this intertextual, revisionary concept may be useful in studying other literatures, Gates nevertheless regards his notion of Signifyin(g), which graphically represents the linguistic difference between white and black pronunciations of the word "signifying," as distinctively black because of his belief that "black writers, both explicitly and implicitly, turn to the vernacular in various formal ways to inform their creation of written fictions. To do so . . . is to ground one's literary practice outside the Western tradition. Whereas black writers most certainly revise texts in the Western tradition, they often seek to do so 'authentically,' with a black difference, a compelling sense of difference based on the black vernacular" (*Signifying*, xxiv, xxii). Indeed, repetition with a (black) difference is another definition Gates offers for Signifyin(g).

If blackness is merely a trope, as Gates asserts in his critique of Addison Gayle in *Figures in Black: Words, Signs and the "Racial" Self* (1987), however, this problematizes his attempt to delineate a specifically black tradition of Signifyin(g). If there is no racial essence, as Gates argues, then the "identifiable black Signifyin(g) difference" that makes African American literature distinctive had to be created by the material conditions in which a particular group of people (arbitrarily) designated as black found themselves. In other words, the black tradition Gates writes about had specific historical and political causes. Despite his protestations to the contrary, beneath his usage of the terminology of the Yale deconstructionists, a major purpose of Gates's project in *Figures in Black* and *The Signifying Monkey,* in fact, is to outline a *history* of black American literature from the eighteenth century to the present. At least in its relationship to white writing, Gates's theory of Signifyin(g) involves a historically based and politically motivated response to the dominant discourse that calls the terms of that discourse, as well as its own, into question.[13] As subsequent chapters will illustrate, black American writing about Africa often endeavors to signify on white texts that assert or assume African Americans and/or Africans have been predestined to inferiority.

Frequently complicating these signifying efforts, however, is the fact that the relationship between black American literature about Africa and white texts about the continent has often been much more ambiguous than the relationship between the discourse of the black and African American writing about Africa would initially appear to be—in large part because of black America exceptionalism. By definition, Africanist discourse should be regarded as part of the discourse of the black, but authors and critics of African American literature have not always recognized this to be the case.[14] Although the link between black Americans and Africa is a key tenet of Ethiopianism, this connection, particularly in the nineteenth century and the first decade of the twentieth, was often perceived to be with the African past but not necessarily with contemporary Africa and Africans. As a result, in writing about the continent and its peoples, black American writers who have attempted to counter white texts that demean African Americans in some cases have consciously or unwittingly parroted Africanist discourse and its negative portrayals of Africa and Africans.

As I argue in *White on Black: Contemporary Literature about Africa* (1992), the three main, often interlocking conventions of Africanist discourse in English have been binary oppositions that contrast Africa and the West, the projection of images onto the perceived blank slate of Africa, and evolutionary language that describes Africans as lagging behind Westerners in terms of moral, intellectual, and/or material development. Africanist writing frequently depicts Africa as a dream or a nightmare and often a dream that becomes a nightmare, an ambivalence that is epitomized in Winston Churchill's description of the continent in his propagandistic travel book *My African Journey* (1909) as a "curious garden of sunshine and nightshade" (65)—a seeming paradise that is actually meretriciously poisonous. Moreover, reflecting the influence of Darwin's evolutionary theories, these texts typically portray Africans as either childlike or living in an era Europeans experienced centuries earlier. Given Ethiopianism's oppositional nature, its monumentalism, its cyclical theory of racial progress, and its reliance on religious mysticism rather than history, economic analysis, and scientific data, the black American literature about Africa that invokes or otherwise engages it at times resorts to the binarism, image projection, and evolutionary language that characterize Africanist texts.

As subsequent chapters will demonstrate, the variety of genres black Americans have used to depict Africa has been impressive, including the African adventure tale, detective fiction, lyric, melodrama, autobiography, anti-utopian novel, pageant, drama, opera, long poem, travel book, and historical novel. However, because specific genres such as melodrama, the African adventure tale, and travel writing have long been used to caricature or otherwise stereotype black characters, African Americans have used them at their peril. A major strength of Gates's Signifyin(g), with its focus on the rhetorical strategies black American authors use to revise the discourse of the black, is its ability to account for not only literary movements and genres that develop in response to earlier ones but also revisions within specific genres.[15] A brief look at an early African American novel will demonstrate some of the discursive and generic pitfalls that depicting Africa can entail.

In the preface to *Negro Culture in West Africa* (1914), a groundbreaking study of the Vai language, George W. Ellis maintains that making accurate information about the continent available to white people will improve race relations: "The view entertained of the Negro African abroad is largely conditioned upon the knowledge possessed of the Negro in Africa. In this thought then the present study may have some bearing upon the interracial understanding between what is [sic] considered the two most divergent and dissimilar ethnic groups" (17).[16] However, although he was well aware that the "Negro [is] substantially different to what is described in modern science and literature" (18), when Ellis himself turned to fiction three years later in *The Leopard's Claw* he apparently failed to realize the extent to which the conventions of the African adventure novel he chose to write would undermine his avowed revisionary goal. Describing Ellis as "one familiar with not only the places and persons concerned but with human actions and motives and with an eye to the exciting in fiction that betrays one long versed in the art of story-telling," the "Publishers' Foreword" to the novel unintentionally identifies the two conflicting impulses operating within Ellis—to report factually what he has experienced firsthand and to tell an action-packed story that will hold his white readers' attention.

Early in *The Leopard's Claw*, Ellis strives for geographic precision, takes the time to explicate certain native practices, and rather pedantically gives the Latin names for various flora and fauna. Nevertheless, the sheer improbability of the plot, involving the melodramatic adventures of a white family who become lost and split up in the West African jungle, as well as the novel's clear debt to Edgar Rice Burroughs' immensely popular *Tarzan of the Apes* (1912), undermines any of the modest revisionary aspirations Ellis may have had for the book. Like Burroughs, Ellis keeps his focus on and evinces an unwavering reverence for British nobility. Again echoing Burroughs, Ellis depicts a great ape that acts as a surrogate mother to young Lucretia Montcrief, who becomes separated from her parents in the bush, and later even creates a Tarzan figure in Lucretia's father. When an accident temporarily deprives Oliver Montcrief, the son of an English earl, of his memory and his ability to speak, he is transformed into a mysterious white man of enormous strength and uncanny survival skills who lives in the West African rain forest until a bump on the head cures his amnesia and aphasia and he, his wife Eva, and his now-grown daughter are reunited after fourteen years apart.

Perhaps a description of one of the awkward and unintentionally humorous passages in *The Leopard's Claw* will serve to illustrate the conflict between Ellis's aims and his chosen genre. In an early chapter, entitled "Jungle Terrors," soon after the aristocratic but cash-poor Montcriefs set out through the bush in search of a platinum mine they hope will make them fabulously wealthy, a leopard snatches the family's new puppy and a crocodile chases Oliver; however, it is the toddler Lucretia who has the most remarkable adventure:

> While [her parents] were busy in the camp, Lucretia became attracted by a beautiful butterfly, which she endeavored to catch. In this way she wandered far from camp. Suddenly she came upon a large elephant which was having its morning meal of rattan buds. The elephant picked up the child and placed it upon its back.
>
> When Lucretia's disappearance was discovered the parents made a search and arrived just in time to behold the spectacle of Lucretia sitting upon the elephant's back and being chased by other elephants.
>
> For a moment the situation was a tense one, as they did not know that this elephant at one time was a pet and a present of a native Indian prince to an African chief. Eva and Oliver climbed a tree, as luck would have it, and just as the elephant passed under them, Oliver reached from a limb and seized Lucretia from its back before the other elephants arrived. (38–39)[17]

Beneath the sensationalism of this scene lie some intriguing tensions. The passage begins with the standard dream versus nightmare binarism of Africanist discourse. Bewitched by the beauty of a butterfly, young white

Lucretia leaves the safety of the camp only to be suddenly swooped up by a huge elephant. Perhaps because he recognized the stereotypical nature of this scene, Ellis attempts somehow to diminish the pachyderm's ferocity by turning it into an Asian elephant, normally smaller and generally considered to be more docile than its African cousin. Yet, in so doing, Ellis only compounds the association of terror with Africa because it is the home-grown elephants in hot pursuit of Lucretia and her mount that pose the real danger. Ellis's remarkable assertion that Lucretia's elephant "at one time was a pet and a present of a native Indian prince to an African chief" suggests a well-established Asiatic-African nexus that not only gives the lie to Western notions of the Dark Continent but also foreshadows Du Bois's novel *Dark Princess* (1928), which concerns efforts to forge links among people of color throughout the world. Apparently constrained by the impulse to satisfy his white audience's desire for melodramatic action, however, Ellis says nothing further on the subject, leaving entirely to conjecture the circumstances which lead to the transportation of this animal from the sub-continent to West Africa.

Despite Ellis's intention to offer his predominantly white readers an accurate account of Africa based on his eight years of diplomatic service in Liberia in *The Leopard's Claw*, his decision to write an adventure story with white people as the main characters results in a poor imitation of popular Africanist fiction, perpetuates a clichéd image of the continent, and at times inadvertently borders on the comic. In its failure to manipulate conventions from popular fiction to serve revisionary ends, the book reveals a great deal about the causes and effects of discourse and genre tensions that have faced African American writers who have attempted to portray Africa.

Uncritically mimicking Africanist fiction, Ellis's novel indicates that firsthand knowledge and the intention to portray Africa accurately do not necessarily guarantee that a black American author will produce a version of the continent that differs significantly from mainstream white depictions. Because white authors writing in the adventure, sentimental, travel, and other genres had long cast black people in certain well-defined, stereotyped roles, African American writers who have chosen these genres have needed to exercise caution. As the chapters that follow will reveal, it has been precisely those writers who recognized the problematic nature of specific literary forms and consciously constructed generic hybrids who have created some of the most effective—in revisionary terms—and memorable black American literary texts about Africa.

2

Double-Consciousness, Ethiopianism, and Africa

Go on and up! Our souls and eyes
Shall follow thy continuous rise;
Our ears shall list thy story
From bards who from thy root shall spring,
And proudly tune their lyres to sing
Of Ethiopia's glory.

PAUL LAURENCE DUNBAR, "ODE TO ETHIOPIA"

Stretch forth thy hand, Jehovah bids thee come
And claim the promise; thou hast had thy doom.
If forth in sorrow, weeping, thou hast gone,
Rejoicing to thy God thou shalt return.

BISHOP L.J. COPPIN, "SONG OF AFRICA"

Ethiopianism's influence can be seen in the turn of the century's best-known characterization of what it is like to be black in America, W.E.B. Du Bois's concept of double-consciousness, which was first published in an 1897 *Atlantic Monthly* article and reprinted in slightly altered form in *The Souls of Black Folk* (1903).[1] The first sentence of Du Bois's two-paragraph definition of double-consciousness[2] begins by blending the author's deliberately imprecise concept of "race"[2] with the prospect of Africa's redemption: "After the Egyptian and the Indian, the Greek and Roman, the Teuton, and the Mongolian, the Negro is a sort of seventh son. . . ." (102). Because each of the first six groups of people has had its moment of glory, the implication is that the "Negro" or "seventh son" is poised to achieve similar greatness.[3] In the second paragraph of his definition, Du Bois introduces the possibility that the thesis and antithesis of white America and black Africa can one day be synthesized to form a better and truer whole: "In this merging [the American Negro] wishes neither of the older selves to be lost. He would not

Africanize America, for America has too much to teach the world and Africa. He would not bleach his Negro soul in a flood of white Americanism, for he knows that Negro blood has a message for the world" (102). Instead of "warring ideals" vying for supremacy, as in the previous paragraph, Africa and America have become "older selves" that will be blended to create a new African American self. On the one hand, Du Bois echoes the pronouncements of predominantly white nineteenth-century developers and missionaries and also the exceptionalism of black American leaders in suggesting that the United States has much "to teach the world and Africa." On the other hand, the phrase "a flood of white Americanism" implies a criticism of white American culture that resonates with his later denunciations in *Souls* of America's rampant materialism and dovetails with Ethiopianism's belief in the imminent decline of the West. Seen in this light, then, the "message" of "Negro blood" will be a spiritualism and purity of motives that will contrast with the greed and short-sightedness of the white world. By thus appealing to a white and a black audience, Du Bois attempts in his definition of double-consciousness to approximate the synthesis of America and Africa he predicts for the future.

Although people of African descent throughout the world shared a desire for the bright future foretold by Ethiopianism, there was little consensus on how it was to be realized. Despite the invocation of Ethiopianism in the definition of double-consciousness, the West African journalist J.E. Casely Hayford, one of Ethiopianism's strongest advocates, responded with disgust to Du Bois's concept, particularly his vision of an eventual synthesis of white America and black Africa. Convinced that Du Bois and African Americans generally had been so tainted by slavery and Western materialism in the United States that they were unfit to participate effectively in the redemption of Africa, in *Ethiopia Unbound* he hyperbolically terms Du Bois's definition "[o]ne of the most pathetic passages in the history of human thought. . . ." (179). Africans do not suffer from double-consciousness, according to Casely Hayford, but black Americans do because of their long exposure to (white) American society and its value system: "It is apparent that Mr. Du Bois writes from an American standpoint, surrounded by an American atmosphere. And, of course, it is not his fault, for he knows no other. To be born an African in America, in that great commonwealth of dollars and the merciless aggrandisement of the individual . . . is to be entangled in conditions which give no room for the assertion of the highest manhood. African manhood demands that the Ethiopian should seek not his opportunity, or ask for elbow room, from the white man, but that he should create the one or the other for himself" (182). For Casely Hayford there is a key geopolitical issue at stake here: whether black Americans like

Du Bois or Africans like himself will be the ones to lead the peoples of Africa and the diaspora to the glorious future Ethiopianism predicts for them. Casely Hayford pointedly rejects Du Bois's African American exceptionalism, especially his contention that because of black Americans' potential to synthesize Africa and America they represent the vanguard of the black world.

In addition to indicating the influence of Ethiopianism and its geopolitical implications on turn-of-the-century African American writing, Du Bois's concept of double-consciousness profoundly confronts the thorny issue of audience. At the start of *Souls*—and at the start of the twentieth century, the century of the color line—Du Bois implicitly addresses what James Weldon Johnson would term "the dilemma of the Negro author" in a 1928 essay. According to Johnson, "the Aframerican author faces a special problem which the plain American author knows nothing about—the problem of the double audience. It is more than a double audience; it is a divided audience, an audience made up of two elements with differing and antagonistic points of view. His audience is always both white America and black America. The moment a Negro writer takes up his pen or sits down to his typewriter he is immediately called upon to solve, consciously or unconsciously, this problem of the double audience" (477). No doubt Johnson, who called *Souls* "remarkable" and claimed its effect upon the black community was greater than any book since *Uncle Tom's Cabin*, had Du Bois's text in mind when he stated that some black writers had accomplished the difficult task of successfully addressing a mixed audience (Rampersad, *Art,* 68; Johnson, 481). What I am suggesting is that double-consciousness as Du Bois conceived it describes not only the "peculiar sensation" experienced by African Americans in general but also the specific challenges facing black writers that Johnson discusses in "The Dilemma of the Negro Author."[4]

Du Bois's definition of African American "twoness" indicates that he was acutely aware of the grave responsibility he was taking upon himself in *Souls* by attempting no less than to portray the largely forgotten history, the present strivings, and the unrecognized potential of his people. How was he to tell the "tale of his tribe" to the dominant white audience accustomed to viewing blacks in only certain limited and often caricatured roles and to the much smaller black audience, which was understandably sensitive about how its people were portrayed? Looked at from this perspective of audience, the concept of double-consciousness enabled Du Bois to see his people as white Americans see them; it also enabled him to see the value in the black experience to which many whites are blind. More important, double-consciousness made it possible for Du Bois to devise a successful means by which to portray this value so that it could be perceived by both white and black readers.

The extent to which African American literary artists who have depicted the continent have attempted to overturn the caricatures of Africa and Africans that dominate white art through a consciously conceived counterdiscourse, and have succeeded in doing so, has much to do with how these writers have responded to specific concerns Du Bois raises in the double-consciousness passage. These are, first, connections between the African American and the African past, present, and future; second, geopolitical considerations involving Africa and America, particularly who will lead the black world; and, third, the complex issue of audience—including the question of which genre or genres to utilize, a concern that Du Bois implicitly addressed in his decision to make *Souls* a compilation of various types of writing.

Interest in Africa among black Americans reached a significant peak in the 1890s and early 1900s, as the Ethiopianist poems by Paul Laurence Dunbar and AME Bishop L.J. Coppin excerpted at the start of this chapter reveal, and soon after the turn of the century some of the earliest African American fictional texts to portray Africa began to appear. Novels by Sutton E. Griggs, Pauline E. Hopkins, and John E. Bruce explicitly invoke Ethiopianism and grapple with the relationship between Africa and early twentieth-century African Americans. Both Griggs and Hopkins portray a black American protagonist who bears a specific bodily marking that attests to his descent from African royalty, the revelation of which forces him to reconsider his beliefs about not only the continent but also the United States. Whereas Bruce remains largely focused on the African present, Griggs and Hopkins only make limited efforts to address the situation in contemporary Africa. Hopkins, in fact, adheres closely to monumentalism, depicting an Ethiopian kingdom of ancient origins that still survives beneath the ruins of Meroe.

Africa appears briefly but significantly in Griggs's *Unfettered* (1902) and *The Hindered Hand* (1905). Although Griggs is a largely forgotten figure today, Hugh Gloster estimates he had more black readers than either Charles Chesnutt or Paul Laurence Dunbar. However, Griggs also hoped that his ideas about the causes and possible remedies for the race problems in the United States that he expressed in his fiction would reach at least those whites sympathetic to the plight of African Americans. Focused on the present moment, that is America's racial crisis at the turn of the century, he lacks Du Bois's awareness of the political stakes involved in attempts to portray Africa and offers no hope of an eventual synthesis like that to be found in the double-consciousness passage. Moreover, he fails to see the connection between Africanist discourse (which he sometimes imitates) and the discourse of the black (which he often seeks to rebut). As a result, Griggs's depictions of Africa are strikingly ambivalent, momentarily positive and then suddenly entirely negative. Although by mixing sentimental fiction and polemical essay in *Unfettered* and *The Hindered Hand* Griggs may have been striving for a kind of nascent generic hybridization, the combination of his desire, at least in part, to appease and appeal to a white audience and his apparently quite limited knowledge about Africa substantially diminishes the revisionary thrust of these novels.

Hopkins's *Of One Blood; Or, the Hidden Self* (1902–1903) and Bruce's *The Black Sleuth* (1907–1909), novels serialized in black periodicals, offer much bolder and more effective portrayals of the continent than those by Griggs; however, their enthusiastic use of Ethiopianism raises some serious questions. Both Hopkins and Bruce use elements from popular fiction in their efforts to educate their readers about Africa, but they concentrate on different time periods. Seeking to counter arguments that people of African descent have no history, Hopkins presents a highly advanced Ethiopian society that still survives below the Nubian desert. In contrast, Bruce focuses on contemporary Africa and uses the perspective of an African student, who later turns detective, to attack America's pervasive racism. Drawing upon conventions from a variety of popular genres, Hopkins and Bruce consciously construct their novels as generic hybrids. Thus, whereas Ellis's *The Leopard's Claw* is little more than a maladroit portrait of white people lost in the jungle and Griggs's novels alternate ineffectively between melodrama and polemic, *Of One Blood* daringly grafts a number of different genres onto the African adventure tale and *The Black Sleuth* far exceeds the standard detective story. Nevertheless, Hopkins's and Bruce's reliance on Ethiopianism's cyclical approach to history is problematic because it closely resembles Africanist writers' frequent depiction of Africa as a dream or a nightmare.

The "Warring Ideals" of Africa and America in the Novels of Sutton E. Griggs

One need look no later than Sutton E. Griggs's *Unfettered* (1902) and *The Hindered Hand* (1905), two of the earliest twentieth-century African American novels to thematize Africa, for vivid illustrations of the mixed feelings black Americans had about their ancestral home. A Baptist minister like his father, Griggs was not only a novelist but also a social and political moralist. Arlene Elder credits Griggs with being the first black author "to center . . . directly on the tensions and ironies within the emerging African-American community" (69). Wilson Moses goes further, asserting that "[w]ith the possible exception of Du Bois, Griggs was the only black novelist of his period who undertook the writing of novels as part of a definite plan to create a national Negro literature" (*The Golden Age,* 173).[5] Apart from Moses, who describes Griggs's style as "splendidly primitive" (*The Wings,* 226), critics have uniformly regarded him as an often clumsy literary artist, whose reliance upon many of the clichés of late nineteenth-century sentimental fiction frequently vitiates the impact of his novels' politically charged subject matter.[6]

An advocate of black self-reliance, Griggs published and distributed all five of his novels between 1899 and 1909 largely at his own expense, establishing his own publishing company in Nashville in 1901 and at times even going door to door among the black community in an effort to develop an audience for his works. Nonetheless, Moses reports that he was endorsed by many Southern whites as a responsible black leader and that his publishing ventures were underwritten in part by white Baptists (*The Golden Age,* 172), which may help to explain why he frequently depicts the participation of enlightened whites as a necessary component of the solutions he proposes to the racial crisis in America in his novels. Attempting thus both to create a market for his novels within the black community and to appeal to a certain kind of white reader, Griggs at a very early period took upon himself the difficult task of writing for a mixed audience, and in his novels he unself-consciously reproduces the dualities of turn-of-the-century American society. Griggs does incorporate a form of Pan-Africanism into these novels, but he does not balance Africa and America as Du Bois attempts to do; rather, Griggs focuses almost exclusively on the present situation in the United States. Griggs's African American exceptionalism is therefore more extreme than Du Bois's. Similar to Africanist writers, he regards Africa more as a literary device than as a real location and consequently fails to question the legitimacy of white portrayals of the continent.

Despite having scant information about and a low opinion of Africa and its people, Griggs grants a significant role to the continent in *Unfettered* and *The Hindered Hand.* His ambivalence about Africa is striking. In fact, from reading these works, one gets the sense of two Griggses struggling for primacy. As a novelist attempting to create a national literature for black America, he seems to be searching beyond both the limitations of expository prose and the borders of his country for a solution to turn-of-the-century America's racial nightmare. Thus, at times Griggs regards Africa as a fictive space replete with possibility, literally and figuratively filled with riches waiting for African American exploitation. On the other hand, as a polemicist for black America hoping to win the support of sympathetic whites, he for the most part keeps his focus firmly on the present situation in the United States, even on occasion abandoning narrative altogether in favor of argumentative essays attributed to his characters. This latter Griggs frequently contrasts African American achievement with African "backwardness," echoing racist characterizations of the continent in order to defend American blacks against charges of inherent inferiority.

Griggs devotes his third novel *Unfettered* almost exclusively to an examination of American racial politics. Even the romance between the two major characters, Morlene Dalton and Dorlan Warthell, is intimately bound to the "Negro Question." In fact, Morlene will only consent to marry Dorlan if he brings about nothing less than an end to the problem of the color line. To satisfy this condition, he produces "Dorlan's Plan," a sixty-five page program for improving the status of blacks in the United States. This Griggs includes as a sequel to *Unfettered*.

Just prior to learning of this mission from Morlene, Dorlan has an extraordinary two-part encounter in a chapter entitled "A Street Parade." Observing a group of black musicians followed by a large crowd of ragged and dirty African Americans of various ages, Dorlan immediately reflects upon them in terms of black-white relations:

> Now these Negroes are moulding sentiment against the entire race. . . . Be the requirement just or unjust the polished Negro is told to return and bring his people with him, before coming into possession of that to which his attainments would seem to entitle him. It is my opinion that there must be developed within the race a stronger altruistic tie before it can push forward at a proper gait. The classes must love the masses, in spite of the bad name the race is given by the indolent, the sloven and the criminal element. . . . Ah! the squalor and misery of my poor voiceless race! What we see here is but a bird's eye view. The heart grows sick when it contemplates the plight of the Negroes of the cities. (160–61)

Dorlan's ambivalence toward this "unsightly mass" of people is clear both in what he says and how he says it. On the one hand, as a "polished Negro" himself, one of Du Bois's "talented tenth," his achievements and aspirations isolate him from the members of the crowd, whom he contemplates, at least initially, in a detached manner. On the other hand, white society's refusal to recognize a difference between blacks like Dorlan and the unwashed flock following the band inevitably links him to this "motley throng." The passage suggests three different motivations behind the program of uplift Dorlan advocates here: self-interest, genuinely charitable feelings, and racial solidarity. Dorlan's diction, moreover, reflects his mixed emotions about the street parade. Even in this aside to himself, Dorlan feels the need to qualify his beliefs with the phrase "[i]t is my opinion," and his shifts from the third person singular to the first person singular to the first person plural suggest his uncertainty about his relationship to the members of the parade.

The second part of this encounter involves what may very well be the initial appearance of an African character in twentieth-century African American fiction. Dorlan suddenly discovers that he is closely related to a group of black people seemingly even more removed from himself than the crowd that has passed before him. Noticing a banner with "a peculiar inscription" held by a man in a dogcart among the musicians, Dorlan shouts, "Hold! here am I" (161). Mysteriously, the man cuts a slit in the arm of Dorlan's clothes, cries aloud for joy over what he finds, and dismisses the band. After Dorlan converses with him in a "strange tongue," the man explains himself: "My name is Ulbah Kumi. I hail from Africa. I am one of an army of commissioners sent out by our kingdom into all parts of the world where Negroes have been held in modern times as slaves. We are hunting for the descendants of a lost prince. This prince was the oldest son of our reigning king, and was taken captive in a battle fought with a rival kingdom. He was sold into slavery. The royal family had a motto and a family mark. You recognized the motto on the banner; you have the royal mark. You also look to be a prince" (162–63). Dorlan confirms Kumi's suspicions, explaining that his grandfather claimed to be an African prince, who passed this knowledge and a secret formula on to Dorlan's father, who in turn passed them on to him. The formula turns out to be the directions to a great treasure that will make Dorlan the wealthiest man in the world.

Rather than rejoicing at this unexpected double legacy of untold wealth and family heritage, however, Dorlan experiences ambivalence once more: "Dorlan's face now wore a pained expression. He had always been profoundly interested in Africa and was congratulating himself on the opportunity now offered to convert the proffered kingdom into an enlightened republic. It now seemed that his own interests and those of his ancestral home were about to clash. He cannot endure the thought of putting an ocean between Morlene and himself. Nor can he with equanimity think of allowing Africa to remain in her existing condition" (165). Like Dorlan's earlier soliloquy on the street parade, this passage reveals a mixture of self-interest, charity, and race solidarity in response to Africa; it is also rife with African American exceptionalism. To Dorlan's surprise, Kumi painlessly resolves this dilemma for him, explaining that there is no pressing need for him to come to Africa; rather, Dorlan can remain in the United States and still be his people's king, working on their behalf from abroad. In addition, Dorlan will be able to use his newfound wealth to finance his program for solving the race problem in America, which, he asserts in his "Plan," will serve as a necessary first step toward the development of Africa: "I have no qualms of conscience in thus applying to the Negroes of America funds derived from Africa, for I firmly believe . . . in the Americanization of the globe, and believe that in due time the Negroes of America are to be the immediate agents of the Americanization of Africa. Money spent in the uplift of the American Negro is, therefore, an investment in the interests of Africa that will pay a glorious dividend" (275). In contrast to Du Bois's goal of a synthesis of Africa and America, the situation of blacks in the United States takes clear precedence in *Unfettered*.

If, as I have been arguing, ambivalence dominates Dorlan's attitudes toward both the black masses and Africa, the same would appear to hold true for his creator, Sutton Griggs. Although *Unfettered* links the fates of African Americans and Africans and asserts the need for cooperation between them, Griggs does not advocate an equal partnership. Not only does he believe that outside influence is necessary to effect the development of Africa—that only someone educated in the West like Dorlan can "convert" its "kingdom[s]" into "enlightened republic[s]"—but Dorlan's decision to finance his plan to uplift black America with African wealth smacks of imperialism, despite the protagonist's claim that to do so will ultimately be in the continent's best interest.

The story of the source of Dorlan's bequest underscores Griggs's low estimation of Africans and the link between Dorlan's scheme and those of European colonialists. After perusing an inventory of his family's treasure, Dorlan asks Kumi, "How could Africans, unlearned in the values of civilized nations, know how to store away these things" (163). Instead of challenging Dorlan's imputation of underdevelopment to his people, Kumi confirms it by explaining that a white person was responsible for amassing the wealth in the first place; moreover, Griggs encodes the white adventurer of Africanist fiction into his depiction of Africa: "A white explorer spent years in our kingdom collecting these things. We deemed them worthless, gave them to him readily and called him fool. He took sick in our country and saw he was going to die. He called your great grandfather, our king, to his bedside, told him that civilization would make its way into Africa one day, and urged him at all hazards to preserve and secrete the treasures that he had collected" (163–64). If Griggs here intends to contrast Africa's lack of a desire for wealth with the West's grasping materialism (in keeping with the spiritual purity version of Ethiopianism), he certainly does not make this as explicit as some other early African American authors do. Griggs's divided stance toward Africa can be seen once more when Kumi states, "We Africans are engaged in a sociological investigation of many questions"—certainly an activity which rebuts the dominant white perception of the continent as backward—but then this African emissary reveals that what they are looking for is an explanation for their own lack of development: "We are seeking to know definitely what part the climate, the surface, the flora and fauna have played in keeping us in civilization's back yard" (165).

The similarity between Dorlan's ambivalent responses to the motley crowd of African Americans at the start of the chapter and the later news of his African legacy can be attributed to more than coincidence. If only by juxtaposition, Griggs seems to be connecting Africa with filth through the shabby street parade. This association is echoed in "Dorlan's Plan" by the unqualified designation of the squalid parts of American towns "inhabited almost exclusively by the poorer, shiftless, more ignorant class of Negroes" where bars and prostitution flourish as "Little Africas" (253). Through these comparisons, Griggs evinces his belief that the continent and its people, like lower class black Americans, are in need of uplifting and civilizing.

Apart from "A Street Parade" and the above-mentioned general references in "Dorlan's Plan," Africa and Africans do not figure in *Unfettered*. Thus, if we look at the use of the continent in the novel solely in terms of plot development, Griggs himself can be said to plunder Africa to help him solve the problem of the novel. Without large sums of money, "Dorlan's Plan" would no doubt remain on the drawing board. The protagonist's unsought-for windfall increases the chances that he will be able to put his ideas into action. Because Griggs believes that Africans cannot progress without outside help and that African Americans can provide them with the greatest assistance, he portrays Dorlan's intention to use his African wealth to upgrade black America in a wholly positive light rather than as a case of black on black exploitation, which someone with a higher opinion of Africa and a more critical appraisal of both the "civilizing mission" and African American exceptionalism might deem it to be.

Griggs uses Africa in a more consistent and conscious, but no less ambivalent, way in his next novel, *The Hindered Hand: or, the Reign of the Repressionist*. Beginning with the epigraph "Princes shall come out of Egypt; Ethiopia shall soon stretch forth her hands unto God," the key Psalms verse that held such resonance for African Americans throughout the nineteenth century and at the turn of the twentieth, this book includes scenes set in Liberia, to which the main character, Ensal Ellwood, emigrates in the last third of the novel. Moreover, in two appendices Griggs discusses his use of

Africa in the book and offers a problematic apology for the continent. As the contrast in titles indicates, *The Hindered Hand* is less sanguine about what the future holds for African Americans than *Unfettered.*[7] Rather than miraculously appearing to underwrite a plan to improve conditions for blacks in America, Africa serves as a refuge in the later novel, a place where African Americans can escape the horrors and frustrations of American racial politics. Once again, however, as the author later explicitly acknowledges, Griggs's Africa is less a real place than a device used to further a plot otherwise devoted to American race relations.

In his novels, as Elder and Moses have noted, Griggs illustrates the conflicting allegiances of black Americans not only through ambivalent characters, such as Dorlan, but also through paired characters who advocate diametrically opposed responses to racism in the United States. In *The Hindered Hand,* the light skin and revolutionary zeal of the mulatto Earl Bluefield contrast with Ensal's dark complexion and more conciliatory disposition. In a highly symbolic scene midway through the novel, Ensal and Earl wrestle on a bridge, the former determined to stop the latter's suicidal scheme to lead five hundred men in the takeover of the state capitol. Ensal, like Dorlan, favors the pen over the sword, composing a thirteen-page appeal "To the People of the United States" on behalf of the country's black population, which is quoted in full in the novel, a copy of which he hopes to send to every American household. Reflecting a racialism[8] that was typical of late nineteenth-century figures such as Alexander Crummell, John E. Bruce, and the early Du Bois, Ensal's document begins by claiming a difference in temperament between the "Anglo-Saxon race" and the "Negro" deriving from the colder and warmer regions that originally produced them, a difference which inevitably led to conflict in the American South during slavery. Emancipation greatly improved conditions for blacks, Ensal asserts, causing them to aspire to participate fully in American society; but, when Reconstruction ended, Southern capitalists, eager once again to exploit African Americans for their labor, combined with resentful poor whites to deny blacks their political rights. The appeal ends with the request that America live up to its ideals by judging people on merit rather than color.

A tragic episode occurs, however, which causes Ensal to despair about the future. A militant black man, Gus Martin, misinterprets the kiss he sees Rev. Percy Marshall, a rare champion of the African American among the Southern white clergy, bestow on Tiara Merlow. Martin kills the minister for this supposed insult to black womanhood, and then is himself shot dead after Tiara convinces him to give himself up. These violent deaths cause Ensal to abandon his cautious optimism about conditions in the South, and the supposed romantic liaison between Marshall and Tiara, whom Ensal had hoped to someday marry, further unsettles him. He resolves to leave the United States for Liberia, committing himself to an effort to develop the entire African continent.

Ensal's sojourn on the continent enables Griggs to develop further the ideas about Africa and its relationship to black America briefly outlined in *Unfettered*. Prior to his departure, Ensal writes a letter of farewell "addressed to a Negro organization devoted to the general uplift of the race, a body that had been founded, and was now presided over by Ensal" (196–97). In it he espouses African American exceptionalism, boasting that "the strongest aggregation of Negro life that has at any time manifested itself on the earth" currently exists in the United States, and notes the "striking coincidence that simultaneous with the turning of the thought of the world to Africa and the recognition of the need therein of an easily acclimated civilizing force, that the American Negro, soul wise through suffering should come forth as a strong man to run a race" (197–98). Warning against assimilation into the white race, Ensal urges African Americans to maintain their ties to Africa and work for racial harmony in the United States so that it can serve as a model for the whole world: "May it continue your ambition to abide Negroes, to force the American civilization to accord you your place in your own right, to the end that the world may have an example of *alien* races living side by side administering the general government and meting out justice and fair play to all" (198, emphasis in original).

Through passages such as this, there is a strong sense that Griggs believes that, in embarking on what he calls "the larger mission of the American Negro," a Pan-Africanist program to uplift Africa with black Americans at the forefront, Ensal is running away from the more important struggle at home. This sense is confirmed when the novel returns to Ensal, who is absent from the book for about seventy pages. In stark contrast with the frustrations often experienced by African Americans who actually worked in Liberia, such as Alexander Crummell, Ensal's African uplift program enjoys remarkable success and notoriety, with the prospect of redeeming all of Africa and creating a powerful worldwide Pan-African movement seemingly at hand. Nevertheless, Ensal suffers from depression until he learns that Tiara has revealed at a trial that Percy Marshall was actually her brother passing for white. Realizing that she is in fact available to him, Ensal abruptly abandons his position in Liberia:

> "Landlady! landlady!" Ensal exclaimed, rushing out of his room in search of that personage. Finding her, he said excitedly, "Put everybody in Monrovia at work packing up my possessions, please. I must leave."

"What can this mean, pray tell. *I understood that you were to devote your life to this work*," said the landlady, much amazed at the sudden turn of affairs.

"What work? Life?" asked Ensal, absentmindedly.

"The uplift of Africa, the redemption of your race," replied the landlady.

"My *race*, dear madam, is to catch the first steamer returning to America. Just now the whole world with me converges to that one point." (273–74, emphasis in original)

As in *Unfettered*, Griggs's protagonist chooses love over Africa, but this time only temporarily. Ensal goes to America to marry Tiara and quickly returns with her to Africa. Significantly, at the end of the novel, there is no further mention of Ensal's program of uplift for the continent; instead, Ensal's mission in Africa has become one of preparing "a home for the American Negro . . . should the good people of America, North and South, grow busy, confused or irresolute and fail, to the subversion of their ideals, to firmly entrench the Negro in his political rights, the denial of which, and the blight incident thereto, more than all other factors, cause the Ethiopian in America to feel that his is indeed 'The Hindered Hand'" (292).

It is tempting, on the one hand, to see Griggs's inclusion of Africa in this and his previous novel as a means to generate interest among his black readers, and, on the other hand, to regard "Dorlan's Plan," Ensal's "Appeal" and the two appendices to *The Hindered Hand*, as polemical essays directed toward his white readers. Echoing the conclusion of *The Hindered Hand*, Griggs discounts the importance of Ensal's civilizing mission in Liberia in his first appendix, "Notes for the Serious." Explicitly acknowledging that he has used Africa as a literary device in the novel, Griggs implies that African American interest in the continent has almost no relevance to the more important struggle at home: "The assigning of the thoughts of the race to the uplift of Africa, as affecting the situation in America, must be taken more as a dream of the author rather than as representing any considerable *responsible* sentiment within the race, which, as has been stated, seems at present thoroughly and unqualifiedly American, a fact that must never be overlooked by those seeking to deal with this grave question in a practical manner" (297, emphasis added). Disavowing a key theme in both this and his previous novel, Griggs here emphasizes only one component of Du Boisian double-consciousness—the American over the African. Moreover, the use of the qualifying adjective "responsible" indicates that Griggs knows that some actions are being taken by members of the African American community to assist and form bonds with Africans—Griggs may have had the emigration schemes and missionary programs of the AME's Bishop Turner in mind—but he believes (or at least feels compelled to assert) that these will either have no effect upon or prove counterproductive to reformist efforts in the United States. Furthermore, in describing Africa as a "dream" cut off from African American reality, Griggs, who appears to have had little knowledge of the continent's past and present, returns Africa to where he presumably found it: the fantasy world of (white) fiction. Griggs thus fails to realize that by uncritically employing Africa as a literary device he is imitating Africanist writers and thereby perpetuating the discourse of the black he is striving so strenuously to refute.

Griggs turns his attention to precisely this world of white fiction in "The Hindering Hand," a second appendix that appeared in the third edition to the novel, described on its title page as a review of the "Anti-Negro Crusade" of the negrophobic writer Thomas Dixon. In this attempt to defend black people against racist characterizations, Griggs again demonstrates his ambivalence toward Africa, making some dubious statements about the continent that reinforce rather than overturn prevailing stereotypes. In a section entitled "Backward Africa," Griggs places the blame for the comparative lack of development of the "Negro race" on the continent's geography, claiming that the African coast's lack of "great indentations" and the presence of "immense falls preventing entrance into its greatest river, the Congo," isolated Africans from the rest of the world, forcing them to "rely on their own narrow set of ideas, while the progress of other peoples has been the result of the union of what they begot with what strangers brought them" (314–15). With no apparent trace of irony, Griggs also echoes white racist accusations of African laziness, aggressiveness, and ugliness, asserting that the "soil of Africa fed the Negroes so bountifully that they did not acquire the habit of industry, and with plenty of time on their hands they warred incessantly. The hot, humid atmosphere made them black and sapped their energies. To save them from yellow fever, nature gave them pigment and lost them friends. Other peoples have hesitated to intermarry with them because of their rather unfavorable showing in personal appearance" (315).[9] It thus appears that the only way Griggs believed he could successfully refute unabashedly racist Southern white writers' rhetoric about innate black inferiority was by conceding the argument about Africa's underdevelopment and then dissociating African Americans from Africans, thereby echoing Africanist discourse in a doomed attempt to counter the discourse of the black. This, of course, was no solution to the dilemma facing black Americans at the turn of the century. The inevitable result of denying Africa in favor of America was to confront once more the fact that the United States refused to recognize African American claims of full citizenship.

Pauline Hopkins's Excavation
of a Usable African Past in *Of One Blood*

Cheikh Anta Diop, an African scientist and scholar, African American academics such as Molefi K. Asante and Ivan Van Sertima, and a white classicist, Martin Bernal, among others, have argued that the roots of Western civilization lay in Africa.[10] This assertion has been bolstered by archaeological findings that suggest that Nubia (the Ethiopia of classical writers) may have been the source for Egyptian and thus, according to one line of thinking, Greek culture.[11] Moreover, articles such as a 1991 cover story in *Newsweek* entitled "Was Cleopatra Black?" attest to the considerable influence of African-centered theories on not only African American but also mainstream American culture, inspiring Lefkowitz's vigorous but superficial attack on Afrocentrism, *Not Out of Africa*. The debate over the origins of Western civilization has been raging for centuries, however, and, as noted in the previous chapter, current advocates of Afrocentrism are by no means the first to suggest that Africa was the source of Greco-Roman culture.

Drawing on classical writers such as Herodotus and Diodorus, eighteenth- and nineteenth-century travel accounts of Ethiopia, and recent reports of excavations at Meroe, Pauline Hopkins sought to lend historical accuracy to the fantastic Africa she created in *Of One Blood; Or, the Hidden Self,* apparently the earliest twentieth-century African American novel to be set partly on that continent. Although for the most part the novel avoids confronting the situation in turn-of-the-century Africa, in *Of One Blood* Hopkins does signify on the conventions of white writing about the continent to produce an Ethiopianist fantasy for her black middle-class audience that restores to Africa its former greatness and addresses contemporary American race issues.

Of One Blood was one of three novels by Hopkins that were serialized in the *Colored American Magazine,* a Boston-based journal with which Hopkins was affiliated for four years and to which she contributed a remarkable number of articles, biographical sketches, short stories, and novels. Although rarely acknowledged as such, she served as *de facto* editor-in-chief of the magazine until she was forced out for not being conciliatory enough in her editorial philosophy shortly after an ally of Booker T. Washington bought the periodical in 1904.[12] As Hazel Carby has noted, Hopkins believed that fiction could reach people unacquainted with history and biography, like many of the middle-class readers of the *Colored American Magazine,* and thus she created fictional histories that served a pedagogic and a political function (Introduction, xxxv).[13]

Because *Of One Blood* involves elements derived from a variety of popular genres—mysticism, revivification, mistaken identity, incest, slavery, exploration, lost cities, amalgamation, passing, racial intolerance, and hoodoo—it frustrates attempts at brief summary.[14] The main plot concerns Reuel Briggs, a brilliant but destitute Harvard medical student who conceals his black ancestry. He reluctantly agrees to accompany the affluent Aubrey Livingston, a Southern "white" fellow student who has somehow learned Reuel's secret, to a performance of the Fisk Jubilee Singers. Sometime later, one of these singers, the very light-skinned Dianthe Lusk, is seriously injured in an accident.[15] Reuel's unconventional medical practices succeed in reviving Dianthe after other doctors have given up. Reuel and Dianthe marry, but he leaves immediately to serve as medical officer on an expedition to Ethiopia, the only job he can find and one which Aubrey has arranged for him. In Meroe, Reuel literally stumbles upon the ancient but still functioning city of Telassar and, similar to Dorlan in Griggs's *Unfettered,* is recognized as the heir to the Ethiopian throne. Meanwhile, the devious Aubrey kills his own fiancée and forces Dianthe to marry him. Eventually the three main characters are revealed to be siblings and thus members of the Ethiopian royal family. Reuel returns to America in time to hear Dianthe's dying words, and, in keeping with an ancient Ethiopian penalty for committing murder, Aubrey kills himself. At the end of the novel, Reuel returns to Ethiopia to serve as king and weds Queen Candace, who appears to be a dark-skinned reincarnation of Dianthe.

Well versed in Africa's past (evidenced in part by her many references to classical accounts of Africa in *Of One Blood*) and more aware of the challenges involved in depicting the continent than Griggs, Hopkins not only avoids but actively strives to counter widely held ideas about African "backwardness" and Africans' lack of history. Unlike Griggs, Hopkins clearly recognizes the interconnectedness of Africanist discourse's stereotyped portrayals of Africa and the plantation myth popular in late nineteenth- and early twentieth-century American literature, which depicted slavery as a benevolent institution responsible for repressing black depravity, and she attempts to rebut both. However, when she discusses contemporary Africa, Hopkins exhibits some of the same ambivalence found in Griggs. Although she worries about the effects of imperialism and colonialism on Africa, she nevertheless presents Western influence as essential to the restoration of Ethiopia's greatness. Likewise, while she seems at times to suggest a connection between a triad of Ethiopian-Egyptian deities and the Christian doctrine of three persons in one God—which dovetails with her assertion that the origins of Western civilization lay in Africa—Hopkins nevertheless depicts her contemporary black American protagonist instructing Africans about Christianity. Hopkins's prognosis about the continent's future—like

Ethiopianism generally—is also problematic. Her cyclical theory of races (which depicts Ethiopia as a once and future dream world) links her inevitably to some of the very writers she attempts to subvert: white authors who wrote fiction about Africa at the turn of the century. Further, Hopkins's emphasis on a distant future that has more in common with the continent's past than its present diminishes *Of One Blood*'s relevance to the situation facing people of African descent at the start of the twentieth century.

In *Of One Blood* Hopkins presents an Africa that contrasts with the popular image of the Dark Continent. As Reuel reaches the interior, he "noticed that this was at variance with the European idea respecting Central Africa, which brands these regions as howling wilderness or an uninhabitable country" (565). Rejecting the assertion that Africans have no history, Hopkins depicts a fully preserved and still functioning ancient Ethiopian kingdom beneath and beyond the ruins of the once great city of Meroe.[16] More than two generations before Jan Vansina's groundbreaking work, which established that in their oral traditions African cultures for many centuries have had an accurate and extensive record of their pasts, Hopkins depicts Reuel learning the history of the Ethiopians through a verse song that is accompanied by music, which she apparently intends to be seen as an analogue to the spirituals sung by the Fisk Jubilee Singers early in the novel.

As indicated by her nonfiction book about Africa, *A Primer of Facts Pertaining to the Early Greatness of the African Race and the Possibility of Restoration by Its Descendants,* which she published at her own expense in 1905, Hopkins was convinced that Egyptian and as a result Western culture derived from Meroe and Ethiopia. Her purpose in this short book was to furnish African Americans with a usable, livable history—not simply an African American past as Du Bois sought to provide in *The Souls of Black Folk* but also a glorious African past (a project with which Du Bois would only begin to concern himself in the second decade of the century when he wrote his pageant *The Star of Ethiopia* [1913], discussed in chapter 3, and his historical study *The Negro* [1915]).[17] Signifying on her classical sources, Hopkins depicts the Ethiopians hailing Reuel as King Ergamenes, the name of an actual Ethiopian ruler who lived at the time of Ptolemy II, the Egyptian Pharoah from 285 to 247 B.C. Similarly, at the end of the novel, Briggs/Ergamenes marries Queen Candace, the name of a long line of female Ethiopian rulers. Hopkins clearly sought to educate her *Colored American Magazine* readers about ancient African history in *Of One Blood,* but she was also concerned about addressing the issue of amalgamation and exposing the hypocrisy of contemporary American racial policies.[18]

It was no coincidence that Hopkins wrote a novel about race relations that had "blood" in the title just six years after the U.S. Supreme Court had legitimized the one drop rule in the *Plessy v. Ferguson* decision.[19] Through a lotus lily birthmark, a convention of the adventure novel, the three major American characters in the book are revealed to be siblings and heirs to the Ethiopian throne: Reuel, who hides his mixed birth; Dianthe, who acknowledges and repeatedly suffers because of her African American heritage; and Aubrey, who is unaware that his mother was black.[20] In fact, the title of the novel has at least three meanings. First, in keeping with the monogenetic biblical passage (Acts 17:26), all human beings are "of one blood" and thus deserve to be treated equally. Second, in America, where slave owners often sexually exploited black women so that a combination of "white" and "black" blood flows through the veins of many Southern and a number of Northern families, miscegenation continues to occur frequently because a large number of people in the United States share this same mixed blood. Incest turns out to be a third meaning of the title; at different points in the novel Reuel and Aubrey unwittingly marry their sister, although the relationship between Reuel and Dianthe is not consummated.

Hazel Carby has argued that through the threatened and actual incest in the novel Hopkins depicts turn-of-the-century America as a hellish environment where happy endings are impossible (Introduction, xlvii). However, Hopkins certainly recognized that the likelihood that significant numbers of African Americans would reach Africa and recover a glorious ancient heritage was quite remote.[21] In a passage from the *Primer* steeped with Ethiopianism, Hopkins encourages black Americans to learn about Africa, take pride in their heritage, and promote international friendship with the continent. She does not, however, believe that emigration to Africa is necessary: "What is the obligation of the descendents of the Africans in America?—To help forward the time of restoration. HOW MAY THIS BE DONE?—By becoming thoroughly familiar with the meager details of Ethiopian history, by fostering race pride and international friendship with the Blacks of Africa. Are we obliged to emigrate to Africa to do this successfully?—No. Friendly intercourse and mutual aid and comfort are all that are necessary at the present time. The future is in God's hands and will take care of itself" (20).

The validity of Kevin Gaines's remark that "[i]nevitably . . . the attempt to transcend the racialized circumstances of enslavement and Jim Crow through an identification with ancient Africa as the source of the race's origins imposed contemporary needs on the nostalgia of the past" (110) can clearly be seen in *Of One Blood*. Hopkins offers her readers not only a fantasy that restores to Africa its former greatness but also a more local and much needed fantasy, one in which a white American character must answer for his country's racial prejudice and legal segregation. Reuel explains the state of American race relations to the Ethiopian Prime Minister, Ai, this way: "There, the dark hue of your skin, your waving hair with its trace of crispness, would degrade you below the estate of any man of fair hue and straight locks, belonging to any race outside the Ethiopian, for it is a deep disgrace to have within the veins even one drop of the blood you seem so proud of possessing" (560). Soon afterward, a rich white accompanying Reuel on the expedition named Charlie Vance must answer to Ai, who has Vance completely at his mercy, for America's racial policies. The flabbergasted Vance answers stammeringly that Africans have always been treated as servants in the United States, which provokes the following response from the Ethiopian: "And yet, ye are all of one blood; descended from a common father. Is there ever a flock or herd without its black member? What more beautiful than the satin gloss of the raven's wing, the soft glitter of eyes of blackest tint or the rich black fur of your own native animals?" (585). Ai's black-is-beautiful philosophy no doubt made this a memorable passage for Hopkins's turn-of-the-century African American readers.

Although Hopkins confidently depicts Africa's former greatness and exposes the falsity of white American racial prejudice, she seems less sure of herself when she discusses contemporary Africa and its relationship with the West. Her attitude toward imperialism and colonialism is ambivalent. Although she makes it clear that the real treasure Reuel finds in Africa is his heritage, his participation in an expedition to find and bring back gold and diamonds from Meroe—at one point Reuel dreams "of fame and fortune he would carry home" (516)—goes largely without comment. Even though at the end of the novel he renounces his desire for plunder, coming to view "with serious apprehension, the advance of mighty nations penetrating the dark, mysterious forests of his native land," he has nevertheless returned to the hidden city of the Ethiopians as a kind of colonialist and missionary, "teaching his people all that he has learned in years of contact with modern culture" (621).[22] Although *Of One Blood* trumpets Africa's past glory, its comments on the current situation reflect an African American exceptionalist worldview.

This same conservative impulse eventually tempers Hopkins's initially bold treatment of religious matters. At times it appears that Hopkins is proposing a radical syncretism with an Ethiopian-Egyptian trinity serving as an ancient African source for the Christian doctrine of Father, Son, and Holy Ghost that is consistent with her claims about the African origins of Western culture. However, while Hopkins will suggest that Adam was black, she remains faithful to biblical sources, adhering to the Hamitic myth and withdrawing her implication that the Garden of Eden was in Africa by explaining that the hidden Ethiopian city of Telassar is not the birthplace of humankind but rather named after the one in Mesopotamia.[23] Here I believe Hopkins is conscious of her staunchly Christian black audience and their often literal interpretation of scripture, which may also explain why in the end a contemporary African American educates Africans about Jesus Christ. However, the relationship between Hopkins's Ethiopians and Christianity is more complex than this. They have heard of Christ and even date events by His birth and yet they need Briggs to tell them of His significance. Perhaps because missionary work was one of the few means by which African Americans gained firsthand experience in and knowledge about Africa, Hopkins is asserting the necessity of maintaining this vital link between black Americans and Africa by assigning Reuel the role of spiritual counselor.[24] In depicting Briggs this way, Hopkins may also have been influenced by another scriptural passage related to Ethiopia, (Acts 8:26–40), in which an emissary of Queen Candace becomes the first non-Jew to be baptized as a Christian. Connecting this biblical text to Ethiopianism, Philip Potter notes that through this Ethiopian convert "the Gospel came to Africa before it reached Europe and other continents outside the Jewish diaspora of the Middle East" and thus Africa is "conspicuously present in God's purpose for the redemption of the world" (158).

Like Hopkins's emphasis on Africa's past, her reliance on future-oriented Ethiopianism also mitigates her novel's relevance to the contemporary geopolitical situation. Reuel learns that Ethiopia was once a dominant power, responsible for great achievements in literature and other arts which were copied first by the Egyptians and later by the Greeks. However, as one of the Ethiopians, echoing Stewart's 1833 "Address," reveals, "Stiff-necked, haughty, no conscience but that of intellect, awed not by God's laws, worshipping Mammon, sensual, unbelieving, God has punished us as he promised in the beginning. Gone are our ancient glories, our humbled pride cries aloud to God in the travail of our soul" (558). Later Ai explicitly links Africa's destined return to glory (which the novel suggests will someday be accomplished through Reuel) to the impending decline of the materialist West when, in addressing Charlie Vance, he warns all white Westerners: "Fair-haired worshippers of Mammon, do you not know that you have been weighed in the balance and found wanting? that your course is done? that Ethiopia's bondage is about over, her travail passed?" (585). Hopkins's cyclical view of races, however, recapitulates a key binary opposition at the heart of white depictions of Africa by presenting the continent as a former dreamworld that will awake from its present nightmare and reclaim its earlier glory. Beyond this, by having Reuel return to the underground city of Telassar at the end of the novel, Hopkins does not offer or even point toward a viable political solution to either Africa's current subjugation by the colonial powers or black Americans' tenuous status in the United States at the turn of the century. Rather, as Claudia Tate has noted, "Much like Ralph Ellison's nameless hero of the *Invisible Man* . . . Briggs resorts to a state of other-worldly suspension to await divine racial intervention" (207).

Although *Of One Blood* does not effectively address the present situation in Africa, the novel occupies a significant position in African American writing about Africa. One of the earliest known fictional accounts of the continent by a black American writer, this generic hybrid claimed Africa as the origin of Western civilization over eighty years before the unfolding of recent debates over Afrocentrism. However, the current political controversy should not obscure the fact Hopkins wrote the serial expressly for a black middle-class audience as a kind of antidote at a time when racism and legal discrimination against African Americans had become pandemic.[25]

John E. Bruce's Ethiopianist Investigation of Anglo-Saxon Race Prejudice in *The Black Sleuth*

During a life that began in slavery in Maryland in 1856 and whose culmination in 1924 was commemorated with a hero's funeral in Harlem by Marcus Garvey's UNIA, John Edward Bruce not only worked as a columnist, editor, novelist, and historian but also served as a conduit linking people of African descent separated by age and geography. A prolific letter writer and a member of several African American organizations, including the Negro Society for Historical Research, which he founded with Arthur A. Schomburg in 1911, Bruce knew key nineteenth-century figures such as Alexander Crummell and Edward Blyden, met and corresponded with Africans who had studied in or visited the United States, wrote for African periodicals and Duse Mohammed Ali's London-based *African Times and Orient Review,* was one of Marcus Garvey's most important contacts when the Jamaican first came to America in 1916, and later became an important liaison between the UNIA and African organizations. Bruce not only sought to educate himself about Africa's past like Hopkins but also had extensive knowledge about contemporary Africa.[26]

One of the only scholars to devote serious attention to Bruce, Ralph L. Crowder regards him as representative of a considerable amount of nationalist feeling that formed a legitimate alternative to the positions espoused by those on either side of the Booker T. Washington/W.E.B. Du Bois controversy ("John Edward Bruce," 48). Crowder offers one explanation for Bruce's relative obscurity today—his refusal, unlike Washington and Du Bois, to court white recognition or approval: "His audience was the Black community and he directed his attention to it alone. He refused to join organizations supported or directed by whites. Thus, Bruce remained outside of 'white American History' and was excluded from its written registry" (62). Another reason that Bruce is largely unknown today may be that he produced no major works elaborating his personal and/or political philosophy, along the lines of Washington's *Up from Slavery* or Du Bois's *The Souls of Black Folk*. Like many African American "street scholars" (to use Crowder's term) after him, Bruce published short books about African American history and political pamphlets, often at his own expense. His only novel in book form, *The Awakening of Hezekiah Jones* (1916), concerning the role of black Americans in politics, has received almost no critical attention. Nearly fifty years after Bruce's death, some of his newspaper pieces and speeches were published in *The Selected Writings of John Edward Bruce,* which helped to generate some short-lived critical interest in the author.

Bruce's serialized novel *The Black Sleuth* was not widely distributed or discussed when first published in a small black magazine from 1907 to 1909 and is virtually unknown today; therefore, it can hardly be called a major work.[27] Nevertheless, this fascinating serial contains one of the boldest attacks on Anglo-Saxon prejudices about people of African descent in early African American fiction. Similar to Pauline Hopkins's *Of One Blood, The Black Sleuth* uses conventions from popular fiction, including the detective story, in a tale that counters the dominant Eurocentric view of the world with an Ethiopianist one. Unlike Hopkins's novel, however, which relies heavily on fantasy and mysticism and emphasizes Africa's past glory, Bruce's serial is largely realistic, focused on the present, and implicitly anticolonial.

If considered solely as a mystery, *The Black Sleuth* is problematic and incomplete because the detective plot does not begin in earnest until the story is more than half over and is never satisfactorily resolved. Although the first chapter mentions the International Detective Agency run by Samuel Hunter, refers to a "case" involving Capt. George De Forrest, and states that Hunter, much to the prejudiced American seaman's chagrin, has decided to put a young African on the case to "run down the thief, or thieves" (2), the detective plot does not start until the eleventh chapter. Moreover, this plot is a bit confusing. Although we are told at the start of chapter 11 that "our hero," the young African Sadipe Okukenu, "round[s] up on foreign shore four of the most skillful swindlers on the continent" (presumably Bradshawe, Crenshawe, Hodder, and their unnamed accomplice whose plot to steal De Forrest's large diamond dominates chapters 11 through 17), their capture has not taken place nor has the gem actually been stolen when the novel stops at the end of chapter 17.[28] Bruce's primary concerns, as indicated by his devotion of nine of the novel's seventeen chapters to what I will call the African abroad plot, are counterdiscursive and didactic. Through the African abroad plot he signifies on the white African adventure tale to expose the narrow-mindedness and inaccuracy of white American prejudices about people of African descent so that black Americans will embrace their African heritage and forge alliances with the people of that continent. Instead of an intrepid white adventurer confronting the savagery and unraveling the mysteries of Africa, in *The Black Sleuth* a brave African student learns firsthand about racial prejudice and violence in the United States.

The African abroad plot and the detective plot are not, in fact, as discrete as they first appear. In the early chapters of the novel, Bruce implies that the father of Mojola and Sadipe Okukenu agrees to allow his sons to journey abroad, to England and America respectively, for politically strategic reasons and not because he wants them to be "civilized" and "Christianized." The Yoruba knows his sons will not be happy in the West, but he sends them on what amounts to spy missions to "learn more about the white man in his native land" (4). Looking at Mojola's sojourn in England and Sadipe's student years in the United States in this light, it becomes clear that the African abroad plot makes the detective plot possible. On the one hand, Sadipe's experiences in the United States, and the South in particular, provide the future detective with important insight into the (white) criminal mind. His encounters with rude, conceited, prejudiced, and acquisitive white Southerners proves invaluable in thwarting the schemes of the confidence men he later pursues, such as Bradshawe and his gang.[29] On the other hand, Bruce suggests that all of the time Sadipe has spent in the West, first as a student in the United States and later as a detective in England and on the European mainland, will help the African protect his people from the designs of colonialists and imperialists when he returns to Africa.

Notable from the start of *The Black Sleuth* is Bruce's use of an expanded, black Atlantic (to use Paul Gilroy's phrase) frame of reference by which white American prejudices and the status quo of racial injustice in the United States can be evaluated.[30] In addition to mentioning the International Detective Agency "with offices in all the great capitals of Europe" and its employment of "hundreds of thief catchers—men of every civilized race" (1), Bruce begins by placing white Americans in distant locations, namely England and Africa, where their attitudes and practices do not always meet with approval. In the first chapter, for example, George De Forrest, the Southern son of the captain of a slave ship, is depicted as being at odds with his environment: "Although he was an American by birth, he was English by adoption, but with the foolish American antipathy and prejudice to people of darker hue" (2).

De Forrest's dislocation intensifies in the second chapter, set in South Africa. Observing the perfect physique of Mojola Okukenu, De Forrest, revealing his slaveholder origins, sees the black man in physical terms only: "'Look!' said the captain to his friends. 'He is as straight as an arrow; what muscles, what a chest development, what a splendid bearing. God! he is a picture'" (3). Later, however, De Forrest is greatly dismayed when he finds Mojola to be both better educated and better spoken than himself, the African being not only a polymath but a polyglot. Bruce does not mince his words in describing for his black American readers the shortcomings of De Forrest and others like him: "The captain had not expected this kind of English from a half-naked 'African savage,' as Negroes in Africa are called by complacent egotists in the white race, who imagine that civilization, which, as Da Rocha[31] says, is a relative term, began and will end with them" (3). It is quite likely that Bruce based his character Mojola Okukenu on the similarly named Majola Agbebi, the Baptist Yoruba leader to whom he was introduced by Edward Blyden during the West African's visit to America in 1903. Shepperson reports that Agbebi's ideas caused Bruce to embrace and cherish fully his own blackness, and that in 1907 (the year *The Black Sleuth* began appearing in *McGirt's Magazine*) Bruce led a group of African Americans in New York who "sought to get 11 October observed each year by Negro Americans as 'Majola Agbebi Day'" ("Notes," 309–10).

In the subsequent interview between De Forrest and Mojola, the Yoruba, echoing Hopkins's *Of One Blood,* contends that the origins of Western civilization are African and espouses Ethiopianist teleology. Much to De Forrest's exasperation, Mojola asserts: "Before your race had a civilization or a religion, mine was, and from it your race has borrowed and stolen all that was best and most useful in art, science, religion, letters, politics and government." (6). Moreover, Mojola predicts that the current imbalance between Africa and the West will be reversed:

> Africans will absorb and assimilate your learning, will study your system of government, and will analyze and dissect whatever is best and most useful to them in your civilization, whatever is rational and reasonable in your religion, whatever is practical and just in your legal jurisprudence, and then construct her own code of morals and ethics for use against the time when "Ethiopia shall suddenly stretch out her hands unto God." She will be equipped with all the learning and wisdom and knowledge of all the races of the earth with whom she has come in contact, and will be ready to take her proper place among the nations. She has no fears as to her future. Her star is in the ascendant. She stands upon the threshold of a future pregnant with magnificent possibilities. (9)

Similarly, subverting De Forrest's earlier emphasis on Mojola's physique, Bruce implies the inevitability of a shift in the political fortunes of the races through the physical and moral contrast between the interlocuters. Unlike the older white seaman with his "big, fat right arm, which was lazily resting on the round table in the cabin" (9), the young, athletic African neither smokes nor drinks alcohol. Mojola also lacks the grasping materialism of Westerners like De Forrest, a collector of curios, whose desire for possessions is emblematic of the white men who continue to pillage Africa. At De Forrest's insistence, Mojola accepts payment for a huge diamond he uses solely for teaching geology but which the captain covets. This transaction causes the African to remark that the "accumulation and hoarding of wealth is an invention of the white man, and Africa is just now the centre of his activity. He is plundering Africa like a buccaneer in quest of gold and diamonds and ivory" (9).

By the end of their encounter, De Forrest claims that Mojola has "converted" him from his previously prejudiced views to a friendly disposition toward blacks. Although the Captain's subsequent doubts about the ability of a "nigger" such as Sadipe to solve his case contradicts his assertion of a change in attitudes, Bruce's purpose has not been to reform racists like De Forrest but rather to "convert" his African American readers from the prejudiced ideas they may have inherited from white society and the discourse of the black to a positive outlook toward themselves and their ancestral home. Anticipating late twentieth-century theorists such as Michel Foucault, Edward Said, and Christopher Miller, who emphasize the role that specific discourses play in the objectification of peoples, Bruce pinpoints the printed sources responsible for erroneous and clichéd perceptions of Africa. In the third chapter, De Forrest finds his prejudiced views about the continent openly contradicted by his senses: "Here, in the heart of Africa, Africa which he had been taught to believe was the home of a wild and barbarous and heathenish people who ate good, white missionaries three times a day and each other, occasionally, *according to the missionary reports and friendly newspapers*. He was standing face to face with one of these heathen and barbarians who was better educated than himself, who spoke purer English, and who had a better general idea of books than he, and a more analytical mind" (7, emphasis added). Bruce, moreover, reverses pervasive Africanist oppositions such as black versus white, light versus dark, and good versus evil. When De Forrest asks Mojola if he was "scared" at seeing a locomotive upon arriving in England, the Yoruba replies that he was only afraid once in his life: "that was when I first saw a man of your race, who came to our country wearing European clothes, the like of which we had never before seen. My people declared it to be their belief that he was the devil, an evil spirit sent to persecute and torment us. We Africans, I must here add, associate the white man with the prince of evil and all that is wicked and bad" (5).[32] Without question this kind of a reversal of racist binarism was notable for Bruce's day.

The dislocation of American characters continues in the fifth chapter when the serial shifts its attention from Mojola to his brother Sadipe, the true protagonist of the novel. This time it is a Northern rather than a Southern white American who finds his beliefs under scrutiny. Unlike De Forrest, the "down-easter" Captain Barnard, "like most of the men from that part of America . . . had a great deal of sympathy for the Negro" (11). Nevertheless, the rhetoric he uses differs only slightly from that of his more blatantly racist fellow American seaman, as, for example, when the Northerner tells Sadipe's father that a sojourn in the United States would be helpful to the young man in uplifting his "benighted race." Like the white Northerner Charlie Vance in *Of One Blood,* Barnard finds himself called upon by an African to answer for segregation and racial injustice in the United States. After asserting to Sadipe's father that "America is the most Christian country on the globe" and that he "could not send Sadipe to a better place than America; it is a progressive country, and black men there enjoy the same rights as white men" (12), the captain is asked about America's past history of slavery and present practice of lynching. As a result, Barnard finds himself as flabbergasted as De Forrest was in the presence of Mojola: "Here in the very heart of Africa he was standing face to face with one of her [sable] sons, who was discussing with him a question of ethics that made him blush for shame for 'the most Christian nation on earth'" (12). In part because of the honesty of Barnard's answer to his question, the elder Okukenu allows Sadipe to travel to the United States.

When *The Black Sleuth* shifts to America in chapters 6 through 10, Bruce enables his readers to see race relations in the United States through the eyes of an African. After a benign eighteen months spent in Maine under the tutelage of Barnard's sister, Sadipe receives a baptism into the fiery realities of American racial prejudice when he travels South to attend the Eckington College for Colored Youth. Insulted by a conductor at the train station in Washington, D.C., and later threatened with physical violence for his defiant refusal to move to the Jim Crow car, Sadipe's horror intensifies when he sees the conditions at the Negro college. In a thinly veiled attack on Booker T. Washington and his Tuskegee Institute, Bruce depicts the open hostility of the white community to the school, the low academic standards of the college, and the cowardice and hypocrisy of its principal, Professor Swift (whose name itself may be a parody of one of Washington's nicknames, the Wizard). When Sadipe learns from Swift of the rigidly enforced segregation within the town, he declares: "This is all very strange, indeed. I had no idea that human beings could be so intolerant of the rights of others, and all this in free America. I cannot understand it, sir" (24). Swift's pathetic response contrasts sharply with the boldness Sadipe exhibited on the train: "Neither can we . . . but we are obliged to submit to these things because we are helpless and can do no better" (24). Sadipe decides to leave almost immediately, writing to a man he met on the train that Eckington "is just an ordinary school, the promoters of which have a most extraordinary ambition to make it a college. Its curriculum does not compare with that of our little village school in Maine" (26). Through the crass prejudice of the local white community, the poor quality of the school, and Swift's accommodationism, Bruce throws an ironic light upon the principal's fund-raising trips in which he tells "northern audiences what a wonderful work he was doing toward the moral redemption and regeneration of the colored race, and how badly his college needed an endowment of $30,000 to put it on its feet, so that it could begin the work of solving on practical lines the race problem which is still with us" (25).

Before Sadipe begins his detective career, Bruce extends the African abroad plot to give the lie to not only white man's burden rhetoric and white American racial prejudice once more but also their acceptance by some black Americans. On the day that Sadipe leaves, he and the other students of the college are invited to attend a talk by Rev. Silas Skinner, a white Southerner who has served as a missionary in Africa.[33] After the speech, Swift praises Skinner's zeal and "self-sacrificing spirit" in carrying "the message of good-will and brotherhood to those who sit in darkness" (30) and then calls upon Sadipe to make a comment. As in the exchange between De Forrest and Mojola, Sadipe's eloquence and superior knowledge contrasts with Skinner's platitudes and misinformation. The African points out that "the so-called 'heathens' of Africa are not nearly so barbarous and inhospitable to the stranger within their gates, nor are they as inhuman and bloodthirsty as the so-called civilized white Christians of the South who burn Negroes at the stake and hang them to trees and telegraph poles, as I have learned that they do, since my sojourn in this country" (30). Sadipe's statement bears a striking resemblance to an assertion made by Prince Momolu Massaquoi, the son of Sierra Leonean royalty who began studying at Nashville's Central Tennessee College at sixteen years of age, when he addressed a meeting of American clergymen in 1894. Despite American talk about the "savage in Africa," Massaquoi, who witnessed a lynching in Nashville in 1892, contended that in the United States there was "more savagery than I have seen in all my days in Africa" (quoted in McCarthy, 148). In Sadipe's rebuttal, which nearly results in a race riot once the white community learns what he has said, he goes on to echo his brother with the Ethiopianist prediction that "the so-called weaker nations" are awakening and their refusal to engage "in cruel warfare to extend their power," as the white nations do, will prove to be their greatest strength (30).[34] Significantly, the African's statements succeed in converting his fellow students— as they presumably converted many of Bruce's black readers—to a new way of looking at Africa and themselves. Through the Skinner episode, Bruce also provides an early condemnation of missionary activity in the continent, a position that will be echoed in the texts of later writers, particularly Langston Hughes, Richard Wright, Lorraine Hansberry, and Alice Walker.

Bruce attributes Sadipe's success as a detective in the later chapters of *The Black Sleuth* to his being African and his having experienced racial injustice in the American South. A racialist like the early Du Bois, Bruce believed that each race possessed inherited characteristics, talents for certain arts, sciences, and endeavors that distinguished it from other peoples.[35] Sadipe's superior memory for faces and uncanny powers of detection derive from his African heritage. Moreover, his knowledge of the white criminal mind and familiarity with Anglo-Saxon prejudice enable him to outwit his foes by donning various disguises and using his status as an Ellisonian invisible man in white society to his advantage.

In contrast to the wily Miss Crenshawe, who uses pencil and paper to sketch the unsuspecting De Forrest in order to be sure to remember his features, Sadipe only needs to look carefully at this seductive thief once and he is able to recall Miss Crenshawe's face forever: "he had photographed her face in his memory, and no matter what her disguise in the future, he would know her" (42). Sadipe specifically attributes this ability to his origins, telling his boss, Mr. Hunter, "an African, and I am told a North American Indian, never forget a face they have once seen" (48).

Sadipe also has such superior powers of observation and deduction that he can read a person's character by carefully attending to his or her words and actions. Sadipe, in fact, sniffs out the criminal conspiracy of Bradshawe and his cohorts even before they have a chance to concoct it. After overhearing inconsistencies in statements Bradshawe makes to another man, Sadipe discovers that the supposed colonel is a fraud and puts him and his gang under surveillance. Similarly, late in the novel when Sadipe penetrates the conspirators' London home disguised as a peddler selling African wares, he tells the fortunes of Miss Crenshawe and the servants in the house with astounding accuracy. However, Bruce is at pains to distinguish the African's ratiocinative abilities from hoodoo and mysticism, which play key roles in Hopkins's *Of One Blood:* Sadipe's success as a soothsayer derives from his powers of detection rather than some occult knowledge.

He tells Hunter that "he did not know one card from another and had merely guessed at the things he had told the girls . . . and their mistress" (61–62).

In addition to dressing as a peddler, Sadipe impersonates a waiter, an African student, and a rich African merchant in his pursuit of the would-be diamond thieves who are themselves experts at disguise. However, it is the combination of Sadipe's innate abilities and his dark complexion that proves to be his greatest weapon against crooks. Sadipe is able to exploit the low opinion most whites have of blacks, which he learned firsthand during his sojourn in the United States, because his skin color "disarm[s] all suspicion as to his true character" (44). Echoing Bruce's own ideas about inherited racial characteristics, Hunter tells his ace detective, "You Africans have many advantages over us Europeans, and there are some things which you can do better than we when you try. Your black face will be an important aid in the capture of [Bradshawe] (if you capture him), and your knowledge of French will come in handy, for in the presence of strangers he always converses in that language, and he will never suspect that you understand that tongue" (49).

Although *The Black Sleuth* does not explicitly state that Sadipe will return to Africa and use the knowledge he has gained from his experiences abroad to help his people, there are at least two hints that this in fact will be the case. The first is the prediction Sadipe's father makes about his son. He tells Captain Barnard: "I have no fear about [Sadipe] not returning to his home here in Africa. The Okukenus will not submit to oppression and injustice in any form, no matter where they are, and if Sadipe is not well treated in your country he will find a way to get back to the land of his fathers" (13). Because everything else that the elder Okukenu has said about his son has been proven accurate, it follows that Sadipe will one day return to fulfill his father's prophecy. Second, given the invocation of Ethiopianism in the novel, it is possible to read Sadipe as an allegorical figure representing his entire continent. Bruce implicitly argues that just as the young Yoruba has succeeded brilliantly as a detective despite having been insulted, threatened with violence, underestimated, and overlooked, so seemingly prostrate Africa will draw upon talents and resources unsuspected in the West to become an autonomous and powerful force in the world.

The boldest portrayals of Africa in early twentieth-century black American fiction appear in novels intended for predominantly black audiences, Hopkins's *Of One Blood* and Bruce's *The Black Sleuth*. Although these texts use conventions from one or more popular genres, Hopkins and Bruce consciously construct them as generic hybrids. Thus, whereas *The Leopard's*

Claw is little more than a rather clumsy depiction of white people lost in the jungles of West Africa, *Of One Blood* grafts a number of different genres onto the African adventure tale and *The Black Sleuth* aspires to be much more than a detective story. With their jarring mixture of sentimental fiction and polemical essay, Griggs's *Unfettered* and *The Hindered Hand* may also strive for a kind of generic hybridization; however, because of his desire, at least in part, to appease and appeal to a white audience, Griggs's novels lack the revisionary thrust of *Of One Blood* and *The Black Sleuth*.

Moreover, because they successfully manipulate conventions from popular fiction to serve revisionary ends, the novels of Hopkins and Bruce far exceed those of Ellis and Griggs in regard to providing their readers with a new way of looking at Africa. Ellis merely imitates the white African adventure tale without questioning its legitimacy. Despite Griggs's revisionary aspirations, he reveals a very limited knowledge about Africa and fails to see the connection between Africanist discourse and the discourse of the black. In contrast, Hopkins and Bruce attempt to educate their black readers about Africa; *Of One Blood* focuses on the continent's ancient history, while *The Black Sleuth* concerns itself with contemporary Africa. Both novelists incorporate Ethiopianism into their works, predicting a glorious future for people of African descent. Neither, however, clearly explains how this will come about. Hopkins, echoing Griggs, implies that black Americans will spearhead Africa's redemption; Bruce, however, does not espouse African American exceptionalism. Although *The Black Sleuth*, unlike *Of One Blood*, directly addresses current conditions in Africa, there is still a gap between the colonial present depicted in Bruce's novel and the bright, autonomous future foretold by Mojola and Sadipe Okukenu. Bruce seems to be suggesting that doubly conscious Africans like Sadipe, and perhaps by extension doubly conscious African Americans such as Bruce himself— that is, people proud of and secure in their African heritage but also knowledgeable about the ways of Westerners—will be the ones to initiate the process of Africa's redemption. However, exactly how soon or by what means this goal will be achieved remains unclear.

3

The New Negro and Africa

Finally, we come to the most sophisticated of all race motives—the conscious and deliberate threading back of the historic sense of group tradition to the cultural backgrounds of Africa. Undoubtably this motive arose in a purely defensive and imitative reaction. But it has grown stronger and more positive year by year. Africa is naturally romantic. It is poetic capital of the first order, even apart from the current mode of idealizing it in reaction from the boredom of ultra-sophistication.

ALAIN LOCKE, "THE NEGRO IN AMERICAN CULTURE"

One three centuries removed
From scenes his fathers loved
Spicy grove and cinnamon tree,
What is Africa to me?

COUNTEE CULLEN, "HERITAGE"

During the Harlem Renaissance period, Ethiopianism continued to affect African American representations of Africa profoundly. In keeping with Marcus Garvey's cultural, religious, and political project, poems, essays, and reviews appearing in the UNIA's weekly newspaper, the *Negro World,* explicitly invoked Ethiopianism.[1] Those writers most closely associated with the New Negro Movement, however—Alain Locke (who announced the "Negro Renaissance" and gave it shape), Langston Hughes, Countee Cullen, and Claude McKay—deliberately sought to distance themselves from the previous generation of African American writing and its monumental approach to Africa. In his essays Locke theorized about the relationship between African and African American art and advocated practical steps to encourage cooperation between Africa and black America. Although they were certainly influenced by Ethiopianism, Hughes, Cullen, and McKay strove to put Locke's more political dictums into practice, often rejecting the previous generation's desire to civilize all things African as well as the monumentalists' "dignified" art (to use Moses' term) in order to celebrate the "urban primitivism" and "counterculturalism" of 1920s Harlem ("More Stately," 43).[2]

Ethiopianism figured not only in the UNIA's African Orthodox Church, but also in its ambitious black literary aesthetic and long-range political objectives. Just as Ralph Waldo Emerson's landmark "American Scholar" nearly a century earlier advocated literary autonomy for the United States, so Garvey's 1924 *Negro World* essay "African Fundamentalism" issued a call for black people to "create and emulate heroes of [our] own" and to "inspire a literature and promulgate a doctrine of our own without any apologies to the powers that be" (4). Echoing and expanding upon the Ethiopianist rhetoric of texts by the previous generation of African American writers, particularly Bruce's *The Black Sleuth,* Garvey asserts, "The world today is indebted to us for the benefits of civilization. They stole our arts and sciences from Africa. Then why should we be ashamed of ourselves? Their *modern improvements* are but *duplicates* of a grander civilization that we reflected thousands of years ago, without the advantage of what is buried and still hidden, to be resurrected and reintroduced by the intelligence of our generation and our posterity" (5, emphasis in original). As this passage reveals, the cyclical view of history associated with Ethiopianist teleology, which figures so prominently in Hopkins's *Of One Blood,* remained intact in Garveyism. Yet, in contrast to nineteenth- and turn-of-the-century promulgators of Ethiopianism (with the exception of Bruce, who would assume a powerful position in the UNIA), Garvey was fiercely anticolonial. He was not, however, anti-imperialist; his ultimate goal was to replace European colonial rule over peoples of African descent throughout the world with a black Empire of his own making that was "united in one *grand racial hierarchy*": "Let no religious scruples, no political machination divide us, but let us hold together under all climes and in every country, making among ourselves a Racial Empire upon which 'the sun shall never set'" (5, emphasis in original). Sensational declarations such as this won Garvey an enormous following during the heyday of his movement; they also incensed black intellectuals such as Du Bois, whose quarrel with Garvey is well known, and George Schuyler, who, in addition to his career as a journalist, wrote more novels in the first half of the twentieth century about Africa than any other black American writer, many of them sharply critical of race chauvinism such as Garvey's.

Alain Locke contributed to the *Negro World*, and several of his well-known statements about African art and culture were compatible with UNIA doctrine; however, his political ideas about the continent differed markedly from Garvey's. In "The Legacy of Ancestral Arts" (1925), although Locke sees no direct African influence on black American art, he predicts that African American plastic artists can and will find inspiration in African sculpture and crafts. The dubious generalizations Locke makes about the art of Africa in this essay—e.g., that it is characterized by rigidity and lacks the spontaneity of African American artistic expression—however, undermine his claims about a lack of continuity between black American and African art.[3] Turning his attention to literature, in "Negro Youth Speaks" (1925) Locke asserts that the younger generation of African American writers "can no longer be twitted as 'cultural nondescripts' or accused of 'being out of love with their own nativity.' They have instinctive love and pride of race, and, spiritually compensating for the present lacks of America, ardent respect and love for Africa, the motherland" (52–53).

Locke makes more specific and more politically pointed statements about the continent and how African Americans should respond to it in his 1924 *Opportunity* essay "Apropos of Africa." Here he begins by lamenting the fact that "politically, economically, scientifically, [and] culturally" Africa has "engaged the Caucasian and primarily the European mind" much more than it has that of the black American (350–51). He attributes this lack of sustained, tangible African American interest in the continent to the legacy of slavery, but predicts that as African Americans gain prosperity they will "exhibit the homing instinct and turn back physically or mentally, hopefully and helpfully, to the land of their origins" just as Jewish and Irish people have done (351). Defining the black American as "the true Pan-African," Locke appears to echo the African American exceptionalism of the previous generation of writers as well as Garveyism by asserting that the African American should assume the decisive role "in constructive Pan-African thought and endeavor" (351).

However, Locke prefaces his program to encourage cooperation between Africans and black Americans with a statement that distinguishes his approach to Africa from that of Garvey and turn-of-the-century Ethiopianists. The central passage of "Apropos of Africa" backs away from African American exceptionalism, emphasizes cooperation, and attacks the paternalism at the heart of efforts to "civilize" the continent: "We now see that the missionary condescension of the past generations in their attitude toward Africa was a pious but sad mistake. In taking it, we have fallen into the snare of enemies and have given grievous offence to our brothers. We must realize that in some respects we need what Africa has to give us as much as, or even more than, Africa needs what we in turn have to give her; and that unless we approach Africa in the spirit of the finest reciprocity, our efforts will be ineffectual or harmful" (352).

Eschewing the hazy, mystical Ethiopianism that often characterized not only the writers of the previous generation but also Garveyism, Locke offers a three point plan that stresses practicality. First, echoing Hopkins's *Primer of Facts,* he calls for "matter of fact information about Africa" past and present to be made widely and readily available (354–55). Second, Locke advocates direct black American contact with Africa and Africans through travel and student exchanges. Third, he sees a need for increased academic interest and activity in Africa, particularly in the fields of art and archaeology. Negro colleges, Locke believes, should spearhead these scholarly efforts. Despite the specificity of this program, Locke often failed in his writing to adhere to his own prescriptions, as James B. Barnes has pointed out. Citing Locke's use of the phrase "the homing instinct" in the same essay in which his practical prescriptions appear, Barnes asserts that "[d]espite his petition for scientific scholarship and his status as a leading and recognized interpreter of what he termed the African heritage or legacy, Locke was often as ambiguous and enigmatic in terms of definition as was the theme he was endeavoring to define" (104). Despite such inconsistency, Locke, particularly in "Apropos of Africa," advocated a new, historically grounded way of looking at and, by extension, writing about Africa.

Authors directly and indirectly connected with the New Negro movement acted upon Locke's recommendations in their poems, dramatic works, autobiographies, and novels. Posing the famous question "What is Africa to me?" Countee Cullen's poem "Heritage" (1925) is rightly cited as a key Harlem Renaissance text about Africa. Implicit within this question is Cullen's rejection of certain received ideas (white and black) about the continent and his desire to find a new meaning for himself. Unlike the previous generation, a number of black authors who wrote about Africa from the late 1910s through the early 1940s actually went to the continent in order to answer Cullen's question for themselves. The initial journeys to Africa by Du Bois and Hughes provide a vivid illustration of this point. When Du Bois experienced the continent for the first time in December 1923, he had reached the age of fifty-five, played a major role in Pan-African activities for over twenty years, and written poetry, fiction, a pageant, essays, and a historical work about the continent. In contrast, at the start of his career as a writer, Hughes reached Dakar as a twenty-one-year-old ship's mess boy in June of 1923—five months before Du Bois arrived in Liberia on a diplomatic mission.

Although the writers affiliated with the New Negro Movement responded to, or, in the case of Hughes, anticipated, Locke's call for direct links to and firsthand information about Africa, not everyone agreed with Locke and Garvey that a specifically black aesthetic should be pursued.

Although, as he later remarked, he knew it was "treason at a time when there was so much talk about African heritage" (*Black and Conservative*, 157), the iconoclastic Schuyler sent a dissenting view to the editors of the *Nation*. After a long delay, the magazine eventually published his "The Negro-Art Hokum" in June 1926 along with Hughes's famous response to it, "The Negro Artist and the Racial Mountain." Schuyler's essay sounds the alarm about the consequences of pursuing a distinctively black arts movement, particularly one organized along the lines outlined by Garvey in "African Fundamentalism," in white racist America. Terming the African American a "lampblacked Anglo-Saxon," whose self-consciousness is identical to that of his white counterpart, Schuyler characterizes the primitivist impulse of much of the art of the Harlem Renaissance as the plot of white racists abetted by black stooges. He concludes by seizing upon the key word "peculiar"—often used to characterize slavery in the nineteenth century and the adjective Du Bois chose to describe the "sensation" of double-consciousness. In contrast to Du Bois, however, Schuyler emphasizes this word's pejorative connotations only: "On this baseless premise, so flattering to the white mob, that the blackamoor is inferior and fundamentally different, is erected the postulate that he must needs be peculiar; and that when he attempts to portray life through the medium of art, it must of necessity be a peculiar art. While such reasoning may seem conclusive to the majority of Americans, it must be rejected with a loud guffaw by intelligent people" (312).

"The Negro Artist and the Racial Mountain" emphasizes the African heritage of black Americans that "The Negro-Art Hokum" so completely discounts. Hughes invokes the spiritual purity variation of Ethiopianism in his description of jazz—"the tom-tom of joy and laughter"—as an anti-toxin for the poison of the "white world, a world of subway trains, and work, work, work" and in his championing of lower class African American peculiarity over "American standardizations" (308, 306). By asserting that "perhaps these common people will give to the world its truly great Negro artist, the one who is not afraid to be himself," Hughes implicitly argues for the existence of a true and distinctive African American self-consciousness (306). In his closing sentences, Hughes denies that an internal struggle bedevils the new generation of African American artists and borrows the imagery of the monumentalists: "We younger Negro artists who create now intend to express our individual dark-skinned selves without fear or shame. If white people are pleased we are glad. If they are not, it doesn't matter. We know we are beautiful. And ugly, too. The tom-tom cries and the tom-tom laughs. If colored people are pleased we are glad. If they are not, their displeasure doesn't matter either. We build our temples for tomorrow, strong as we know how, and we stand on top of the mountain, free within ourselves" (309).

Brimming with defiance and self-confidence, this statement nonetheless fails to address the issue of audience raised in Johnson's "The Dilemma of the Negro Writer" two years later. Reflecting on the Harlem Renaissance period in an article written the year before he died, Hughes acknowledges the very real question of how the black artist who cannot gain an audience, white or black, is to function by juxtaposing his idealistic declaration of black literary independence in 1926 with the failure of *Fire!!* magazine shortly thereafter. Saying "Amen" to "The Negro Artist and the Racial Mountain," Wallace Thurman, Aaron Douglas, John P. Davis, Bruce Nugent, Gwendolyn Bennett, and Zora Neale Hurston joined with Hughes to launch what they intended to be "a Negro quarterly of the arts to *epater le bourgeois,* to burn up a lot of the old stereotyped Uncle Tom ideas of the past, and to provide us with an outlet for publishing not existing in the hospitable but limited pages of *The Crisis* or *Opportunity*" ("The Twenties," 35). Ignored by white newspapers and magazines and attacked by the black press, *Fire!!* folded after one issue, leaving the seven members of the editorial board with a substantial debt to pay. Clearly whether to pursue a specifically black aesthetic was not the only issue facing African American artists during the Harlem Renaissance. The questions of who the audience for their works was and what genres and methods they should employ to reach that audience remained pertinent, especially for those writers who depicted Africa in their literary texts.

Reflecting their generation's desire to pursue new approaches to Africa, black American writers after 1920 began to depict the continent in dramatic works and autobiographies with greater frequency. Like Hopkins's *Of One Blood* and Bruce's *The Black Sleuth,* much of the African American drama of the Harlem Renaissance period—particularly those plays and pageants that depicted Africa—was written for a black audience and was intentionally didactic. The plays about Africa written during the 1920s and 1930s tended to be short, most of them being limited to one act. Likewise, even though the pageants of the period sometimes lasted as long as two hours, with their emphasis on spectacle these works were short on speaking lines. In contrast, Shirley Graham's *Tom-Tom* (1932) stands as a unique hybrid. Intended for a mixed audience, this three-act opera possesses a complexity and power unprecedented among African American dramatic works about Africa of the day. Depicting three decisive moments in black history and set in both Africa and the United States, *Tom-Tom* combines the spectacle of pageantry with character development and a tightly constructed plot. In addition, Graham, who later wrote a master's thesis entitled "The Survival of

Africanism in American Music," heeds Locke's call for both direct connections with African art (by incorporating authentic African rhythms into her musical score and linking these to both nineteenth-century spirituals and twentieth-century jazz) and an end to condescension toward the people of Africa.

Building upon the excellent recent scholarship on the slave narrative, Paul Gilroy asserts the counterdiscursive dimension of both nineteenth- and twentieth-century African American autobiographical writing in *The Black Atlantic.* Between World Wars I and II, black American authors turned to autobiography in order to challenge the white historical record on Africa and problematize Africanist discourse and its pervasive influence. Harry Dean's 1929 "autobiographical narrative," entitled *The Pedro Gorino* in the United States and *Umbala* in England, resembles the monumentalist writing of the previous generation. Subtitled *The Adventures of a Negro Sea-Captain in Africa and on the Seven Seas in His Attempts to Found an Ethiopian Empire,* it outlines his Pan-African family history, touches upon his life up until the age of fifteen in the 1860s and 1870s, and describes in detail his experiences as a sailor, businessman, and sometime secular missionary in southern Africa at the turn of the century. Although as rife with Ethiopianism as Hopkins's *Of One Blood,* Dean's book is grounded in his actual experiences on the continent; thus, as far-fetched as his desire to "found an Ethiopian empire" may have been, he did take practical steps to realize this goal. A decade later, Langston Hughes moves much further away from the monumentalists than Dean in *The Big Sea* (1940), the first volume of his autobiography covering his life up until 1930. By opening the book with a description of his initial experience of Africa—a subject to which he returns later in the book—Hughes indicates the great impact this journey had upon his life and work. Unlike the previous generation of black Americans who wrote about Africa and several of his contemporaries, Hughes never refers to the African past; instead, he matter-of-factly reports what he saw on the continent and the impressions this made upon him.

Drawing on the long history of American and more importantly African American relations with Liberia, black American novelists in the first half of the twentieth century periodically devoted their attention to the West African nation, beginning with Griggs's *The Hindered Hand* (discussed in the preceding chapter). Henry F. Downing's *The American Cavalryman* (1917), Gilbert Lubin's *The Promised Land* (1930), and George Schuyler's *Slaves Today* (1931) continued this trend. Although these books avoid the Ethiopianist teleology of Griggs, Hopkins, and Bruce, none is an unequivocal, revisionary success. Downing's novel offers a largely clear-sighted portrayal of the republic's problems and suggests that black American investment and immigration represent the best hope for saving the country, yet its dependence on an African adventure plot, which casts its protagonist in the role of the heroic outsider who rescues a white woman imperiled in the African jungle, vitiates the political assessment it provides. Likewise, *The Promised Land,* a story of mass African American migration to Liberia, can hardly be deemed effective. Subtitled "A Visionary Tale," this short novel about African Americans quickly converting Liberia into a modern, prosperous nation is less a work of fantasy or science fiction than an exercise in wishful thinking. With much better though still somewhat mixed results, Schuyler in *Slaves Today* uses an extended analogy linking antebellum slavery in the American South with contemporary labor practices in Liberia to yoke together a journalistic exposé of Americo-Liberian corruption and a melodramatic tale of native suffering.

Given the continued domination of Africa by European nations between the World Wars, it is not surprising that Liberia, one of only two independent nations on the continent, figures prominently in black American novels written during this period. Settled by African Americans in the nineteenth century and still governed by their descendants through a political system modeled on that of the United States, the West African country was the continent's only black republic for more than a century and became its sole black-ruled state after the Italian takeover of Ethiopia in 1936. Because of the country's unique status, as I.K. Sundiata observes, "[e]ven early in its history Liberia was seen as a symbol of black achievement or as a black failure" (3).

At the mercy of market forces, dependent on foreign capital, victimized by Western prejudice, threatened by English and French encroachment on its territory, and fragmented by ethnic and class differences, Liberia endured severe economic and political challenges in the late 1800s that continued into the twentieth century. Largely as a result of lobbying by Booker T. Washington, according to Louis Harlan, the United States intervened to avert an economic collapse in 1912 when it became the general receiver of customs for Liberia, African American army officers were dispatched to direct the country's Frontier Force, and a $1,500,000 loan to the republic from a combination of British, French, German, and American banks was approved. It was in 1929 that Liberia faced its most serious political crisis. The League of Nations established a three-person Commission of Inquiry, which included the African American social scientist and editor Charles S. Johnson, to investigate longstanding accusations that the settlers were exploiting the native population. The most sensational charge was that Americo-Liberian government officials were essentially selling members of the indigenous population to the Spanish for work on cocoa plantations on the island of Fernando Po (now Bioko and part of Equatorial

Guinea) off the coast of Cameroon. Two immediate consequences of the Commission's findings were the resignations of the president and vice president and a temporary halt in the efforts begun earlier in the century by the settlers to consolidate power in the hinterlands (Kieh, 33). In the long run, however, the crisis not only failed to decrease the exploitation of labor within the country but resulted in increased power for the executive branch (Sundiata, 159, 157).

The scandal received widespread attention in the United States, in large part because of the efforts of George Schuyler, who went to Liberia to report on the situation firsthand. Schuyler roundly condemned the Americo-Liberians in a series of articles printed in a number of mainstream newspapers. Fearing that the crisis might cost Liberia its sovereignty, Du Bois, George Padmore, and Nnamdi Azikiwe, who would later serve as president of Nigeria, offered spirited defenses of the country and its ruling elite.[4] Early in his apology for Liberia, Azikiwe portrays the first settlers as pioneers who overcame incredible odds: "The difficulties encountered by the founders of this future black republic have been unequalled in the history of any nation, excepting perhaps the trying experiences of the Puritans in the *Mayflower* days" (448). Since that time, according to Azikiwe, Liberians have faced similar challenges. Thus, although he concedes that the revelations about forced labor are disheartening and asserts that changes must be made, he argues that the scandal should not be allowed to overshadow Liberia's many achievements

Downing not only casts a black American officer overseeing the Liberian Frontier Force as his protagonist but makes the country's financial problems shortly before the First World War a recurrent theme in *The American Cavalryman*. Apparently only concerned about Liberia's historically significant position as an independent black African country with close ties to the United States, Lubin, unlike Downing, eschews topical references, never alluding to the escalating Fernando Po scandal or to the aborted attempt Marcus Garvey made to transport African Americans to the West African nation in the early 1920s in *The Promised Land*. In stark contrast, *Slaves Today*, written soon after Schuyler returned from reporting on the forced labor crisis, focuses on the current situation in Liberia, only referring to the country's founding and its formative years to contrast the lofty ideals of the original settlers with the greed and cruelty of their descendants.

Shirley Graham's Forging of Dramatic Links between African and African American Art and Experience in *Tom-Tom*

Revisionary depictions of Africa in black American drama lagged somewhat behind those in African American fiction. Owing a clear debt to minstrelsy, which had a stranglehold on nineteenth-century American theater in general and the portrayal of blacks in particular, *In Dahomey* (1902) and *Abyssinia* (1906), two early black American musical comedies set in Africa, featured the famous team of George Walker and Bert Williams, credited with popularizing the cakewalk. With lyrics by Paul Laurence Dunbar and others, book by Jesse A. Shipp, and music by Will Marion Cook, *In Dahomey* concerned two detectives, Shylock "Shy" Homestead (Williams) and Rareback Pinkerton (Walker), hired by the Dahomey Colonization Society (probably based on the controversial ACS) to find a missing treasure. According to one description of the play, all the characters "end up in Dahomey where they are nearly executed. They decide there's no place like home" (Hatch and Abdullah, 211).[5] The musical contained songs such as the "Coboceers' Entrance"—"We are the loyal subjects of King Eat-Em-All, / The ruler over all our states both great and small" (Cook, 23)—and "On Broadway in Dahomey Bye and Bye"—

> If we went to Dahomey suppose the King would say,
> "We want a Broadway built for us; we want it right away."
> We'd git a bunch of natives say ten thousand or more,
> Wid Banyan trees build a big department store.
> We'd sell big Georgia possums some watermelons too
> To git the coin for the other things we'd like to do.
> If we couldn't have real horse cars we'd use zebras for a while.
> On the face of Broadway clock use a crock-o-(dial).
> On Broadway in Dahomey bye and bye. (Cook, 42–43)

Walker and Williams also starred in and helped to write the book for Alex Rogers and Jesse Shipp's *Abyssinia*. Just as *In Dahomey* parodied the resurgent back-to-Africa movements of the day, such as that of Bishop Turner of the AME Church, the later play was no doubt designed to capitalize comically on the fact that many African Americans identified with the venerable African kingdom of Abyssinia or Ethiopia. Such feelings of kinship had recently intensified after Menelik's 1896 defeat of the Italians. Featuring a cast of over one hundred, lavish costumes and lighting effects, a manmade waterfall, and wild animals, *Abyssinia* "told of the misadventures of Rastus Johnson (Walker) and Jasmine Jenkins (Williams), a pair of Kansas rascals, returning to the land of their forefathers, Abyssinia, accompanied by numerous female cousins, a Baptist minister, and an Oriental cook" (Riis, 113).

Although *In Dahomey* and *Abyssinia* were the best-known and most extravagant early twentieth-century theatrical productions to feature depictions of Africa, they were by no means the only ones. James Hatch and Omanii Abdullah mention an earlier musical comedy, *The Sultan of Zulu* by James T. Vaughn and Alex Rogers, but apparently no descriptions of this play are extant. In addition, Thomas L. Riis reports that Sissieretta Jones starred in the Black Patti Troubadours shows *A Trip to Africa* (1910) and *In the Jungles* (1911), playing an African princess in the former, the story of the rescue of a missionary from a tribe of Zulus, and Queen Le-Ku-Li of the Gumbula tribe in the latter (146–47).

It would not be until shortly before the First World War that the first significant noncomic African American drama about Africa would be staged, W.E.B. Du Bois's pageant *The Star of Ethiopia.* Entitled *The Jewel of Ethiopia* when Du Bois wrote the first draft in 1911, it was later published as *The People of Peoples and Their Gifts to Men* in *The Crisis* in November 1913. The previous month a cast of 350 performed the Ethiopianist pageant four times before a combined audience of fourteen thousand people in New York City as part of the National Emancipation Exposition (celebrating the fiftieth anniversary of Lincoln's proclamation abolishing slavery). Du Bois's pageant was staged three more times bearing the title *The Star of Ethiopia:* in Washington, D.C. in October 1915; in Philadelphia in May 1916; and in Los Angeles in May 1925. The adaptability of *The Star of Ethiopia* was quite remarkable. In addition to the name changes, the content of the pageant differed in each of its four venues. For example, because it was part of the Emancipation celebration, Du Bois included Lincoln in the New York performances in 1913. Similarly, the version performed in Philadelphia, which was shown before the Centennial General Conference of the AME Church, stressed "the religious development of the Negro" more than the other productions by prominently featuring "the twelve apostles of Negro Christianity (de Luna Victoria, Hosier, Allen, Jones, Leile, Chavis, Carey, Nat Turner, Vesey, Varick, Gloucester and Payne)" (Du Bois, "'The Star of Ethiopia' A Pageant," 162).

Du Bois believed that with *The Star of Ethiopia* "[t]he great fact has been demonstrated that pageantry among colored people is not only possible, but in many ways of unsurpassed beauty and can be made a means of uplift and education and the beginning of folk drama" ("The Drama Among Black Folk," 93), and without question the primary motive behind the pageant was pedagogic. Trained at Harvard and the University of Berlin, Du Bois had taught at various schools and served for a decade as the general editor of Atlanta University's landmark series of sociological investigations into African American culture. In 1911, however, Du Bois decided to attempt to reach a larger and more diverse audience when he founded and assumed the editorship of *The Crisis,* the official organ of the N.A.A.C.P. In

The Crisis and in his historical study *The Negro* (1915), Du Bois sought to provide African Americans with a long and continuous history of which they could be proud. Likewise, in *The Star of Ethiopia,* Du Bois linked the origins of human civilization, the achievements of ancient Egypt, and the greatness of more recent African empires to the experiences of black people in the United States. Additionally, Du Bois sought to sow the seeds for a thriving African American dramatic community with the pageant, a goal which he was to work toward in a more concrete way when he served as producer of the N.A.A.C.P.'s Krigwa Players Little Negro Theater in Harlem from 1925 to 1927.

Given the paucity of serious dramatic works by black Americans before 1920, the number of African American plays and pageants that were written, produced, and published during the 1920s and 1930s is striking, attesting to African American writers' increased access to black and white audiences during the Harlem Renaissance. Moreover, many of these works had African themes, indicating the burgeoning interest in the continent during the period. Most of the dramas concerned with the continent were either one-act plays, some of which were staged in small theaters such as that at Howard University, or relatively brief pageants that in some cases were performed in several cities with large casts before substantial audiences. Others, however, were apparently only performed on the primary and secondary school level, which appears to be the case of most of the historical dramas in Willis Richardson's *Plays and Pageants from the Life of the Negro* (1930) and Richardson and May Miller's *Negro History in Thirteen Plays* (1935). As with Du Bois's *Star of Ethiopia,* education and uplift were the primary goals of these anthologies. Richardson explains in his introduction that he envisioned *Plays and Pageants* as "a collection to be used in schools"; therefore, he excluded certain works because of an excessive use of dialect and others because of subject matter that might be deemed inappropriate for younger audiences (vii). Similarly, *Negro History* listed the age groups for which the plays were thought to be suitable and also included an introduction by Carter Woodson, founder of the *Journal of Negro History,* declaring that the volume "must be considered another step of the Negro toward the emancipation of his mind from the slavery of the inferiority complex. The Negro has discovered that he has something to dramatize, and in spite of mocking onlookers he has the courage to undertake the task" (v). Thelma Duncan's one-act play *The Death Dance* (1923), Richard Bruce's ballet *Sahdji* (1927), Richardson's one-act dramas *The Black Horseman* (1929) and *In Menelik's Court* (1929), Miller's single-act play *Samory* (1935), and pageants linking ancient African and modern African American history, such as Dorothy C. Guinn's *Out of the Dark,* Frances Gunner's

The Light of Women, and Edward J. McCoo's *Ethiopia at the Bar of Justice,* all possess a certain amount of historical value and varying degrees of artistic merit, but none of them can be called major literary texts.

Shirley Graham's groundbreaking opera *Tom-Tom* was the first full-length work for the stage to confront directly the relationship between Africa and black America. A unique hybrid—a single-act play that was converted into a three-act opera by a composer with knowledge of African music—*Tom-Tom* recalls in its title and most important symbol key passages of Hughes's "The Negro Artist and the Racial Mountain." It also responds to Locke's appeal to African American artists to avoid paternalistic attitudes toward Africa and to turn to themes and forms from the continent for inspiration. In her music for the opera, however, Graham goes even further, refuting Locke's questionable assertion of a lack of continuity between African and African American art. Echoing in somewhat muted fashion the previous generation's monumentalism but also providing an answer to the new generation's key question, "What is Africa to me?" Graham wrote in *The Crisis* in 1933: "Firmly, I do believe in the innate artistic soul of the Negro. Age-old wisdom purified and beaten down by suffering, pain and hurt to which we are constantly exposed, whimsical fancy, soaring high hopes, all these and more like smothering coals lie planted in our beings. This is our heritage, first handed down to us when our forefathers guarded the headwaters of the Nile—a sacred trust" ("Black Man's Music," 178). By presenting the connections among African life prior to its disruption by the European slave trade, the plantation slave system in the South, and the hopes and fears of contemporary African Americans living in Harlem, Graham in *Tom-Tom* produced a substantial and sophisticated dramatic work that aspires to and achieves more than the overt didacticism of not only Du Bois's *Star of Ethiopia* but also the pageants and one-act plays about Africa published in the 1920s and 1930s.

Unjustly forgotten until quite recently, *Tom-Tom* began like many of the dramas of the period as a one-act play, which Graham wrote and produced while working as a music instructor at Morgan College in Baltimore from 1929 to 1931. Graham sent the play to Rowena and Russell Jelliffe, directors of the Gilpin (later the Karamu) players in Cleveland in 1931. Although unable to use the play, the Jelliffes remembered it the next spring when Laurence Higgins consulted them in his search for an African American opera to be included in his "Theater of Nations" series, which was to present operas from various cultures at Cleveland Stadium during the summer of 1932. According to Kathy Perkins, Graham, who by this time was studying music at Oberlin College from which she would receive her B.A. and M.A., took a leave of absence and spent three months in a hotel room with a piano converting her short play into a three-act, sixteen-scene opera. A cast of nearly five hundred performed *Tom-Tom* twice, on June 30 before ten thousand spectators and July 9 before an audience exceeding fifteen thousand people; moreover, the opera was broadcast over NBC radio. A brief notice about *Tom-Tom* in the Music section of the August 1932 issue of the *Crisis* reported that "To secure realism for its jungle reproductions, producers have imported from Africa, Indoxiz Chiakazia, native voodoo man. Elaborate staging plans call for elevated trains, subways, automobiles, cabarets, sailing vessels that explode, hundreds of dancers, pantomimenists [sic], warriors, headhunters, gigolos." Credited with being the first opera written by an African American to be performed with a professional cast,[6] *Tom-Tom* received substantial media attention, and the reviews, apart from some complaints about technical problems, were generally quite favorable (Perkins, "The Unknown Career," 9).

A lengthy review article by Norine West in the *Pittsburgh Courier* provides a wealth of information about the music of *Tom-Tom*. Instead of the traditional recitative of European opera, Graham employed the long chant of early African American preachers. The music of the first act was inspired by African themes and rhythms over five hundred years old that were collected by her uncle, father, and brother, all of whom lived and worked in Liberia for several years. Graham learned other rhythms and themes from Senegalese and Martinicans she met while studying music in Paris in 1926. In an effort to achieve authenticity during the performance, African marimbas, six African tom-toms, pebble-filled gourds, clanking anklets, and hand-clapping were used. Through her title and her efforts to link African rhythms, African American spirituals, and American jazz, Graham was signifying not only on the use of tom-toms in Eugene O'Neill's *The Emperor Jones,* which the notice in the *Crisis* mentions, and Vachal Lindsey's "The Congo," but also on Hughes's description of jazz as the "tom-tom of joy and laughter" in "The Negro Artist and the Racial Mountain." Without intending to ignore or minimize Graham's achievement in rendering authentic African music and illustrating its profound influence on African American and American music, I want to focus here on the literary aspects of Graham's libretto, which was published for the first time in 1991. Addressing the African American past, present, and future as well as geopolitical considerations involving Africa and America, *Tom-Tom* powerfully depicts the tensions responsible for as well as both the disadvantages and the benefits of double-consciousness. Graham both historicizes and positively interprets this key concept of W.E.B. Du Bois, the man who served as her mentor during the 1930s and 1940s and who was her husband from 1951 until his death in 1963.

Although the conflict in *Tom-Tom* is not always or merely America versus Africa or assimilation versus separatism, oppositions abound in the opera. Graham continually presents theses and antitheses; in contrast to Africanist writers, however, at the close of the opera she offers a Du Boisian synthesis that may resolve the conflicts. It is the blending of this recurrent and evolving pattern of oppositions on the one hand and the presence in each of the three acts of the same four major characters—the Girl, the Boy, the Mother, and the Voodoo Man—on the other that gives the opera its continuity and coherence.

Graham stages a struggle for the soul of the black community in each act of *Tom-Tom*. The first act pits the traditions of the Voodoo Man, who has selected the Girl to be sacrificed to the gods in order to stop the encroachments of the slave catchers, against the Boy, who, smitten by the beauty of the Girl, violates her purification rites and encourages her to escape and fall in love with him. Although the Voodoo Man publicly rebukes the Boy in the name of the gods, both men later risk their lives to reach the tom-tom so as to alert neighboring villages of the arrival of Bantu kidnappers. In act 2, set in the American South, the Voodoo Man, known as Bad Sam on the plantation, clings to his ancient African gods, refusing to accept the Christian religion of Uncle Ben, the preacher, embraced by most of the slaves. Heeding Locke's call for an end to condescension toward Africa, Graham presents the religions of Uncle Ben and Bad Sam as equally valid paths of faith for African Americans, unlike nineteenth- and early twentieth-century Ethiopianists who privileged Christianity over African religion. In what at first appears as a startling role reversal, act 3 finds the Boy, now transformed into a minister of a large Harlem congregation and thus an upholder of what have become traditional religious beliefs, denouncing the unconverted Voodoo Man's plans to transport African Americans to Africa. However, when the angry mob mortally wounds the Voodoo Man following the sinking of his Africa-bound ship due to overcrowding, the Boy vows to carry on the Voodoo Man's mission in America.

Along with the conflicts over values, a recurrent theme in the opera is the prospect of separation that confronts the Girl and her Mother. At first horrified that the Girl has been selected to be sacrificed, in the first act the Mother quickly swells with pride because the gods have chosen her daughter for such an honor. When in act 2 she learns that the Girl has been sold to an unscrupulous master, the Mother prepares to take her daughter's life and thereby condemn herself to what she believes is eternal damnation rather than to allow the Girl to be degraded. In the final act, despite the protestations of the Girl, who loves her mother but wants to remain in America and keep her job as a singer in a Harlem cabaret, the Mother decides to go to Africa and leave her daughter behind because of the crass materialism and immorality she sees in the United States.

The cabaret scene in act 3 illustrates Graham's ability to present conflicting characters' conscious and unconscious motivations empathetically. On the one hand, the Mother's objections about her daughter's job and American society in general, which dovetail with the spiritual purity variation of Ethiopianism, appear to be confirmed by the exploitive aspects of the club that reinforce a caricatured image of Africa, such as the dancers' native costumes and the primitivism of the Girl's song. On the other hand, the blues number sung by the Girl not only owes a debt to the authentic African rhythms and themes of the first act but, echoing Hughes's statements about jazz in "The Negro Artist and the Racial Mountain," offers a critique of mainstream American culture's hectic pace and disregard for the past and reflection:

> No time for flowers, no idle hours
> No time to sit and think,
> No time for friends, no days that end
> With just the sun a-settin' and the sighin' of the wind.
> No . . . time.
> They tell me somewhere there are rivers
> They tell me somewhere there's a moon
> Maybe you have seen the moonlight shining on the trees,
> Maybe you have sailed upon the rivers.
> But I dance! I sing!
> No time to dream, no time to hope,
> No time to say good-bye. (278–79)

Significantly, the last line from Girl's song also comments upon the rushed and apparently final exchange between the mother and daughter in the previous scene.

Graham ends her first two acts with events that have an epistemic impact upon Africans and their descendants in America; similarly, she implies that the occurrences that close the play signal one more paradigm shift for the black community. The arrival of slave catchers at the conclusion of the first act alters forever the tradition-bound lives of the villagers, who are faced with the horrors of the Middle Passage and New World slavery. Similarly, the liberation of the plantation by Union soldiers at the end of act 2 ushers in a totally new era of freedom and frustration for the slaves. Likewise, Graham apparently intends the sinking of the overcrowded Afro-Pan-African line ship and the angry crowd's fatal attack on the Voodoo Man at the end of the opera to represent another sea change in the lives of her characters. Included in an opera staged just five years after the deportation of Marcus Garvey, these events suggest that the option of mass African American repatriation in Africa no longer exists and black Americans must therefore focus their attention on the United States. In addition, they distinguish Graham's ideas about Africa from the black American exceptionalism of earlier writers, who envisioned African Americans leading Africans to a brighter future. However, the Boy's change of heart about the Voodoo Man in the opera's final moments indicates that synthesis is possible, that black Americans can live in America without sacrificing their African heritage:

> VOODOO MAN: It doesn't matter now, my boy. I've failed. I've
>   failed. Always, through the ages I have failed.
> BOY: Forgive me.
> VOODOO MAN: Now even my tom-tom will be silent.
>   (*The stick falls from his hand. The BOY catches it*)
> BOY: No! Black Man. No! Your tom-tom shall be heard.
>   (*He strikes a mighty blow upon the tom-tom*)
>   Who will go with me
>   Not to distant lands,
>   But here, beating the tom-tom
>   We'll find kingdoms unknown. (285)

The end of the opera seems to assert that when seen in a historical perspective African American double-consciousness can and should be regarded as a boon rather than a burden, that in their long and continuous past black Americans have not only a cause for pride but also a source of strength.

As the passage quoted just above makes clear, Graham closely associates the opera's most important symbol, the tom-tom, with Africa. In act 1's presentation of Africa, the tom-tom serves the largely practical function of communication, uniting villages and warning of danger but also allowing people to express themselves through music and dance. Just as Africa has become a memory on the plantation in the second act, so the tom-tom has lost its utilitarian function. Its rhythms are still fresh in the minds of certain slaves, such as the Voodoo Man, but most experience their African musical heritage indirectly through spirituals. No longer a reality or even a vivid memory for black Americans in early twentieth-century Harlem, in act 3 Africa becomes an idea, a dream, a symbol of the way things ought to be. Likewise, at the end of the opera, the tom-tom represents both hope for the future and continuity with the past.

A word that epitomizes "twoness," comprised of two equal halves whose individual integrity is maintained by the presence of a hyphen, "tom-tom" graphically illustrates the possibility of synthesis. By not only vividly presenting the hybridity—the "two souls, two thoughts, two unreconciled strivings" and "two warring ideals"—at work within the black community but also placing these conflicts within a historic continuum, Graham argues for the constructive potential of the African and American heritages contained within the "dark body" of black America. Although her score serves to debunk Locke's dubious contention that there is a lack of continuity between African and black American art, Graham's assertion of what Africa means to contemporary African Americans links her to his explicitly antimonumentalist and antipaternalist prescriptions in "Apropos of Africa." Moreover, in its title and most important symbol, Graham's opera invokes key passages of Langston Hughes's "The Negro Artist and the Racial Mountain."

Harry Dean and the Dream of an Ethiopian Empire

In *The Black Atlantic* Paul Gilroy claims that in the writing of Frederick Douglass and other former slaves "a new discursive economy emerges with the refusal to subordinate the particularity of slave experience to the totalising power of universal reason held exclusively by white hands, pens, and publishing houses. Authority and autonomy emerge directly from the deliberately personal tone of this history. . . . What Richard Wright would later identify as the aesthetics of personalism flows from these narratives and shows that in the hands of slaves the particular can wear the mantle of truth and reason as readily as the universal" (69). The counterdiscursive potential of the personal narrative, which, as Gilroy notes, has continued to be a key feature in black American autobiography, was embraced by Harry Dean and Langston Hughes when they sought to write about their experiences in Africa.

Harry Foster Dean serves as a transitional figure between the first and the second generation of twentieth-century black American authors who wrote about Africa. He wrote his autobiographical curiosity *The Pedro Gorino* with the assistance of Sterling North (who would later write *Rascal*) when he was an indigent sixty-four-year-old man in poor health. Although published in 1929, the book concerns events that took place in the nineteenth century and the early years of the twentieth century. Dean's advocacy of black American emigration to Africa links him with nineteenth-century figures such as Alexander Crummell and Henry McNeal Turner, and his dream of founding a black empire in Africa recalls not only the Ethiopianist fantasies of the turn-of-the-century novelists Griggs and Hopkins but Garvey's ultimate objective as stated in "African Fundamentalism." Dean's firsthand experience on the continent, active participation in the southern African political and religious movement known as Ethiopianism, and anticolonialism, however, distinguish him from the monumentalists.

Apart from George Shepperson's helpful introduction to the 1989 reissue of the British edition of Dean's book and a 1973 master's thesis on Dean by John S. Burger, very little has been written about the author of *The Pedro Gorino*. Those who do comment upon Dean describe him as dynamic but embittered; they also question the veracity of his autobiography. In a brief review of *The Pedro Gorino* in *The Crisis*, W.E.B. Du Bois recalls meeting Dean in London in 1900 at the time of the first Pan-African Conference: "Dean was bitter. He wanted to lead a black army across the straits of Gibraltar. I saw his point of view, but did not think the scheme was practical."[7] Du Bois's assessment was that the "book is the interesting and in its final chapters, fascinating story of Dean's dream. Perhaps his dream goes in some respects beyond the facts, but it is all worth reading" ("The Negro in Literature," 376). Sterling North echoes Du Bois in a letter written thirty-six years after the publication of *The Pedro Gorino:* "Dean was a colorful and attractive figure. The fact that he wouldn't show me his diaries and letters [while they were writing the book together] may have meant that he was slightly romanticizing his past. His dreams may have surpassed his c[a]pacities. But I remember him kindly" (Letter to Dr. Robert I. Rotberg). Shepperson likewise admits that when he first read Dean's autobiography he had "an uneasy suspicion that there was more fiction than fact in his book" (vii). Reconsidering the narrative almost forty years later, Shepperson expresses more confidence in Dean's truthfulness because in the interim some of the author's assertions about South Africa at the beginning of the century had been verified. "Perhaps Harry Dean possessed at times a tendency to exaggerate or to romanticize, and there was an occasional touch of gullibility about him," writes Shepperson, "but I do not believe that he ever consciously lied or intended to deceive" (vii).

Although Burger found it impossible to verify many of Dean's claims, he concurs with Shepperson on the veracity of *The Pedro Gorino* in his thesis, "An Introduction to Harry Dean Pan-Negro-Nationalist."[8] The people Dean wrote about were in South Africa when he claimed they were, but Burger found no mention of him in their writings (although Burger speculates that they may not have named Dean in order to protect him from government censure). Echoing Shepperson, North, and Du Bois, Burger suggests that Dean's memory may have failed him at times and that he may have "embellished" many of the incidents in the book "for the sake of interest and readability" (10). In his final assessment, however, Burger gives Dean the benefit of the doubt: "In so far as the validity of general information available is concerned, it is the author's opinion that much is true but requires further verification. There are many indications in regard to events and persons named which point toward confirmation of Dean's role as an active participant in the black nationalist movement in Africa, details which lend credence to Dean's claims" (10–11). Burger was apparently unaware of a letter to the editor published in the *Colored American Magazine* in 1903 written by A. Kirkland Soga, a native South African editor whom Dean mentions in *The Pedro Gorino,* that not only proves Dean was in South Africa at that time but indicates that Dean was both familiar with and deeply impressed by Pauline Hopkins's work: "Dear Miss Hopkins:—Our attention has been drawn to your work in the *Colored American Magazine* by Mr. Harry Dean, a young American travelling in this country, who gives us a very flattering account of your work on behalf of the colored race" (quoted in "Editorial and Publishers Announcements," 467). Although Soga's letter does not explicitly state that Dean was familiar with Hopkins's *Of One Blood,* it suggests that there is a strong possibility that Dean read this Ethiopianist serial in the magazine.

Roughly covering the first forty years of Dean's life, *The Pedro Gorino* comprises four books; the first concerns Dean's family history and his early life and the latter three describe Dean's activities in South Africa around the time of the Boer War. Although the title of the British edition, *Umbala* ("it is true"), directly addresses questions about the book's veracity, *The Pedro Gorino* is a more appropriate title.[9] Almost assuming the role of the protagonist at times, Dean's sailing ship, *The Pedro Gorino,* was purchased in Stavanger, Norway, in 1900, sailed to Cape Town, and used for various commercial ventures until Dean was forced to leave South Africa; moreover, the vessel embodies Dean's dream of founding a black African empire. Dean thus anchors his autobiography upon the chief and originary symbol Gilroy chooses for his black Atlantic model. "I have settled on the image of ships in motion across the spaces between Europe, America, Africa, and the Caribbean as a central organising symbol for this enterprise and as my starting point," explains Gilroy. "The image of the ship—a living, micro-cultural, micro-political system in motion—is especially important for historical and theoretical reasons. . . . Ships immediately focus attention on the middle passage, on the various projects for redemptive return to an African homeland, on the circulation of ideas and activists as well as the movement of key cultural and political artefacts" (4). It would be hard to imagine a better description of the multifaceted role Dean's ship plays in his narrative.

Book I, "My First Voyage," sets the tone for the rest of the work by indicating Dean's pride in his black heritage and desire to help his race. It also portrays Dean as a romantic figure seemingly sprung from the pages of

Robert Louis Stevenson. North's preface to *The Pedro Gorino* cultivates the image of Dean as a larger-than-life figure, describing him as a man who had "circumnavigated Africa eighteen times, crossed it from east to west three times and from north to south once" (*The Pedro Gorino,* xi).[10] North recalls Dean telling him on their first meeting: "I look like a poor old man . . . but I am a prince in my own right back in Africa. I know things that would make the King of England tremble on his throne. I know facts that would make the imperialists of every nation blush with shame" (*The Pedro Gorino,* viii). Following the opening chapter devoted to the early Pan-Africanist Paul Cuffe, the next five chapters briefly describe Dean's childhood and then detail his three-year journey around the world on his uncle Silas Dean's ship, a voyage which ended when he was fifteen.

More concerned with establishing the accuracy of Dean's purported adventures in South Africa, neither Shepperson nor Burger fully investigates the first and in many ways the most important claim in Dean's book: the author's assertion that he is the great-grandson of the black sea captain and businessman Paul Cuffe (1759–1817). Burger reports that in his notebooks Dean refers to a biography he wrote about Cuffe and that Dean had transferred photographs of letters written by Cuffe onto glass plates, which he used in lectures he gave about black history.[11] Indeed, the first chapter of *The Pedro Gorino* certainly shows evidence of research on Dean's part into Cuffe's life.[12] However, Dean's account of Cuffe differs greatly from those of other biographers. One of the most striking discrepancies is Dean's account of Cuffe liberating slaves from a South Carolina plantation and transporting them to Freetown in Sierra Leone. None of Paul Cuffe's biographers mentions this incident. It does serve, however, to portray Cuffe and Dean as kindred spirits—daring black sea captains prepared to strike a blow against white oppression. Moreover, Dean quotes in full a short letter written to Paul Cuffe by his "youngest son, John Cuffee" from prison in York, Pennsylvania, asking for assistance from his "father" (17–18), and Dean claims that this same "John Cuffee" was his maternal grandfather. Yet Paul Cuffe did not have a son named John, as Lamont Thomas's genealogy of the Cuffe family in his biography clearly indicates (161). Cuffe did, in fact, receive the letter Dean reprints; however, it came from a thief named Bailey who at various times had impersonated Paul Cuffe and Cuffe's brother-in-law (Sherwood, 208–10; Thomas, 116).[13] Dean apparently found the letter in Cuffe's papers at the New Bedford Public Library, but he must have overlooked Cuffe's reply in which he berates the impostor for betraying his race: "If the Great evil that thou hast embarked upon, were only against me as an individual . . . I should not have to lament the Cause so much. But this is a national Concern. It is a Stain to the Whole Community of the African race. . . . The manumission of 1,500,000 Slaves depends upon the faithfulness of the few who have obtained their freedom. Yea, . . . but the Whole Community of the African race, which are according to best accounts 30,000,000" (quoted in Thomas, 116).[14]

Both questions and ironies abound. Was Dean perhaps descended from Paul Cuffe's nephew John (the son of Cuffe's older brother John), who was born in 1799?[15] If this is so, then perhaps Dean mistakenly believed that the letter to Paul Cuffe from his "son, John Cuffee" in Cuffe's papers was written by his grandfather. Or did Dean fabricate the ancestral link to Paul Cuffe because he regarded the early Pan-Africanist as the perfect antecedent for his own efforts to "establish an Ethiopian Empire"?[16] In any event, by claiming to be the grandson of the "John Cuffee" who wrote a letter to his "father" from prison, Dean, an ardent black nationalist who devoted his life to assisting and defending people of African descent, unintentionally affiliates himself with a man whom Paul Cuffe himself denounced as a traitor to black people everywhere.

Whether Paul Cuffe was actually a blood ancestor of Dean's or not, he certainly served as a powerful spiritual forefather for Dean, with whom he shared not only a love for the sea but also ideas about the development of Africa, education, and black self-reliance. A builder, captain, and owner of ships, Cuffe was the wealthiest black person in America by the early 1800s and left an estate of almost $20,000 at his death (Thomas, 22, 118). Cuffe's vessels had traded and whaled successfully along the African coast long before he set sail in late 1810 in his brig *Traveller* on what Thomas terms a "civilizing mission" to Sierra Leone (46). Five years later he transported thirty-eight American blacks to the British colony in the same vessel—"the first black-initiated emigration movement from the Western Hemisphere to the shores of Africa" (Thomas, 100). A firm believer in education, Cuffe established a racially integrated school for children in Westport, Massachusetts, in the 1790s; personally instructed the members of his predominantly black crews, including Africans recruited in Sierra Leone; and gave lectures on Africa to black audiences in the United States. Cuffe was convinced that "black maritime trade was essential for the advancement of Africa" and, despite his concerns about the racist motivations behind white support for the back-to-Africa movement, believed that American blacks would be better off in Africa, where they could "rise to be a people," as he wrote in an 1816 letter (Thomas, 104, 119, 108).

As a youth on his uncle's ship, named *Traveller the Second* after Cuffe's vessel, Dean learned the rudiments of sailing, experienced Africa for the first time, and began concocting a plan for the rehabilitation of the black race. Building on the theme of family heritage introduced in the initial chapter, in the fourth chapter Dean feels "burdened with [the] great responsibility" of having been chosen by his Uncles Silas and Solomon (whom he meets in San Francisco after rounding Cape Horn) to carry on the sea life. Dean recalls that "[i]t seemed that all my seafaring ancestors were watching me from their graves on the land and in the dark sea, trying to determine if their faith had been misplaced" (43–44). After stops in Hawaii and various ports in Asia, the young Dean is delighted when the boat reaches East Africa. Demonstrating an interest in the continent's history that links him with the monumentalists, Dean explains that "I had always been interested in Africa because of the stories I had been told, and because it was the continent from which my ancestors had come. . . . I wanted to see for myself the remnants and ruins of its glorious past" (55).

Soon after departing from Cape Town, *Traveller the Second* stops at Saldanha Bay, where Dean's uncle tells him a story that profoundly affects his attitudes toward Africans and whites. According to Silas Dean, the sailors on a Dutch ship named the *Full Moon* that had come into Saldanha Bay to get water kidnapped sixteen little girls and four young boys and sold them into slavery at Jamestown in 1619, thus initiating the slave trade in America.[17] To the young Dean's question as to why the Hereros did not chase the Dutchmen and recapture their children, his uncle replies: "Not a ship among them . . . [t]hat has been the downfall of our race" (57). From that day forward Dean commits himself to providing black people with vessels and the knowledge necessary to carry out maritime trade. When Dean reaches Liberia a short time later, its independence further fuels his dreams: "My knowledge that Liberia was the one bit of land in all Africa still held by its rightful heirs made me think of its importance as a base for operations. The dark continent held a new interest for me, and the troubles of my race had taken on a new significance. Even at that early age I was dreaming of an Ethiopian Empire" (59).

Like Cuffe and Crummell, both advocates of emigration to Africa, and like nineteenth- and turn-of-the-century black American Ethiopianists generally, Dean saw the need for African American leadership in not only the economic and but also the cultural development of Africa. Early in Book II, Dean recalls his exceptionalist resolve to "instigate a movement to rehabilitate Africa and found such an Ethiopian Empire as the world has never seen. . . . It would be greater than the empires of Africa's past . . . for although these kingdoms must have numbered their subjects in the hundreds of thousands, their store of knowledge was limited. I dreamed of an empire infinitely more cultured. Africa would again lift up her head. Her fleets would sail the sea. Her resources would once more enrich her own children" (69–70).

Book II, "The Pedro Gorino," describes Dean's acquisition of a seventy-foot, two-masted vessel with which he tries to establish a black-owned and -operated shipping company based in southern Africa; it also includes his incredible account of being offered Portuguese East Africa by the colonial governor's secretary for a mere fifty thousand pounds. The story behind the name of Dean's "freak topsail schooner" is significant to Dean's nation-building project in Africa. It was originally called *Pellar Guri* after a girl of that name who rallied "all the peasants of Norway" to defeat a robber baron trying to capture the land. "From this united effort," according to a page of illuminated script affixed beneath the name, "rose the kingdom of Norway" (73). The folktale that Dean refers to actually surrounds a girl named Prillar Guri, reputed to have played a role in the defeat of a group of Scottish mercenaries who were traversing Norway on their way to Sweden in the early 1600s.[18] However, a West Indian member of Dean's crew thought the name was *The Pedro Gorino* and painted this on the prow. When informed of his error, the sailor replied that *Pellar Guri* was no name for a black man's ship and so the Spanish name stuck. Thus, Dean's ship is fortuitously christened with a name that is oddly appropriate to his quixotic project of establishing an autonomous black African nation in the wake of Europe's Scramble for Africa.

Dean explains his decision to use Cape Town—"the most strategic point in that part of the world"—as a base for operations by depicting himself as a kind of spy in enemy country: "while awaiting my chance to help the Ethiopian race I could not do better than take up a position in the very midst of the Imperialists and learn their game firsthand" (80). Not long after establishing a lucrative shipping business, Dean, to his amazement, is taken for an intelligence agent of the American government by colonial officials in Lourenço Marques (now Maputo), who offer him all of Portuguese East Africa "for the ridiculously low figure of fifty thousand pounds sterling" (114). The offer, which Dean later believes is made because of Portuguese fears that the British will take over what is now Mozambique in a bold scheme to flank the Boers, triggers a manifest destiny-type fantasy for Dean: "The possibilities opened before me like a flower: Delogoa Bay, future maritime headquarters for native Africa; Lourenço Marques, a new centre of culture for the coloured race; Portuguese East Africa, a national home to which the wandering Ethiopians the world over might come and live in peace. Who could tell? With such a foothold an enterprising colony might expand until it had recaptured the whole continent" (114–15). After claiming that he then wrote "[e]very prominent Ethiopian in America" requesting funds to be used to purchase the colony but was unanimously turned down, Dean hyperbolically declares, "Thus the bright bubble burst, and the greatest chance the 'negro' has ever had to rehabilitate Africa came to nothing" (122).[19] Echoing Casely Hayford's thoughts about the effects that living in the United States has had on people of African descent (discussed in chapter 1), Dean places much of the blame on the pernicious influences of America's climate of oppression and "false ideals" (123). He then directly chides those African Americans who refused to heed his call to liberate Africa and themselves: "In your blindness and rustic unsophistication you reminded me of the native Somali, who, if you were to offer him a thousand bright gold sovereigns for a quart of goat's milk, would refuse, but if you were to offer him three cents worth of shell money would gladly sell it" (123). Despite his numerous refutations of white misconceptions about Africa and Africans in the book, Dean here engages in the exceptionalism and paternalism that so many earlier black American Ethiopianists exhibited toward the continent's inhabitants. Reminiscent of Othello's comparison between himself and the "base Indian [who] threw a pearl away / Richer than all his tribe" in his final speech, Dean's telling analogy seeks to point out to the uncooperative African Americans the error of their ways by asserting that they are no better than a lowly African.

In Book III, "Segow Faku, King of the Pondos," Dean recounts his efforts to build schools, unify tribes, and establish an ongoing trading concern in Pondoland, a recently subdued nation in eastern South Africa bordering the St. John river.[20] The final book, "The Net Draws Tighter," tells of Dean's work in Basutoland (now Lesotho), his efforts to establish a dialogue among the native leaders in South Africa, and his harassment by government officials that culminated in his expulsion from the country. Still hoping to raise fifty thousand pounds to buy Portuguese East Africa, Dean conceives of a plan to link Pondoland, Basutoland, and Port St. John by a system of roads, which would enable the Pondos, Pondo Mesis, and Basutos to ship and receive goods to and from Cape Town and the rest of the world via *The Pedro Gorino*. Dean also believes that through his educational efforts he will succeed in sowing the seeds of unrest among these native people, stating with characteristic exceptionalism and exaggeration: "Very soon now I should be in a position to do more for my race than any coloured man before me. . . . [My enemies] could not undermine the influence I was already gaining with the natives. They could not undo my work once I had instilled the desire for liberty in those fertile Ethiopian minds" (204).

Yet despite two attempts on his life by government agents and his earlier excoriation of "the Imperialists as . . . vulgar murderers and thieves whose egotistical, crafty, and cunning nature holds no respect for intellectual or moral values" in a letter to a friend (174), Dean underestimates the wiliness of his foes who run him into debt, destroy his property, and eventually deport him. Thus, Dean's "bright dreams" come "crash[ing] about

[his] head" and he is "driven from [his] motherland by foreigners and usurpers" (255, 256). Although nostalgia pervades Dean's book, it becomes particularly acute in the final chapter. In Books II, III, and IV, Dean mentions the need to have power installed in *The Pedro Gorino* so that it will be able to compete with motorized boats; however, he keeps putting off this modernization even though he can readily afford it. Ironically, at the time that Dean encounters intense government harassment that leads to an insurmountable financial crisis for him, his ship is in dry dock awaiting the installation of power. Even though his vessel will no doubt be confiscated to pay his debts, Dean takes some consolation in the fact that the boat will remain as it has always been. In a passage that signifies on Conrad's lament about the end of the sailing era in *An Outcast of the Islands*,[21] Dean, speaking for himself as well as his sailors, states on the final page, "we were all thinking that perhaps it was best to leave her thus, and never hear the angry rumble of an engine in her vitals, or see the wild, free spirit of her broken and surly, and the ship plunging on without regard to wind or waves. And that was the last I ever saw of *The Pedro Gorino*" (256).

Dean's resistance to modernization in regards to his ship, the most powerful symbol of his dream of an "Ethiopian Empire," accords perfectly with the tensions inherent in the Ethiopianism invoked by the first generation of twentieth-century black American writers to depict Africa. On the one hand, these authors often believed that Western and in particular American technology imported to Africa by African Americans would set in motion forces that would culminate in the rehabilitation of the continent. On the other hand, these writers denounced what they regarded as the rampant and corrupting materialism of European and American culture and occasionally predicted that only a resurgent Africa could redeem the West from the worldly path it had taken. Although throughout the book Dean argues that people of African descent require ships to compete globally (a position he would maintain all of his life), he apparently fears that by blindly imitating white modernization efforts blacks may be coopted by the inauthentic ideals of the Western world, may have their "wild, free spirit[s]" broken, and may sacrifice the lofty goals to which he has always aspired for the sake of material gain.

From Life to Literature in *The Big Sea*

Melodramatic maybe, it seems to me now. But then it was like throwing a million bricks out of my heart when I threw the books into the water. I leaned over the rail of the S.S. Malone *and threw the books as far as I could out into the sea—all the books I had had at Columbia, and all the books I had lately bought to read.*

By opening *The Big Sea* with this memory, Langston Hughes emphasizes his desire for a break with both his personal past and his literary heritage—white and black. Where Arnold Rampersad sees ambiguity in Hughes's dumping of his books—"this radical gesture implies either adolescent, anti-intellectual rebellion or the achievement of Prospero-like wisdom. Or perhaps something else" (*Life,* 376)—I see a symbolic action that accords perfectly with Hughes's central theme: the need to experience life directly in order to be able to write about it effectively.[22] Hughes underscores the process of converting lived experience into art on the book's final page when he revises his epigraph ("Life is a big sea / full of fish. / I let down my nets / and pull") to read "Literature is a big sea full of many fish. I let down my nets and pulled. I'm still pulling" (335).

Like Hughes's decision to sign on for a six-month voyage on a freighter stopping at thirty-two ports along the West Coast of Africa from Dakar to Luanda, his discarding of the books he had purchased during and since his disappointing year at Columbia University signals his desire to see the world for himself and not through the eyes—or words—of others. Hughes, in fact, describes getting rid of his books not once but twice in *The Big Sea,* returning to the incident at the end of his first section, "Twenty-One," as a means of summing up his life to this point. As he looks at the volumes after boarding the ship, "they seemed too much like everything I had known in the past, like the attics and basements in Cleveland, like the lonely nights in Toluca, like the dormitory at Columbia, like the furnished room in Harlem, like too much reading all the time when I was a kid, *like life isn't, as described in romantic prose*" (97, emphasis added). This action of hurling the books with great force—not simply tossing them lightly aside—is all the more significant because Hughes chose Africa as the place to experience for himself. More than any other part of the globe, as Countee Cullen remarks in "Heritage," the continent is "a book one thumbs." Rarely having experienced Africa for themselves, most white and black American writers prior to 1920 who wrote about the continent had to rely on other peoples' books and their own imaginations in constructing their Africas. Even the depictions by those who had actually visited or lived on the continent, like that in Ellis's *The Leopard's Claw* (see chapter 1), were greatly influenced by the pre-existing discourse about Africa. Rather than allowing previous writers' visions of the continent (and the world in general) to color his own perceptions, Hughes deep-sixes them. Although he probably did not recognize the socio-political symbolism of his gesture as he leaned over the railing of the freighter (actually called the *West Hesseltine*) in 1923, sixteen years later Hughes certainly wrote the description of his very first glimpse of the continent so that it vindicates his deep-sea divestiture: "when I saw the dust-green hills in the sunlight, something took hold of me inside. My Africa, Motherland of the Negro peoples! Africa! The real thing, to be touched and seen, not merely read about in a book" (10). Rejecting the monumentalism of the previous generation of black American writing about Africa, Dean's *Pedro Gorino,* and even the imagery of his own 1926 essay "The Negro Artist and the Racial Mountain," Hughes keeps his attention riveted on contemporary Africa, never invoking the continent's past in *The Big Sea.*

Reviewers both white and black differed over whether *The Big Sea* was honest or reticent, particularly as it was published not long after Richard Wright's politically charged bestseller *Native Son* (Rampersad, *Life,* 388–89). Although for the most part Hughes avoids attacking America's racial policies in the autobiography, he holds little or nothing back in the pages concerning Africa, frequently denouncing the colonial practices and lamenting the effects of imperialism he witnessed firsthand. Hughes states bluntly, "The white man dominates Africa. He takes produce, and lives, very much as he chooses. The yield of earth for Europe and America. The yield of men for Europe's colonial armies. And the Africans are baffled and humble. They listen to the missionaries and bow down before the Lord, but they bow much lower before the traders, who carry whips and guns and are protected by white laws, made in Europe for the black colonies" (102).

Even in describing the people on his ship, Hughes emphasizes the exploitation of Africa. Except for the sailors, everyone brandishes some sort of equipment with which to change or profit from the Africans: white missionaries bring the Word—"Bibles and hymnbooks"—with which to convert the natives; a black West Indian tailor and Garveyite carries "bolts of cloth, shears, and tailoring tools," believing that he can civilize the Africans by getting them to wear proper clothes; and the Captain comes armed with "invoices and papers having to do with trade" (8). Although he and the other seaman arrive empty-handed, Hughes realizes that they, too, participate in the process of robbing Africa of its treasures and degrading its peoples. Hughes refers to the months spent in Africa as a "sailor's holiday" and a "picnic" for himself and his mates because a Liberian crew comes aboard and performs almost all of their duties for them (105), yet Rampersad reports that Hughes was shocked to learn that these Kru men received only two shillings per day for all their hard and in some cases life-threatening work (*Life,* 77). Clearly Hughes also has misgivings about having joined the other sailors in buying up a town with cigar coupons that the local people mistook for French francs. Likewise, although he apparently visits the local brothels with his shipmates on a regular basis, the sailors go too far for Hughes one night when two girls paddle out to the ship hoping to make some money: "Thirty men crowded around, mostly in their underwear, sat up on bunks to watch, smoked, yelled, and joked, and waited for their turn. Each time a man would rise, the little African girl on the floor would say: 'Mon-nee! Mon-nee!' But nobody had a cent, yet they wouldn't let her get up. Finally, I couldn't bear to hear her crying: 'Mon-nee!' any more, so I went to bed. But the festival went on all night" (108).[23]

Throughout the description of the journey, Hughes's feelings for the Africans he encounters vacillate between pity and communion. On the one hand, as a sailor on an American ship, he at times looks at the local people as a detached and privileged outsider, expressing sympathy for their poverty, disease, and helplessness. On the other hand, because Hughes has suffered from prejudice and legal segregation in the United States, exhibitions of white intolerance—such as that of the Third Engineer in Hughes's own mess room and the presence of "Europeans Only" signs throughout colonial Africa—cause him to identify with the native people. His light skin and straight hair further complicate Hughes's relationship with the locals, who much to his chagrin treat him as a white man. The Africans greet his assertion that "[o]ur problems in America are very much like yours . . . especially in the South. I am a Negro, too" with laughter, head shakes, and cries of "You, white man!" (102–3).

His liminal status—as a "black" in the eyes of white Americans and European colonials and a "white" in the eyes of Africans—becomes most apparent in the chapter entitled "Burutu Moon." It begins with a sentence that casts Hughes in the role of Tantalus, reaching out for something he desires greatly but failing to attain it: "Sometimes life is a ripe fruit too delicious for the taste of man: the full moon hung low over Burutu and it was night on the Nigerian delta" (117). Learning from Tom Pey, one of the Kru men on his ship, that the local people will soon be engaging in an Omali dance, Hughes states his intention to go, but Pey warns him not to because "White man never go see Ju-Ju. Him hurt you! Him too awful! White man never go!" (118). Later they meet an old Muslim trader named Nagary who shows them an impressive collection of treasures from the interior. Hughes's joy at having glimpsed the continent's grandeur is quickly cut short, however, when he and Pey pass a group of local prostitutes who service foreign sailors. Returning to the docks, Hughes regards the vessels in the harbor as "[t]all, black, sinister ships" (120). On board his own boat that night, with the drums of the Omali dance he has not witnessed reverberating around him and the moon "like a gold ripe fruit . . . too sweet for the taste of man" shining above him, Hughes finds it difficult to sleep (120).

Late in *The Big Sea* Hughes makes a statement that once again places him between the white Western and black African worlds. In describing his painful break in 1930 with his white patron Charlotte Mason (whom he does not name in the book), Hughes affiliates himself with urban black America and thus separate from both "primitive" Africa and white America: "She wanted me to be primitive and know and feel the intuitions of the primitive. But unfortunately, I did not feel the rhythms of the primitive surging through me, and so I could not live and write as though I did. I was only an American Negro—who had loved the surface of Africa and the rhythms of Africa—but I was not Africa. I was Chicago and Kansas City and Broadway and Harlem. And I was not what she wanted me to be. So, in the end it all came back very near the old impasse of white and Negro again, white and Negro—as do most relationships in America" (325). As David Chinitz has noted, Hughes never completely repudiated primitivism even though he had moved away from it after the publication of *The Weary Blues* and "The Negro Artist and the Racial Mountain" in 1926. In the preface to a research paper he wrote at Lincoln University, Hughes indicates the differences he sees between "primitive" and "civilized" people: "In the primitive world, where people live closer to the earth and much nearer to the stars, every inner and outer act combines to form the single harmony, life. Not just the tribal lore then, but every movement of life becomes a part of their education. They do not, as many civilized people do, neglect the truth of the physical for the sake of the mind. Nor do they teach with speech alone, but rather with all the acts of life. There are no books, so the barrier between words and reality is not so great as with us. The earth is right under their feet. The stars are never far away. The strength of the surest dream is the strength of the primitive world" (quoted in *The Big Sea,* 311). Commenting on these lines, Hughes writes: "This meant, I suppose, that where life is simple truth and reality are one" (311). As a black person living in America, Hughes knows that life in the United States is never simple and that truth and reality seldom correspond. Anticipating to an extent an idea propounded by structuralist and post-structuralist theorists, Hughes sees "civilized" people as inhabiting a fallen world in which human beings are trapped in discourse. Given this premise, however, because he was born into "civilized" American society, even Hughes's act of throwing his books into the sea could not enable him to experience the prelapsarian condition of those people who, he claims, are not caught up in language.

In contrast to "Burutu Moon" where Hughes feels cut off from others and divided within himself, in his description of his break with his patron he positively asserts his African American identity. Anticipating the black American travel writers who began journeying to the continent with some frequency in the 1950s, Hughes did not go to Africa to find a new place to live (like nineteenth- and early twentieth-century émigrés), uncover the continent's past glory (like Pauline Hopkins's Reuel Briggs), redeem the continent (like Sutton Griggs's Ensal Ellwood), or found an empire (like Harry Dean) but rather to experience firsthand a land with special significance for people of the diaspora like himself. Echoing the conclusion of Graham's *Tom-Tom,* Hughes, though well aware of America's shortcomings in the era of Jim Crow, regards the United States as his only home.

Saving a "White" Woman (and Liberia, Too) in Henry F. Downing's *The American Cavalryman*

Like Ellis's *The Leopard's Claw,* Henry Francis Downing's *The American Cavalryman* attempts to tell a thrilling tale that draws on its author's considerable experience in and knowledge about West Africa. Although more politically engaged and ambitious than Ellis's novel, Downing's book also suffers from genre tensions that keep it from being truly revisionary and artistically successful. Unlike *The Leopard's Claw* with its rather vague jungle setting and focus on white characters, nearly all of the action of *The American Cavalryman* occurs in Monrovia or the Liberian hinterlands, the protagonist is an African American, and the other major characters are Americo-Liberians or Liberian natives. Moreover, the novel refers to specific locations in and around the Liberian capital, provides some limited historical background, and enumerates the problems besetting the country. However, Downing's decision to make his book a "Romance," a melodramatic story involving an American girl missing for twenty years who at the last minute is rescued from certain death in the heart of the jungle, greatly diminishes the impact of the novel's assessments of conditions in Liberia and its occasional observations about race relations in the United States.[24]

Born before Griggs, Hopkins, Bruce, and Du Bois, probably in 1846, in New York, Downing might seem an odd choice for a chapter on the New Negro and Africa. However, his extensive experience in and with Africa and his three books and an essay wholly or partly devoted to contemporary conditions in Liberia make him a transitional figure, like his fellow sailor Harry Dean. Downing divided his long, eventful life among three continents. Before reaching the age of thirty, he had seen action in the American Civil War, traveled around the world, spent three years in Liberia working for the government and living in the rural areas, and served in the U.S. Navy's Asiatic Squadron. Returning to New York in 1875, Downing held various jobs and became involved in politics. Grover Cleveland rewarded him for his support by appointing him U.S. Consul to Luanda in Portuguese West Africa, where he served from 1887 to 1888 when he resigned apparently because his efforts to encourage trade between the two countries proved fruitless. Downing continued to promote business ventures with Africa, first in New York in the early 1890s and then in London, where he lived from 1895 to 1917. In England, he worked as a commercial agent for Liberia, attended and presented a paper at the Pan-African Conference of 1900, and became friends with Samuel Coleridge-Taylor and Duse Mohamed Ali. Around 1913 he embarked on a new career as an author, writing at least nine plays for the London stage and contributing essays and serial fiction to Mohamed Ali's *African Times and Orient Review.* Shortly before returning to New York, Downing published *The American Cavalryman: A Liberian Romance.* Prior to his death in 1928, Downing wrote two brief nonfiction books, *Liberia and Her People* and *A Short History of Liberia.*[25]

All but two chapters of *The American Cavalryman* take place in Liberia. Capt. Paul Dale, a cavalry officer who served in the Philippines and is currently on loan to Liberia to direct its recently formed constabulary force, rescues the beautiful, fair-skinned native girl Lupelta from slavers and brings her to Monrovia to learn English, hoping to send her to America to be educated and eventually to marry her. However, Lodango, the Imbunda chief, wants Lupelta back so she can become his wife. Resentful of Dale and Americans generally, the Liberian president and his nephew conspire to send the Captain away on a mission so that Lodango can steal Lupelta. After learning of the abduction of Lupelta and Hulda, the mulatto stepdaughter of the president who is attracted to the American, Dale sets out in search of them, only to be drugged and kidnapped. Freed by his servant, Dale receives a letter from Monrovia informing him of the president's trickery and that Lupelta is white. Accused of being a witch, Hulda is commanded to undergo an ordeal ceremony; however, Lupelta offers to drink the sassa-wood in her place. Just before she drinks the poison, Dale arrives with reinforcements and Lupelta and Hulda are saved.

The American Cavalryman's assessment of Liberia echoes those to be found in Downing's *Liberia and Her People* and his 1913 *African Times* essay "Liberia": internally, a handful of corrupt, incompetent Americo-Liberians, the descendants of freed slaves who emigrated from the United States in the nineteenth century, exploits a backward native population that still practices polygamy, slavery, and witchcraft; externally, Liberia is crippled by foreign debt, threatened by European rapacity, and largely ignored by the United States. All three works assert that only African Americans can intervene to remedy the country's dire situation.[26] Rife with evolutionary language, the novel distinguishes "civilized" Americans such as Dale from "savage" Liberian natives, with the Americo-Liberians falling somewhere in between.[27] The initial depiction of the Liberian president drinking whiskey with his feet up on his desk is designed to illustrate the dissipation and crassness of the ruling class. However, while Dale notes their mismanagement, asserting that "under the right supervision" the natives could be transformed into productive workers (87), he does not hold the Americo-Liberians entirely responsible for the country's failures. As he explains to his African American second-in-command, Lieutenant Brown, "Because of their ignorance, they have failed to use opportunity wisely. One should not expect children to perform duties such as experienced persons would have found it exceedingly difficult to accomplish. Liberia's present misfortunes are the outcome of the false training of a ruling class lacking in moral and mental virility" (150–51).[28] Fleshing out Dale's argument, Brown asks, "You mean that a people fresh from a condition of enforced servitude, uneducated, inexperienced and without pecuniary capital, were not likely to succeed in building up a successful republic?" (151). "Exactly," replies Dale, who then proposes the following solution: "If a few hundreds of our people skilled in farming and other industries, would come over, the country would be bucked up" (151).

The end of the novel takes this exceptionalist argument to the extreme, sanguinely suggesting, like Griggs in *The Hindered Hand,* that one properly qualified black American can make the difference. With his military training and knowledge of agriculture, Dale epitomizes the type of person Downing believed should come to Liberia.[29] At the very end of the book, he has been given a five-year leave to pursue his "plan to develop the agricultural resources of Liberia" (306). Although he expects some opposition to his development project from the ruling class, Dale confidently asserts that the native population will welcome it and suggests that its implementation will save the nation from foreign encroachment and bankruptcy: "The so-called leaders, who now fatten on the State, doubtless will wish me further, but the majority will rejoice. Anyhow, if I succeed, the country will be saved from being absorbed by some European power, and that will be something gained" (306).[30]

The American Cavalryman thus appears to subscribe to a corollary of the Fortunate Fall doctrine, discussed in chapter 1. Dale here suggests that African Americans, who have ancestral affinity and historical links to the republic, have gained the requisite qualifications to insure Liberia's continued existence through converting to Christianity via the horrors of slavery, experiencing emancipation, and acquiring agricultural and vocational skills in postbellum America. However, the melodramatic African adventure plot becomes so dominant by the second half of the novel that Dale is relegated to the role of the heroic outsider who rescues a white woman from dangerous African natives. Downing's decision to rely so heavily on romantic conventions consequently vitiates the significance of *The American Cavalryman's* diagnosis of Liberia's ills and prescription for its recovery.

The novel's opening and closing chapters, both set in New York, expand the scope of Downing's text to include black-white relations in the United States. In chapter 1, "An Output of the Bleachery," John Calvert, "one of New York's wealthiest and most influential citizens" (11) but also the son of an octoroon, receives some information that causes him to begin to come to grips with his past. Dale's mother, Sarah, who happens to be Calvert's half-sister and disapproves of his passing for white, calls to ask a favor. Expressing her concern over a letter from Dale that reveals his interest in a fair-skinned native girl (later revealed to be Lupelta) and recalling Calvert's kindness in helping Dale get admitted to West Point, she asks him to write her son and advise him against such an entanglement. When Sarah mentions that the name of the girl's mother is Reesha, Calvert recalls the disappearance of his two year-old daughter and her nurse (none other than Reesha who kidnapped Lupelta) twenty years previously while he was working in West Africa as a lowly agent for a trading company. In the final chapter, set three years after the events in Liberia, Dale now married with a young son, has been promoted to Major, received the Spingarn Medal, and written a book about Liberia.[31] The only mystery that remains concerns whom Dale has married. Not until the novel's final page is it revealed that Lupelta has convinced her father to finance Dale's plan and Hulda is his wife.

If *The American Cavalryman's* overweening adventure plot minimizes the impact of its assessment of Liberia, it renders largely incomprehensible the book's intermittent references to American racial attitudes and practices, particularly passing and miscegenation. The first chapter presents Calvert as a person consumed with racial self-hatred, someone who denies his own racial ancestry and treats black Americans as his inferiors. Chided by his sister for keeping his origins secret, Calvert states he is not alone: "America is a Bleachery, and I am one of its peculiar outputs. The country is full of my kind" (15), suggesting that miscegenation, which along with passing the novel appears to decry, has been widespread. Dale's interest in Lupelta, the native girl later discovered to be "white" (though her grandmother was an octoroon), complicates matters. Lupelta's uncertain racial status—but not the happy outcome of the novel—parallels the tragic mulatto syndrome used so frequently in turn-of-the-century white and African American fiction.[32] Despite Sarah Dale's opposition to her son's relationship with the presumably African girl, his interest in Lupelta is presented as acceptable so long as she has been properly educated and he follows through with his intention to marry her. Once she is declared to be "white," however, Dale stifles his feelings for her—after the rescue, "[t]he American longed to take Lupelta in his arms. But she was white!" (301)—and turns his attention to Hulda. Unlike Hopkins's *Of One Blood*, in which siblings unwittingly marry as a result of the widespread miscegenation that occurred during slavery, Downing's novel does not stress or even mention the threat of incest posed by a union between Dale and Lupelta, who are first cousins. The final chapter clearly depicts the protagonist's decision to marry Hulda as the right one, which seems to underscore the novel's disapproval of miscegenation. Although there is a kind of justice in Calvert underwriting Dale's plan to save Liberia, a hereditary debt being paid though not publicly acknowledged, the novel fails to emphasize or comment upon this.

The novel also suffers from a curious presentation of dialogue. Unlike Ellis, who wrote a well-respected book on the Vai language, Downing was not a linguist. The narrator gives notice early on that "no attempt will be made to write the [English] language as it was brokenly spoken by Lupelta, or by any other person civilized or savage, who appears in these pages" (27)—perhaps because Downing believed that rendering such nonstandard and/or pidgin English would be unflattering to his Liberian characters (or is he merely concerned about compromising the dignity of his "white" heroine?). However, because he believes that "there are certain peculiarities of speech common among the natives, which must be retained" (27), when the indigenous people speak among themselves in their own tongues, Downing consistently translates these conversations into ungrammatical and at times idiotic and laughable English: "Waupau is head with know in it, Tongha is body with guts in it. Wow!" (183); "Waupau's head is full of cunning too much. Waupau's head is making softly catch monkey!" (186); "Waupau will send the don't know out of Tongha" (188); and so on. It is, of course, much more common practice to translate conversations in other languages into standard English. Furthermore, authors have succeeded in effectively rendering West African pidgin or creole.[33]

In a rare critical discussion of *The American Cavalryman,* Robert Bone makes some dubious statements that warrant comment here. Including Downing in a group of "assimilationist" early black novelists "who treat the color line as nonexistent or unimportant," Bone refers to the novel as a "success-fantasy" with Dale adhering to the heroic model of the white "Empire Builder" (49). However, Dale's hands-off posture toward Lupelta upon learning she is "white" indicates that the color line exists not only in the United States but even in the African bush. Moreover, the novel predicts but does not depict the success of the agricultural program proposed by Dale, who is much closer to the hero of a white African adventure story than a black American Cecil Rhodes (a characterization that might more accurately apply to Dorlan Warthell in Griggs's *Unfettered* and Reuel Briggs in Hopkins's *Of One Blood* than Downing's protagonist).

With the exception of *The Leopard's Claw,* which focuses on white characters and strives to be apolitical, *The American Cavalryman* is unique among African American novels about Africa published before 1920 in its failure to invoke a central tenet of Ethiopianism—the prediction that people of African descent are destined (once again) to assume a leadership position among the nations of the world. There are neither references to Africa's past greatness nor predictions that Africans will rival Europeans and Americans. The survival of Liberia—made possible by black American investment and immigration to the country—is the boldest prognostication of Downing's book. Despite its exceptionalism and paternalism, the novel's movement away from monumentalism and its emphasis on conditions in contemporary Africa anticipate some of Locke's prescriptions for New Negro writers. However, although the book includes an informed assessment of Liberia's woes that contrasts with Griggs's *The Hindered Hand* and looks ahead to George Schuyler's *Slaves Today* (1931), its reliance on an African adventure plot greatly reduces its political significance and revisionary impact.

Exporting Manifest Destiny and Economic Prosperity to Africa in Gilbert Lubin's *The Promised Land*

Gilbert Lubin's fifty-nine-page novella *The Promised Land* tells the story of three prominent African American citizens—a lawyer named Black, a Baptist minister named Jones, and an African Methodist minister named Wesley—who conceive a plan for transporting large numbers of black Americans to Liberia. After receiving every encouragement from that country's consul general to the United States, they travel to Liberia to determine whether their plan is practicable. There they are welcomed by the president, who offers to give each immigrant twenty acres of unoccupied land provided he or she agrees to become a citizen. While Black stays to make arrangements for placing those who decide to come, Jones and Wesley return to Washington, where they outline their plan to Mr. Prince, an African American Congressman. Prince makes an impassioned speech that persuades Congress to pay for the émigrés' passage to Liberia and provide them with some capital so they can get settled in their new country. Jones and Wesley address congregations throughout the South, attempting to convince blacks to relocate to Liberia. Not only is their recruitment campaign a complete success but the emigration scheme results in such prosperity for Liberia that the country doubles in size, outstripping the prediction made in Downing's *The American Cavalryman* that black Americans will be responsible for turning the country around.

Lubin attempts to address questions concerning the plausibility of his narrative in his preface. Although he states that "[f]or the most part [the novel] is purely imaginary," he proceeds to list some facts that attest to the book's accuracy, namely that Liberia is a free republic, that there are Liberian consulates in the United States, and that an African American does serve in the House of Representatives.[34] Overall, however, in contrast to Downing's novel and Schuyler's *Slaves Today, The Promised Land* contains very few references to either specific events in Liberia's past or present conditions in the country, which suggests that the author may not have known a great deal about the West African republic. In addition, Reverend Wesley's statements that there are "about twenty thousand former American slaves and their descendants" in Liberia (15) and that the soil is "very fertile" (16) substantially overstate the case.[35]

More important, Lubin's depiction of the positive reactions of not only the American and Liberian governments but also the African Americans themselves to the prospect of mass emigration conflicts with the historical record. Even assuming that the majority of white Americans would welcome the departure of the African American population and that this could be implemented without chaos ensuing, there is little to suggest that Prince's argument that the American government has a duty to underwrite the emigration plan because of its complicity in the slave trade during the previous century would convince the members of Congress to appropriate the hundreds of millions of dollars necessary to transport the country's black population to Liberia.[36] Likewise, the Liberian government's refusal to allow Marcus Garvey to carry out a comparatively modest plan to settle three thousand immigrant families within its borders calls into question the president's open-armed reception of black Americans in *The Promised Land*. In 1920 Garvey dispatched a group of UNIA officials to meet with the Liberian government to discuss his plans eventually to transfer his headquarters and transport large numbers of black Americans to Liberia. Although negotiations went well initially, by July of 1924 President C.D.B. King had so turned against the Garveyites that three UNIA official who arrived in Monrovia were quickly arrested and deported. Sundiata suggests that the Liberian government rejected Garvey's initiatives because of its fears that a strong UNIA presence in Liberia would both complicate its delicate relations with England and France because of Garvey's announced intentions to liberate Africa and pose a threat to the already tenuous position of the Americo-Liberian ruling elite (112–14).[37] Similarly, Lubin's portrayal of black America's ready acceptance of Black, Jones, and Wesley's emigration program ignores the intense and longstanding opposition of prominent black leaders, including Frederick Douglass, to the back-to-Africa schemes of the ACS, Bishop Turner, Garvey, and others.[38] The mass exodus in *The Promised Land* anticipates later African American fiction, such as William Melvin Kelley's *A Different Drummer* (1959) and Derrick Bell's "The Afrolantica Awakening" (1992). However, in contrast to these works, Lubin's novel does not depict the effects that the departure of the black population has on America.

Although almost wholly devoid of the millenarian Ethiopianism that figures largely in novels by first-generation writers, Lubin's book (like Downing's) exhibits the condescension toward Africa that Locke chided earlier writers for. Wesley's espousal of the Fortunate Fall doctrine in the first chapter—"It is true that we have much for which to thank the white men. They brought our forefathers from a state of barbarism to one of civilization" (14)—is typical of the attitude toward the African past expressed in the novel.[39] Throughout the book Wesley asserts his pride in his race; however, it becomes clear that by his "race" he means African Americans rather than people of African descent in general. Reflecting on the progress made by black Americans since the end of the Civil War, Wesley declares, "No race in history has made such a remarkable improvement in so short a time" (49). Aligning himself with several black leaders of the previous century, Wesley implies that the experience of slavery and its aftermath in the United States has had positive results for African Americans, elevating them above even the most dignified of Africans: "My father though a king and my mother a queen, in their native country, were captured and made to bear the stigma of slavery. But I am a free man" (49). Although this revelation of royal African ancestry links Wesley to Dorlan Warthell in Griggs's *Unfettered* and Reuel Briggs in Hopkins's *Of One Blood,* the minister discounts the significance of his parents' status because it failed to protect them from the degradation of enslavement. As not only a free but also a "civilized" person, Wesley suggests that he is better than his parents.

In the late eighteenth and the nineteenth century, African American leaders such as Paul Cuffe and Alexander Crummell were concerned about liberating Africa from what they regarded as barbarism and paganism. Around the turn of the century, however, some Ethiopianists began to adopt the emancipation of the continent from the colonial powers as an ultimate if not immediate objective. While they might seem to be strange bedfellows, Ethiopianism and manifest destiny at times came together—as in Blyden's "Call of Providence," Garveyism, and Harry Dean's dreams of a black African empire—to form a hybrid philosophy envisioning an African American-led movement that would start in one corner of Africa and eventually liberate the whole continent. *The Promised Land* hints at such a scenario in the third chapter when the Liberian president tells his American guests, "To be sure we have but one star [on our flag] instead of forty-eight, but we may have more later on. We remember that the United States started with only thirteen" (29). In summing up the fate of the immigrants and their new country on the book's final pages, Lubin indicates that the process of decolonizing Africa is already underway: "Very shortly all of the desirable unoccupied land in Liberia was cleared; then taking for their slogan 'Africa for the Africans' they reached out into the surrounding countries. They bought out other settlers and had land annexed to the republic of Liberia. Thus the country became practically twice its original size" (58–59). In contrast to most of the first generation writers, who invoked Ethiopianism's prediction that spiritual and moral strength would enable people of African descent to overcome white world dominance, Lubin (like Dean) sees economic prosperity as the key to Africa's rehabilitation.

Realism, Melodrama, and Allegory in George S. Schuyler's *Slaves Today*

Unlike Downing, who rather than effectively manipulating the white African adventure tale is manipulated by it, and Lubin, who apparently gave little thought to generic considerations or their implications, George Schuyler consciously constructs a generic hybrid in *Slaves Today*. Although critics have noted the alternation between realism and melodrama in the novel, they have failed to account for its allegorical dimension, which Schuyler achieves by signifying on the African American slave narrative. Although the greatest revisionary success by far among these three black American novels about Liberia, *Slaves Today* reverts at a key moment to a major motif of Africanist discourse, which somewhat diminishes its revisionary impact.

Commissioned to write not only a series of articles on the situation in Liberia by the *New York Evening Post* but also a book on the subject by the publishing firm of Brewer, Warren, and Putnam, Schuyler arrived in Monrovia in February of 1931. Having carefully researched his subject, Schuyler knew that he could not openly investigate the charges against the government, and so he pretended to be on vacation. During his three-month sojourn, Schuyler traveled extensively and interviewed a number of people, including survivors of the Fernando Po slave camps, President Edwin Barclay, and W.D. Hines, the resident manager of the country's largest employer, the Firestone rubber plantation. His articles began appearing in the *Post* and other mainstream white newspapers in June and were reprinted in African American newspapers, including the *Pittsburgh Courier* in September and October. Written in only two or three months while Schuyler was recovering from malaria and attempting to fulfill his many journalistic responsibilities, *Slaves Today* was published in October 1931 (Peplow, 85, 99).

To date the most in-depth reading of *Slaves Today* appears in Michael

W. Peplow's *George S. Schuyler*. In discussing the novel, Peplow refers to the "Monrovia Thread," which exposes the corruption and depravity of Americo-Liberian officials from the president on down, and the melodramatic "Zo-Pameta Thread," named after an indigenous couple whose marriage is interrupted by a governmental raid and who subsequently endure slavery on Fernando Po and concubinage in the harem of an Americo-Liberian district commissioner respectively. Although Peplow extols the effectiveness of certain scenes, he regards *Slaves Today* as a flawed novel because of the one-dimensionality of many of the characters and what he sees as Schuyler's inability to integrate his two narrative threads successfully. Characterizing the book as a potboiler, a "muckraking novel" that should be judged by "journalistic" rather than literary standards, Peplow nevertheless correctly describes the book as "the first attempt at a realistic assessment of Africa by a black writer" (99). He also credits Schuyler with going beyond the less heretical New Negro writers who expressed doubts about "the significance of Mother Africa," such as Cullen in "Heritage" and Hughes in "Afro-American Fragment," by "deromanticiz[ing] Africa completely" in *Slaves Today* (87).

Schuyler deromanticizes Liberia by equating it with dictatorships elsewhere. Although he was accused of betraying the race for his articles about slavery in Liberia, the foreword to *Slaves Today* puts an entirely different slant on Schuyler's loyalties: "If this novel can help arouse enlightened world opinion against the brutalizing of the native population in a Negro republic, perhaps the conscience of civilized people will stop similar atrocities in native lands ruled by proud white nations that boast of their superior culture" (6). What seems implicit in this statement is Schuyler's awareness that George Putnam would never have sent him to a European colony to report on the treatment of the natives there, nor presumably would Schuyler as a black journalist have been granted entry into— much less mobility within—one of these colonies. Schuyler was angered by the many attacks upon him for his condemnation of the Liberian government, which he believed were motivated by black race chauvinism. In a 1933 *Pittsburgh Courier* column he defended his calls for outside intervention in Liberia by declaring, "I have neither said nor intimated that Negroes per se were incapable of self-government. I have stated over and over again that intervention is necessary in Liberia because it is impossible for self-government to function when elections are stolen by force. Liberia is a self-perpetuating dictatorship of a half dozen families, who do as they please and use the army to stay in office. Those who are progressive and liberal have no chance of getting to power. I condemn such dictatorship, whether it be in Mississippi, Peru, Germany, or Russia" ("Views and Reviews," 1 July 1933).

Schuyler sees no difference between a black dictatorship exploiting blacks in Africa and either white exploitation of blacks in the American South or white exploitation of whites in other countries. People who would make excuses for the dictators because of their skin color elicited only scorn from Schuyler: "I loathe the hypocrisy of those Negroes who are willing and eager to cover up the misdeeds and cruelties of other Negroes just because they are Negroes, even though the victims be Negroes" ("Views and Reviews").

Introducing one of the novel's major themes, Schuyler states in his preface to *Slaves Today,* "Slavery . . . exists under various euphemisms today in practically all parts of Africa, the East Indies and the South Seas. It is found as well in the colonies of the European powers as in the Negro-ruled states of Abyssinia and Liberia" (5). He finds its existence in the black republic particularly ironic, however, because freed slaves had founded the country in the previous century. To drive home this irony and to illustrate his contention that every state must guard against the corrupting effects of absolute power, Schuyler constructs an elaborate analogy between the Southern United States before the Civil War and contemporary Liberia. For this reason certain passages in the novel recall antebellum abolitionist works, particularly slave narratives. Casting the Americo-Liberians as brutal Mr. Coveys (from *Narrative of the Life of Frederick Douglass*) and lecherous Dr. Flints (from Harriet Jacobs's *Incidents in the Life of a Slave Girl*) and the indigenous population in the role of Southern slaves, this extended comparison, in fact, ties together the Monrovia and Zo-Pameta Threads, which Peplow regards as discrete.

Schuyler heightens the depravity of the Liberian ruling elite by connecting them with not only the Southern slave owners (whose comfort was predicated on the unremunerated labor of their servants and who sexually exploited the women over whom they ruled) but also the slave catchers who kidnapped and shipped Africans overseas to work on large plantations. His description of Zo and Pameta's village before and after the arrival of District Commissioner David Jackson and his Frontier Force troops recalls Olaudah Equiano's moving account of the effects that being kidnapped and thus separated from his family and village as an eleven year-old boy had upon him. Like Equiano, Schuyler depicts the orderliness, morality, and harmony in the village of Takama. All of this is suddenly shattered, however, when Jackson arrives and arrogantly demands the taxes that are owed by the village to the government. When Chief Bongome cannot produce the required amount, Jackson publicly beats him in front of the shocked villagers. Their attempt to defend the man whom they regard as a father results in a massacre when the troops open fire. The new bride Pameta is taken as a concubine by Jackson to teach the village a lesson, and when Zo later goes in search of his wife he is captured and shipped off to Fernando Po. In recounting Zo's kidnapping, transportation to Fernando Po, and experiences on the island, Schuyler emphasizes the links between the trans-Atlantic and the Liberian slave trade. For example, a ship called the *Santa Clara* takes Zo and other shanghaied natives to the Spanish colony on a voyage that recalls the horrors of the Middle Passage: forty men are crowded into the fore part of the ship, there are only two portholes, the smell is appalling (154).

Schuyler both implicitly and explicitly links the Americo-Liberians to white Southern slaveholders. To give the reader a sense of the size of Liberia he compares "this vast tropical territory" to "the American state of Virginia" (100), the cradle of the Confederacy. More often, however, he directly points out the irony of the ruling elite's actions: "Their forefathers had come here to this expanse of jungle to found a haven for the oppressed of the black race but their descendents were now guilty of the same cruelties from which they had fled. The Americo-Liberians were to rule; the natives to obey" (100–101). Schuyler's focus on Americo-Liberian sadism and licentiousness, particularly the whippings inflicted on the indigenous people and the government officials' sexual exploitation of native women such as Pameta, resembles the often graphic depictions of slaveholders' violence and lust found in many slave narratives. Likewise, Florence Jackson's jealousy of the women her husband exploits and the cruelty she directs toward these unwilling concubines signifies on the African American slave narrative, particularly those by women, such as Harriet Jacobs, who depicts Mrs. Flint in a similar manner. In addition, Schuyler's statement late in *Slaves Today*—"It is no uncommon sight in Monrovia to see a well-dressed Americo-Liberian child going to school followed by a ragged youngster of perhaps his age carrying his books. Both might be of exactly the same color but nevertheless a great gulf separates them. As there were social classes far removed from each other in white countries, so there were in this black republic" (232)—is reminiscent of Jacobs's poignant description of the two sisters, one black and one white, whom chattel slavery will soon separate and confer completely different fates upon: "I once saw two beautiful children playing together. One was a fair white child; the other was her slave, and also her sister. When I saw them embracing each other, and heard their joyous laughter, I turned sadly away from that lovely sight. I foresaw the inevitable blight that would fall on the little slave's heart. I knew how soon her laughter would be turned to sighs" (29). Borrowing another theme from the slave narrators as well as Downing's *The American Cavalryman,* Schuyler also stresses the hypocrisy of the Americo-Liberians whose intense Christianity never interferes with their greedy and immoral pursuit of wealth, power, and sexual gratification.

In attempting to account for the Americo-Liberians' depravity in one of the novel's key passages, however, Schuyler momentarily abandons not only his analogy between the ruling elite and Southern slaveholders but even his belief that absolute power corrupts absolutely. He writes of Florence Jackson: "She often smiled cynically at the living irony that is Liberia. Her forefathers, freed Negroes from Maryland, had come to Liberia filled with Christian ideals, trained to Anglo-Saxon customs and suffused with the true spirit of pioneers. They had planned to establish in Africa a replica of America. Instead of conquering Africa, she realized that they and especially their descendents, had been conquered by Africa. One by one they had adopted the worst habits and customs of the aborigines they exploited and despised" (229). In depicting the ruling elite as having succumbed to the corrupting influences of Africa and Africans, Schuyler here invokes a theme frequently employed in white writing about Africa. Although he clearly means to continue his relentless condemnation of the Americo-Liberians in this passage, Schuyler instead absolves them somewhat of responsibility for their actions by portraying them as "going native."[40] Rather than being guilty of gross moral failing and of corrupting the indigenous population—which is how Schuyler has presented them in the book up until this point—here the ruling elite comes off as merely constitutionally weak, unable to resist the moral contagion that Africa represents. Taken to its logical conclusion, this passage suggests that the Americo-Liberians' corruption makes them the most quintessentially African people in the book.[41]

Despite this significant lapse into a motif often used by white authors to depict Africa as a nightmare world, the central thesis of *Slaves Today* remains unchanged. Deliberately avoiding Ethiopianist teleology and the monumentalism of the previous generation and Garveyism, as well as the romanticism of many of his contemporaries, Schuyler asserts that slavery in particular and dictatorship in general are evils to be rooted out and defended against no matter where they may occur or who may be dominating whom. Implicit within this argument is Schuyler's belief that those who would excuse the people responsible for such oppression because of the skin color of the parties involved are short-sighted race chauvinists, a position he would return to and elaborate in later works, some of which will be discussed in chapter 4.

During the New Negro era, Ethiopianism continued to exert considerable influence on black American writing about Africa; however, some of its basic tenets were challenged or abandoned. Although Garvey and the UNIA repeatedly invoked Ethiopianist teleology and although expressions of African American exceptionalism appear in books such as *The American Cavalryman, The Pedro Gorino,* and *The Promised Land,* several other texts, including Locke's "Apropos of Africa," Cullen's "Heritage," Hughes's *The Big Sea,* and Schuyler's *Slaves Today,* deliberately diverge from the monumentalism and condescension often found in nineteenth- and the turn-of-the-century depictions of the continent. Unlike earlier authors who tend to be ambivalent toward or even supportive of European colonialism, second generation writers are uniformly anticolonial, although not always anti-imperial, as texts by Garvey, Dean, and Lubin that advocate the establishment of some type of a black empire in Africa attest. In addition to avoiding monumentalism and exceptionalism, each of the three most notable texts of the New Negro era, Graham's *Tom-Tom,* Hughes's *The Big Sea,* and Schuyler's *Slaves Today* breaks new ground in some way. The first serious, full-length, non-didactic black American drama to be set partly in Africa, Graham's opera meditates on the relationship between African Americans and the continent in an artistically and historically profound way. Anticipating African American literary travelers who began journeying to Africa with regularity in the 1950s, including Richard Wright, Hughes devotes not only the opening but a significant portion of his autobiography to his experiences in Africa in the early 1920s. Focusing, like Hughes, on the present rather than the past, Schuyler conceives his novel as a generic hybrid, using an allegory of American slavery to unify the realistic and melodramatic strands of his condemnatory portrait of contemporary Liberia.

4

The African American Literary Response to the Ethiopian Crisis

All you colored peoples
No matter where you be
Take for your slogan
AFRICA BE FREE!
Be a man at last
Say to Mussolini
No! You shall not pass.

LANGSTON HUGHES, "BALLAD OF ETHIOPIA"

The Black Shirts slump on the camels,
Haggard and granite-eyed;
No longer the gypsying Caesars
Who burnt-faced breeds deride:
In the river Takkaze their vanity
Lies with the Caesars who died.

MELVIN TOLSON, "THE BARD OF ADDIS ABABA"

Whereas the first generation of twentieth-century black American writers to depict Africa uniformly embraced Ethiopianism, during the second generation writers such as Locke, Graham, Hughes, and Schuyler consciously rejected some, most, or all of its basic tenets. On the subject of colonialism and imperialism, turn-of-the-century writers such as Griggs, Hopkins, and even the early Du Bois were at best ambivalent,[1] though John E. Bruce took a clearly negative stand. During the Harlem Renaissance period, in contrast, Hughes and Schuyler were unequivocally anticolonial and anti-imperial while diehard Ethiopianists like Garvey and Dean sought to replace European colonialism with some form of black imperial rule. In the literature inspired by the Italo-Ethiopian War and its aftermath, a staunch anticolonialism and anti-imperialism was grafted upon a specialized form of Ethiopianism centered around the beleaguered East African kingdom of Abyssinia.

The Italian invasion and occupation of Ethiopia figure not only in several poems by Langston Hughes but also in a lengthy prose fragment and poetry by Melvin B. Tolson and serial novels by George Schuyler. Early in the war, Hughes adopted a racial approach to the besieged nation; late in the conflict and after the Italian takeover, he looked at the Ethiopian situation from a Communist point of view. Set in East Africa just before and during the war, Tolson's unfinished novel "The Lion and the Jackal" (1935?)[2] and a companion piece, "The Bard of Addis Ababa," included in his first published book of poems *Rendezvous with America* (1944), take a decidedly pro-Ethiopian stance and evince an impressive familiarity with Ethiopian history, culture, and geography. Like Hughes, in the wake of the Italian victory, Tolson's position toward the Ethiopian conflict shifted from a racial to an economic approach, as revealed in "Caviar and Cabbage" columns Tolson wrote in the late 1930s and early 1940s. Thus, both writers initially embrace but then move away from the new version of Ethiopianism greatly intensified if not occasioned by the Italian aggression.

Novels by the first generation of African American writers to depict Africa reflect the powerful influence of Ethiopianism on the black American imagination. Hopkins portrays a once and future Ethiopian kingdom in *Of One Blood,* and Griggs and Bruce invoke the biblical prophecy of a renascent Africa in their novels. *The American Cavalryman, The Promised Land,* and *Slaves Today* eschew the Ethiopianist teleology and ambivalence toward colonialism of the previous generation; however, Downing and Lubin's novels loudly trumpet African American exceptionalism. Although not primarily devoted to Ethiopia, George Schuyler's "The Black Internationale: Story of Black Genius Against the World" and "Black Empire: An Imaginative Story of a Great New Civilization in Modern Africa" (1936–1938 and published for the first time in book form in 1991 as *Black Empire*), which began running in the wake of the Ethiopian defeat, cannot properly be understood outside of the context of the Italian invasion and conquest. These truly remarkable serials portray Liberia as the base of operation for a technologically sophisticated and politically ruthless African American-led movement to seize control of Africa from the European colonialists, including the Italian occupation force. Capitalizing more explicitly on the intense African American response to the Italian defeat and takeover of Ethiopia, Schuyler depicts a wealthy black American assisting an Ethiopian princess in a scheme to restore Haile Selassie's regime to power in "Revolt in Ethiopia: A Tale of Black Insurrection Against Italian Imperialism" (1938–1939 and published as part of *Ethiopian Stories* in 1994). In hindsight many observers came to recognize what Schuyler was able to see so clearly in these serials: that Italy's act of belligerence against an independent African nation signaled the Axis powers' intention to dominate Europe and much of the rest of the world.

Like Hopkins's *Of One Blood* and Bruce's *The Black Sleuth*, Schuyler's serials feature bold and intriguing depictions of Africa. Schuyler deftly combines science fiction and political satire in the *Black Empire* novels to produce cautionary tales about the regimentation, brutality, and race chauvinism of totalitarian regimes. Although he abandons science fiction and anti-utopia in favor of a rather formulaic adventure story in "Revolt in Ethiopia," his final *Pittsburgh Courier* serial set in Africa, Schuyler once again targets fascism—in this case, Mussolini's takeover of the oldest independent nation in Africa, which the League of Nations and the major powers failed to stop. Significantly, in each of these three serials, Schuyler quite deliberately—and, in the case of the *Black Empire* novels, subtly, one might even say mischievously—uses Ethiopianism to manipulate his black American readers.

The Italo-Ethiopian War and Black America

Menelik II (1844–1913), who became emperor in 1889, significantly expanded Ethiopian territory, modernized the army, and consolidated the power of the royal family. After forming alliances with Britain and France against Italy, he routed the Italians at the Battle of Adowa, which led to the formal recognition of Ethiopia's independence in the 1896 Treaty of Addis Ababa. After his death, Menelik was succeeded by his grandson, Lij Iyasu, a Muslim, who wanted to change Ethiopia's official religion from Coptic Christianity to Islam. Tafari Makonnen (1892–1975) overthrew Iyasu in 1916, replacing him with Menelik's daughter Zauditu and naming himself next in the line of succession. In 1928, Ras Tafari was crowned king and after the death of Empress Zauditu in 1930 assumed the title Emperor Haile Selassie (Mighty of the Trinity) I, a position he held until he was ousted in a military coup in 1974. Between 1916 and 1935, Ras Tafari took steps to abolish slavery, made some efforts to upgrade the army, and sought to centralize the Ethiopian government. He also succeeded in getting Ethiopia admitted to the League of Nations in 1923, despite objections by Italy (McCann; Gann; "Haile Selassie").

Seeking to avenge the crushing Italian defeat nearly forty years earlier, Benito Mussolini's fascist army invaded Ethiopia on 3 October 1935. The Ethiopian forces offered some strong resistance, particularly during their "Christmas offensive" along and around the Tekkaze River in the north (Del Boca, 72); however, the Italians, relying on superior weaponry and chemical warfare, pushed steadily deeper into the country and entered Addis Ababa on 5 May 1936. Four days later, Italy announced its annexation of Ethiopia. Just prior to the takeover, Haile Selassie fled to French Somaliland, eventually making his way to Geneva in July 1936, where he made an impassioned plea for his occupied country before the League of Nations and warned of the consequences if the world failed to intervene.[3] Although this speech was well received, the League was powerless to act. Britain and France, the major colonial powers in Africa, quickly recognized Italian rule in Ethiopia; however, other countries, including the United States and the Union of Soviet Socialist Republics, did not. During the occupation, the fascists began building an extensive system of roads, banned miscegenation, and instituted segregation. The Ethiopians responded to Italian rule with fierce resistance. Following an unsuccessful attempt on the life of Marshall Rodolpho Graziani in February of 1937, the Italians put to death thousands of Ethiopians, including many members of the young, educated elite. That same year hundreds of monks were killed at the monastery of Debra Libanos. Nevertheless, a revolt broke out in Gojam in 1938 that was led by some of the younger, educated Ethiopians who had escaped the purge of the previous year. Italy entered World War II on the side of Germany in June of 1940 and shortly thereafter conquered British Somaliland. Haile Selassie traveled to Khartoum to coordinate resistance to the Italians with the British, reentered Ethiopia early in 1941, and returned to Addis Ababa on 5 May. The total liberation of Ethiopia was not complete, however, until January of 1942 (Turner, 38–39; Schwab, 33; Del Boca, 212–26).

At the turn of the century, in the wake of the Battle of Adowa, the popularity of Ethiopianism reached a peak among African Americans. Its influence—and the identification of black Americans with Menelik II's country in particular—can be seen, as several observers have noted, in the many black churches founded around 1900 with the word Ethiopian or Abyssinian in their names. The harsh conditions facing African Americans during this period also played a significant role. As Robert G. Weisbord explains: "Confronted by a deteriorating rural economy and a hardening of white racism, some American Negroes seized upon the theory that their ancestry could be traced to the once-glorious Ethiopian kingdom. The theory had no basis whatsoever in fact, but quite understandably it had great appeal for a downtrodden people who had been forcibly separated from their cultural heritage. They wanted to tie themselves ethnically to Africans who had successfully preserved an independent nation and an independent Christian church in the face of the European scramble" (231). Actual contacts between African Americans and Ethiopians in the first three decades of the twentieth century occurred infrequently at first but gradually increased. Some black Americans visited Ethiopia, primarily on business ventures, during this period, and in 1919 and 1927 Ethiopian delegations traveled to the United States. Haile Selassie's coronation in 1930 generated new interest in Ethiopia among African Americans, and, in response to Ethiopian appeals for skilled workers, professionals, and technical advisers, several black Americans left the economically depressed United States for Ethiopia between 1930 and 1935, although most of them were to return before the outbreak of the war.

In two recent books devoted to the African American response to the Italo-Ethiopian War, Joseph E. Harris and William R. Scott emphasize the intensity and the massive scale of black American identification with and moral support for Ethiopia. According to Scott, "The pro-Ethiopian crusade of African-Americans represents an extraordinary episode in modern U.S. black history. A mass impulse, its scope was broad and its force intense, exceeding in size and vigor all other contemporary black freedom protests" (210). The black press covered the conflict at length, roundly condemning Italy's aggression. No African American publication devoted more attention to the war than the *Pittsburgh Courier,* which in 1935 had the largest circulation of any black newspaper. The *Courier* presented Italy's invasion and the major powers' tepid response as a conspiracy designed to bolster white imperialism and keep black people in submission. The paper dispatched J.A. Rogers to the front, the only correspondent from a black American paper to report on the battles firsthand. Rogers achieved a journalist coup when the *Courier* on 7 March 1936 published his exclusive interview with Haile Selassie, the first granted to a foreign reporter (Buni, 245–47; Weisbord, 237–38). Scott suggests that as a result of all the news coverage, African Americans in 1936 knew more about Ethiopia's history and culture than that of any other African country. Several organizations were formed to raise money for Ethiopia, although the amount of money collected was quite small and very little of this actually found its way to Addis Ababa. During the war and immediately following Italy's victory, tensions between African Americans and Italian Americans escalated, resulting in riots in Brooklyn, Harlem, and Jersey City, New Jersey. In a 1945 *Chicago Defender* article, Langston Hughes recalled the racially charged atmosphere during "that tense week some years ago when Italy invaded Ethiopia and the police department flooded Harlem with men. . . . [T]hey were almost entirely white cops who glared at the Negroes and were glared at by the colored people" ("V-J Night," 157).

A major obstacle to concrete, long-lasting cooperation between African Americans and Ethiopians was the perception, apparently not without some basis in fact, that members of the Ethiopian ruling class did not regard themselves as black people and were reluctant to associate with African Americans. Two major supporters of the Ethiopian war effort later condemned Haile Selassie and the ruling elite's racial attitudes. When the exiled Haile Selassie refused to meet with him, Marcus Garvey, long a champion of the Ethiopian cause, attacked the ruler, warning that "The Negro Abyssinian must not be ashamed to be a member of the Negro race. If he does, he will be left alone by all the Negroes of the world" (quoted in Isaacs, *The New World,* 153).[4] Likewise, Willis N. Huggins, who had headed the major African American fund-raising effort on behalf of Ethiopia, subsequently criticized the Ethiopian regime. Despite efforts at damage control by Rogers and others as well as by Ethiopian representatives themselves, the combination of the rumors of Ethiopians' disavowal of racial kinship and the swift defeat of the country dampened African American enthusiasm for Haile Selassie's cause considerably.

Harris and Scott differ markedly on the long-term significance of the African American response to war in Ethiopia. Regarding the black American reaction as "a watershed in the history of African peoples," Harris sees a clear link between it and the freedom movements in the United States, the Caribbean, and Africa following World War II (xi, 159). Scott, in contrast, noting that despite extensive coverage in the black press the restoration of Haile Selassie to power in 1941 generated little interest among the African American masses, does not see the connection: "During the era of the civil rights revolution in America and the rising tide of black power all over colonized Africa, a generation of black Americans who had not been nurtured on the gospel of Ethiopianism or the veneration of the Ethiopian state tended to look beyond racially ambivalent Ethiopia toward other openly avowed black African nations for inspiration in their own liberation struggle against white oppression" (219–20).[5] The truth appears to lie somewhere between Harris's and Scott's widely divergent positions. Although key figures in the effort to aid Ethiopia during the war later proved instrumental in founding the Pan-African Federation, which organized the Fifth Pan-African Congress held in Manchester in 1945, these men, who included George Padmore and Jomo Kenyatta, were West Indian and African rather than African American, and their base of operation was London rather than New York (Hill, Introduction, 37).

Langston Hughes and Melvin Tolson's Shift from a Racial to a Marxian Approach to the Ethiopian Conflict

A gradual move from a racially based to an economic reading of the Italo-Ethiopian War can be seen in the six poems that Langston Hughes published between September 1935 and September 1938 that either directly address or in some way allude to the conflict. In his biography of Hughes, Rampersad observes that Hughes responded to the Ethiopian crisis in two different ways: "Hughes seemed sometimes to endorse the communist view, sometimes the more racial perspective" (322). The dates of the poems are significant, however, because they reveal a progression, rather than an inconsistency or alternation, in Hughes's thinking. In the two poems published before the Italian invasion, Hughes clearly adopted the racial perspective, but once the fate of Ethiopia was sealed he espoused the Communist view.

In "Call of Ethiopia," a nineteen-line lyric published in *Opportunity* in September 1935, Hughes's calls on "all Africa" to "arise" and "answer . . . the call of Sheba's race" (11, 13), concluding with the lines, "Be like me, / All of Africa, / Arise and be free! / All you black peoples, / Be free! Be free!" (15–19). This Pan-Africanist recruiting pitch recurs in "Ballad of Ethiopia," a fourteen-stanza poem published the same month in the Baltimore *Afro-American* that contains more topical references and employs a more belligerent tone. The speaker, personifying the black race throughout history, calls upon his reader to "Take as your slogan: / AFRICA BE FREE" (23–24) and then, echoing the sorrow song, issues a warning: "O nobody knows / The trouble I've seen— / But when I rise I'm / Gonna rise mean" (29–32). After recalling Joe Louis's defeat of the Italian fighter Primo Carnera, the speaker boasts, "Mussolini's men / They may swing their capes— / But when Harlem starts / She's a cage of apes!" (37–40), calls for black unity, and ends with the admonition, "Listen, Mussolini, / Don't you mess with me!" (55–56). These two poems resemble racially inflected poems inspired by the war published elsewhere in the world. For example, "A Poem on Ethiopia," appearing in Accra's *Vox Populi on* 21 September 1935, concludes, "From East and West, South and North / To Ethiopia we'll come, a fighting band / To drive imposters out of the Black Man's land; / If we win not, we will die trying / To keep our land, and freedom flag flying / Greedy man, let your war madness cease / The Ethiopian wants his land, and peace" (quoted in S.K.B. Asante, 217).

Beginning with the 132-line "Air Raid over Harlem," published in *New Theatre* in February 1936, Hughes looks at the Ethiopian conflict and its significance for African Americans in more than just racial terms. Subtitled "Scenario for a Little Black Movie," this poem implicitly and explicitly connects conditions in doomed Ethiopia with those in Depression-era Harlem. Two-thirds of the way through, the speaker not only continues to link Italian oppression of blacks in Africa with white oppression in America, particularly that of the police in Harlem, but pinpoints capitalist greed as the source of both instances of oppression:

BLACK WORLD
Never wake up
Lest you knock over the cup
Of gold that the men who
Keep order guard so well
And then—well, then
There'd be hell
To pay
And bombs over Harlem. (91–99)

This stanza suggests that if African Americans were to become aware of how capitalism exploits them and try to do something about it, then they would be just as likely to be the victims of the white world's firepower as the Ethiopians. Nevertheless, the speaker proceeds to imagine Harlem "waking," "see[ing] *red*," and "shak[ing] the whole world with a new dream"— a Marxist dream of "Black and white workers united as one / In a city where / There'll never be / Air raids over Harlem / FOR THE WORKERS ARE FREE" (103, 108, 110, 122–26, emphasis added).

The three relatively brief poems concerning Ethiopia that Hughes published in the wake of the Italian victory likewise consider the takeover of Ethiopia from a Communist viewpoint. "Broadcast on Ethiopia," which appeared in the July/August 1936 issue of *American Spectator* concerns 4 May 1936, the day Haile Selassie fled his country but also the day Communists gained seventy-five seats in the French Parliament. The poem refers to the defeated nation as a "Tragi-song for the newsreels" (6); reveals the African American disillusionment with the racial aloofness of the Ethiopian ruling class and asserts that the Ethiopians did not stand a chance, "Haile / With his slaves, his dusky wiles, / His second-hand planes like a child's, / But he has no gas—so he cannot last" (7–10); and laments that "Civilization's gone to hell!" (35). Yet because "Italy's cheated / When *any* Minister anywhere's / Defeated by Communists" (27–29, emphasis in original), there is cause for hope in the French election results. "White Man," published in *New Masses* in December 1936, begins by emphasizing the racial perspective but suddenly shifts to the Marxist view. The speaker, identifying himself as "a Negro," directly addresses the "White Man": "You take all the best jobs / And leave us the garbage cans to empty" (4–5); "You enjoy Rome— / And *take* Ethiopia" (12–13, emphasis in original); "Let Louis Armstrong play it— / And you copyright it / And make the money" (14–16). The last third of the poem, however, suggests that the real source of exploitation lies in class rather than race differences. Stating "I hear your name ain't really White / Man" (21–22), the speaker asks, "Is your name in a book? Called the *Communist Manifesto*? / Is your name spelled / C-A-P-I-T-A-L-I-S-T / Are you always a White Man?" (28–32). Finally, in "Song for Ourselves," published in the *New York Post* on 19 September 1938, the speaker links "Czechoslovakia! Ethiopia! [and] Spain!," recently overrun or currently beset by German, Italian, and Spanish fascists respectively, as victims of "the long snake of greed" (7, 10).

Melvin Tolson's fiction, poetry, and political commentary about Ethiopia in the late 1930s and early 1940s follow a similar path from racial identification to global economic analysis. The fifteen chapters of Tolson's incomplete "The Lion and the Jackal" are divided into two books. The title refers to Haile Selassie and Benito Mussolini respectively, although neither actually appears in the manuscript. The action begins in Djibouti, Ethiopia's French colonial neighbor, on 1 October 1935, two days before the Italian invasion. The major figure in Book I is Abba Micah Soudani, a renowned poet and patriot, who is a close friend of the emperor. In Book II the scene shifts to Ethiopia itself as a motley group of passengers travels by train from Djibouti to Addis Ababa on the day the war begins. The novel then jumps ahead to late December 1935 after the Italians, despite the setback of the Ethiopian counteroffensive in the vicinity of the Tekkaze River, have pushed deep into the country, and Soudani's son, Lionel, a lieutenant in the Ethiopian army, emerges as a key figure in the story. At the end of the manuscript, the outcome of the conflict remains very much in doubt as Lieutenant Soudani speculates that guerrilla tactics may be the most effective means of defeating the Italians.

Although there are no African American characters in the manuscript, Haile Selassie has an American advisor, and two white Americans ride the French train to the Ethiopian capital. One is a journalist who has come to report on the conflict. The second, a missionary who identifies himself as a descendant of John Brown, offers to take up arms against the invaders. Here implicitly and elsewhere in the novel much more openly Tolson equates fascism and slavery. The manuscript does allude to the "Black Condor," John C. Robinson, the African American pilot who served as the leader of Ethiopia's small air force in the war, as well as to the flamboyant Hubert Fauntleroy Julian, also known as the Black Eagle of Harlem (but referred to by one of Tolson's characters as "the big-mouth, Colonel Peacock" [89]). West Indian by birth and a Garveyite during the 1920s, Julian first came to Ethiopia in 1930 to organize Haile Selassie's air force, but left the country soon after crashing the emperor's best plane. He returned shortly before the war and once more served as aviation chief, only to anger the ruler yet again and lose his position to Robinson.[6] Most intriguing of all are references in "The Lion and the Jackal" to rumors among the Ethiopians that a group of five thousand African Americans, "freed and led by the great Dedjazmatch [General] Abraham Lincoln, were on their way to Addis Ababa, with tanks and bombers" (19).

Not enough of "The Lion and the Jackal" exists to determine for certain where Tolson intended to go with the story; however, it does not contain his only thoughts on the Italo-Ethiopian War. Allusions to the conflict are scattered throughout *Rendezvous with America,* and "The Bard of Addis Ababa" is completely devoted to the early months of the Italian invasion.[7] Like Tolson's unfinished novel, this 112-line poem adopts the racial approach. Each of the three sections of "The Bard" provides evidence that the poem derives from and/or was written in conjunction with "The Lion and the Jackal." The description of the accouterments of the Bard in section one identify him as Abba Micah Soudani. In the second section, the Bard's exhortation to the Ethiopian soldiers to "Rise up, ye warriors, do or die" (55 and 73), linking their cause to a wide variety of freedom movements mentioned in *Rendezvous* (especially that of the American soldiers at Valley Forge), and his prediction of defeat for Italy—part of which serves as an epigraph for this chapter—appear exactly as they do in "The Lion and the Jackal." Finally, the celebration of Ethiopia's Christmas offensive in the third section closely resembles that of the second half of Book II of the novel.

After the Italian conquest, Tolson abandoned the racial approach to the war. Writing about the then-concluded conflict in a "Caviar and Cabbage" column in the *Washington Tribune* entitled "Drama: 'The Tragedy of Ethiopia,' May 28, 1938," Tolson offers a coldly economic analysis that differs markedly from the passionate partisanship of "The Lion and the Jackal" and "The Bard of Addis Ababa." Like Hughes, Tolson blames capitalism for Ethiopia's defeat and for the undermining of international law, yet he is less cynical about the exiled Emperor than Hughes in "Broadcast on Ethiopia," describing Haile Selassie begging for assistance at the League of Nations as a tragic figure worthy of Shakespeare. Whereas at the end of the novel and "The Bard" Ethiopia's fate has not yet been determined, Tolson claims in the column to have predicted a swift Italian victory on the day the conflict began because "spears and old-fashioned guns are no match for mechanized modern warfare" ("Drama," 105). Tolson makes no distinction between Italy's occupation of Ethiopia and Britain and France's colonial rule in Africa and elsewhere; rather, referring to these countries as "The Unholy Three," he states, "England and France and Italy now exploit 500,000,000 colored people. For what? For dollars. For profits in gold and oil and rubber and agricultural products" (106). Although his global economic analysis differs significantly from the Ethiopianism of the first and

some members of the second generation of black American writers to depict Africa, his prediction for the future is somewhat reminiscent of
Ethiopianism's cyclical view of history. Tolson suggests that the capitalists
have been sowing the seeds of their own destruction, "But at home the
masses of the population in these countries tear out their lives against economic injustices. That's the cancer that will eat away these dishonorable
governments" (106), and he concludes the column with the assertion that
"The white man—I mean the big white man—has messed up the world.
He's had two thousand years to make good. He's had the best soil of the
earth at his command. Nature and fortune have smiled upon him. But he
started out wrong. Because he started out to exploit" (106). Although he
echoes many late nineteenth- and early twentieth-century Ethiopianists in
asserting that the West is destined to fall, Tolson differs from them by failing to express any hope that this will result in a better world for people of
African descent. Instead, with bitter sarcasm he can only urge his readers to
"laugh" at the "worst of all possible worlds" white people have created
(107, 106).[8] As will be discussed in chapter 5, Tolson would modify his
prediction about the future and Africa's role in it in the *Libretto for the Republic of Liberia*.

George Schuyler's Strongest Attacks on Race Chauvinism in the *Black Empire* Novels

*I knew it was hokum. I knew Binks had rigged up this robot and I
knew approximately just how it worked, and yet for the life of me I
could not but enter into the spirit of the thing and obey the commands of the voice.*

GEORGE S. SCHUYLER,
"THE BLACK INTERNATIONALE:
STORY OF BLACK GENIUS AGAINST THE WORLD"

If any work by George Schuyler can be called typical, it might be his 1927
essay entitled "Our Greatest Gift to America." After skewering those African Americans who take every opportunity to enumerate their people's contributions to the United States, he states that they have missed the greatest
gift of all—flattery. For not only does the presence of blacks in America
raise the self-esteem of even the lowliest whites in the country, enabling
them to feel they are better than somebody, but African Americans themselves reinforce such prejudice by trying to act and dress just like white
people. Along the way Schuyler points out what he sees as the absurdity of
the monumentalist approach to Africa, poking fun at the "self-appointed
spokesmen of the race who will even go back to the Garden of Eden, the

walls of Babylon, the pyramids of Egypt and the palaces of Ethiopia by way of introduction, and during their prefatory remarks they will not fail, often, to claim for the Negro race every person of importance that has ever resided on the face of the earth" (122). Dispensing his barbs democratically, Schuyler creates not only the ludicrous black spokespersons "Prof. Hambone of Moronia Institute" and "Dr. Lampblack of the Federal Society for the Exploitation of Lynching" but also insipid white supremacists such as "Cyrus Leviticus Dumbbell" and "Dorothy Dunce."[9] Beneath this humor, however, lies a very serious issue that informs most of Schuyler's works: race chauvinism and its deleterious consequences. On the one hand, Schuyler believed that white race chauvinism not only gives the Dumbbells and Dunces a false sense of self-importance, it also breeds feelings of inadequacy in the black population, who turn to hair straighteners and skin lighteners to look more like whites. On the other hand, black race chauvinism, such as that promoted by Schuyler's frequent target, Garvey, makes it nearly impossible to discuss rationally mistakes or crimes committed by blacks, intensifies divisions between the races, and plays into the hands of white racists who have constantly asserted African Americans' inherent differences from white people.

To expose the hazards and lunacy of race chauvinism Schuyler envisions the invention of a process that turns dark skin white and depicts the comic effects this has on both whites and blacks in America in his most famous novel, *Black No More* (1931), which Ishmael Reed hailed as the "first science fiction novel written by an Afro-American" ("George S. Schuyler," 195). As noted in the previous chapter, Schuyler also targets race chauvinism in the largely realistic *Slaves Today*. By dwelling on the greed and cruelty of Americo-Liberian officials, he makes an issue of what he regarded as the hypocrisy of African American leaders who kept silent about this case of black exploitation of black people that parallels the colonial practices of European countries. Although the *Black Empire* serials lack the humor of *Black No More*, Schuyler returns to political satire and science fiction in these novels. Once again he takes aim at black race chauvinism, specifically Garvey's announced intention to found a black empire and the refusal by many African Americans to denounce atrocities that would be roundly condemned were they committed by whites.

Abandoning the realism of *Slaves Today*, Schuyler nevertheless again uses Africa as a setting and once more targets dictatorship and race chauvinism in his fascinating, futuristic serials "The Black Internationale" and "Black Empire," which originally appeared in the *Pittsburgh Courier* from 1936 to 1938 under the pen name Samuel I. Brooks.[10] The publication of *Black Empire* in 1991 did much more than make available to scholars and the general public these virtually unknown novels about a successful African American-led conspiracy to liberate Africa from the European colonial powers and establish a black empire that will unify the continent. The volume also included a sixty-five page afterword on Schuyler and the significance of the novels written by the volume's editors, Robert A. Hill and R. Kent Rasmussen, as well as an annotated bibliography of Schuyler's fiction written for the *Courier* between 1933 and 1939 under a variety of pseudonyms. This combination of previously unavailable texts and new information, coupled with a substantial 1992 *New York Times Book Review* essay about the writer and the *Black Empire* novels by Henry Louis Gates Jr., should have the effect of rescuing Schuyler from unwarranted obscurity and forcing critics to come to grips with this complex writer whose career stretched from the 1920s to the 1970s.

The serials give expression to Garvey and Dean's black nationalist dream of a powerful, black-ruled state that can compete with the white powers. However, in contrast to not only Dean, who relied on a small, unmotorized ship and the trade it could generate to pursue his dream, but also the first generation of twentieth-century African American authors to depict Africa, who asserted that the superior morality and spirituality of people of African descent would redeem the continent, Schuyler enlists advanced technology, military might, and terrorist strikes to make the Black Empire a fictive reality. The Black Internationale wrests Africa from the colonial powers and withstands the subsequent assault launched upon it by the white world in large part because of its technical superiority—television, fax machines, high altitude airplanes, autogiros, solar power, atom smashers, hydroponics, germ warfare, and Strategic Defense Initiative-type ray guns are among the gadgets and new technologies featured in the serials.[11] In addition, as the Black Internationale's leader, Dr. Henry Belsidus, is fond of pointing out, his organization succeeds because of its ruthlessness.

Gates's "A Fragmented Man: George Schuyler and the Claims of Race" offers an insightful and largely persuasive reading of the author and his work that will certainly be the point of departure for future interpretations of Schuyler's corpus. Although Gates recognizes and strives to account for Schuyler's complexity, his reading of the writer as a literary schizophrenic who created a conservative public persona for himself while expressing extreme leftist views through the pseudonymous Samuel Brooks does not completely mesh with the facts.[12] Gates uses Du Bois's notion of double-consciousness to frame the divided self argument he makes about Schuyler. After recounting the highlights of Schuyler's life, Gates quite accurately states: "his career was not a simple drift from left to right but a complicated, painful journey filled with the sort of 'double-consciousness' that continues to raise disturbing questions about what racism does to people in America" ("Fragmented," 31). According to Gates, the *Black Empire* novels reveal that Schuyler's fragmented self reached schizophrenic proportions: "We now know that Schuyler had already begun to create powerful fictions more compelling in their nationalist mythologies than anything Marcus Garvey or Elijah Mohammed ever dreamed of. For Schuyler had matched his growing conservative and antinationalist public persona with an underground alter ego . . . Samuel I. Brooks" ("Fragmented," 42).

I am in complete agreement with Gates's statement that the *Black Empire* novels "are particularly important for what they teach us about Schuyler's complicated responses to the pressure of ideological conformity among blacks—and the failure of received ideological stances or political programs to account for this complexity" ("Fragmented," 43). However, in contrast to Gates's reading of the author as a schizophrenic, I view Schuyler as a black writer who responded to white racism and the pressure to toe the line within the black community by creating a variety of personae for himself (Samuel I. Brooks being just one of these). Schuyler donned and doffed these masks so that he could both "avoid monotony" (quoted in Hill and Rasmussen, "Editorial Statement," xviii), as he told a colleague, and, like the protean narrator of Ralph Ellison's *Invisible Man,* create space for himself in which to address the complex issues facing black Americans.

As compelling as Gates's argument for a split personality is, a close analysis of Schuyler's journalism from the 1930s, his other fiction written for the *Courier,* and the *Black Empire* serials themselves produces a much murkier picture. Gates's acknowledgment that the writer used the Brooks pen name as early as 1928 and that columns bearing Schuyler's name from the period when the *Black Empire* novels were running in the *Courier* contained many of the same anticolonial sentiments weakens his argument for schizophrenia. Both the serials and many of the writer's other contributions to the *Courier,* moreover, can be profitably read within the context of the African American response to the Italo-Ethiopian War and its aftermath. The conflict completely dominated the pages of the *Courier;* in some issues more than ten articles were devoted to the war. The paper commissioned Schuyler's friend, J.A. Rogers, whom it described as "the best-informed man in the world on Africa," to report on the battles. Week after week the Psalms verse "Ethiopia Shall Stretch Forth Her Hands to God" ran in big letters at the top of the *Courier's* Church section. The newspaper also advertised a new column by W.E.B. Du Bois that began on 8 February 1936 by claiming that each week it would provide background on the Italo-Ethiopian War. During the conflict, Schuyler wrote one or more editorials in support of Ethiopia almost every week. In addition, he often discussed the war in his

"Views and Reviews" column in the *Courier,* encouraging readers to con-tribute to Willis Huggins's defense fund for the besieged nation. Most no-table of all of Schuyler's nonfiction from this period is his 1938 *Crisis* essay "The Rise of the Black Internationale," included as an appendix to *Black Empire,* which not only recalls the title of the first *Black Empire* serial ("The Black Internationale") but also declares that "to combat the White Internationale of oppression [i.e., colonialism] a Black Internationale of liberation is necessary" (336).[13] Schuyler's emphasis in this essay on the role science and technology have played in Europe's domination of people of color and the role they can play in the liberation of these oppressed people also links it to the *Black Empire* novels, which are chocked full of descriptions of futuristic devices and new approaches to farming, diet, and health care employed by the Black Internationale.

A careful look at Schuyler's other fiction written for the *Courier* dur-ing the 1930s further undermines Gates's assertions about the writer's frag-mented self. The record shows not only that in his journalism in the middle to late 1930s Schuyler became increasingly anticolonial, but also that Schuyler using his own name wrote action-packed, science fiction fantasies about conspiracies to take over Africa that closely resemble the *Black Em-pire* novels attributed to Samuel I. Brooks. Schuyler's "Strange Valley: A Novel of Black and White Americans Marooned in the African Jungle," a thirteen-installment serial that ran in the *Courier* from 18 August to 10 November 1934, reads like a trial run for the *Black Empire* novels. It fea-tures a black American doctor, Augustus Cranfield, who in a remote sec-tion of the West African rain forest slowly amasses the wealth, soldiers, and arms necessary to fight a war designed to liberate Africa from the colonial powers.[14]

With their often stirring black nationalist rhetoric, the *Black Empire* serials almost beg to be read straight—that is, as expressing how Schuyler (or, as Gates would have it, Schuyler as Brooks) really believed blacks should respond to colonialism and white oppression in America in the wake of the subjugation of the oldest independent African state by a minor European power. Like Gates, Hill and Rasmussen in their afterword read the novels this way. To do so, however, one must disregard Schuyler's repeated refer-ences to the cold-blooded brutality and regimentation of Belsidus's Black Internationale and the mixed feelings of the serials' narrator, Carl Slater, about the organization he finds himself forced at gunpoint to join. Early in the first serial, Belsidus tells Slater, "I have dedicated my life . . . to destroy-ing white supremacy. My ideal and objective is very frankly to cast down the Caucasians and elevate the colored people in their places. I plan to do this by every means within my power. I intend to stop at nothing, . . .

whether right or wrong. Right is success. Wrong is failure. I will not fail because I am ruthless" (10). Patricia Givens, a kind of black prototype for *Goldfinger's* Pussy Galore, heads the Black Internationale's air force and eventually marries Slater. Matter-of-factly, she outlines Belsidus's program and its cynical attitude towards those he is supposedly liberating: "The masses always believe what they are told often enough and loud enough. We will recondition the Negro masses in accordance with the most approved behavioristic methods. The [Black Internationale's newly created] church will hold them spiritually. Our economic organizations will keep control of those who shape their views. Our secret service will take care of dissenters. Our propaganda bureau will tell them what to think and believe. That's the way to build revolutions. . . ." (47). Slater makes numerous statements expressing his reservations about Belsidus's organization. Of his participation in the Black Internationale's activities, Slater says: "I confess that I was a little taken aback. I had not bargained for anything like this. To be associated with cold-blooded murder was bad enough; to commit it was worse" (68). Similarly, at the start of the second serial, Slater describes the Black Internationale as "an organization which in its rise to power had known no law save that of expediency, no mercy except to people of color, an organization so ruthless in attaining its object that . . . sometimes even I shivered at the memories of the past" (145).

Although Gates does describe Belsidus as a "fascist superman," he makes no further comment about the methods the Black Internationale uses to achieve its goals—mass hypnosis through drugs and staged spectacles, germ warfare, euthanasia, and so forth—nor their implications. In contrast to Gates, John A. Williams, in his foreword to *Black Empire,* is troubled by the "grimmer side" of the serials, declaring that "Dr. Belsidus, in the final analysis, is a dictator, a fascist" (xiv). Nevertheless, he also reads the serials straight, believing Schuyler to be advocating the Black Internationale's take-no-prisoners approach, which Williams finds consistent with the writer's later extreme right-wing views and what he regards as Schuyler's elitism.[15] That Williams on the one hand can marshal evidence from *Black Empire* to argue that it dovetails with Schuyler's subsequent ultra-conservatism and Gates on the other can find support in the serials for his assertion that they reveal Schuyler to have been a closet leftist and black nationalist in the middle to late 1930s indicates the complexity of the *Black Empire* novels and their often elusive creator.

Furthermore, Schuyler's lone statement about the serials and their popularity—"I have been greatly amused by the public enthusiasm for 'The Black Internationale,' which is hokum and hack work in the purest vein. I deliberately set out to crowd as much race chauvinism and sheer improbability into it as my fertile imagination could conjure. The result vindicates my low opinion of the human race" (quoted in Hill and Rasmussen, "Afterword," 260)—cannot be dismissed as easily as Gates dismisses it. Even though the comment was made in a private letter to a fellow staff member of the *Courier,* Gates reads it as the public George Schuyler running down the work of his "other self," Samuel Brooks. In contrast to Gates's reading of the comment, I suspect that Schuyler associated himself as the author of the serials with the mastermind Belsidus and the young narrator, Carl Slater, whom Belsidus manipulates easily, with what Schuyler seems to have regarded as his naive *Courier* reader. This interpretation brings new meaning to certain passages in the serials, such as the epigraph I have chosen for this section, wherein Slater, who wants to resist the Reverend Binks's Church of Love ceremony, which he knows to be "hokum," nevertheless succumbs to "the spirit of the thing" and "the commands of the voice" (61). In many ways, this passage appears to sum up Schuyler's attitude toward Ethiopianism in its many forms. He considers it to be a dangerous, anti-intellectual myth with an incredibly powerful hold over the African American imagination, yet he is not above using it in his own fiction to produce specific effects.

It is also worth noting that particularly during the 1930s Schuyler often decried political systems that denied people personal freedoms, Communist and fascist alike. For instance, on 3 December 1937, while the second *Black Empire* serial was running in the *Courier,* Schuyler wrote: "What seems to have escaped the generality of writers and commentators is that [Communism, Fascism, and Nazism] are identical in having regimented life from top to bottom, in having ruthlessly suppressed freedom of speech, assembly, press and thought, and in being controlled by politicians. . . . What is new about these three forms of government is that all are controlled by politicians with a reformer complex; ex-revolutionaries who have gained power and have nobody to curb their excesses" (quoted in *Black and Conservative,* 240). This passage accurately describes Belsidus's organization in the United States and the kind of government he establishes in Africa. Thus, it seems quite possible that Schuyler, instead of creating a utopia in the *Black Empire* serials, wrote an anti-utopian text reminiscent of his earlier science fiction novel *Black No More* to expose the dangers of race chauvinism once again.[16] If this is the case, then for Schuyler the irony of the *Black Empire* novels and the public response to them may have been that the empire Belsidus creates is just as fascistic and repressive as the colonial governments he ousts.[17]

In the *Black Empire* serials, as in *Black No More,* race chauvinism and its consequences are a major theme, as Schuyler himself remarked. In *Black*

No More, Max Disher becomes the perfect white supremacist because he has experienced racial intolerance firsthand. As he tells his friend Bunny, "I've learned something on this job, and that is that hatred and prejudice always go over big. These people have been raised on the Negro problem, they're used to it, they're trained to react to it. Why should I rack my brain to hunt up something else when I can use a dodge that's always delivered the goods?" (147).[18] Similarly, Belsidus and the Black Internationale create chaos throughout the United States and trigger World War II in Europe by using terrorism and playing upon white people's religious and ethnic prejudices, not to liberate black people in America, Africa, and elsewhere but rather to revenge themselves on the white world and establish their own repressive regime. Certainly if the *Black Empire* novels are read as Gates, Williams, and Hill and Rasmussen have read them—as utopian fantasies rather than anti-utopian cautionary tales—then Schuyler must be seen as both perpetuating Africanist stereotypes about the continent and its peoples and harkening back to the exceptionalism of earlier black American writing by depicting an African American-led elite effecting the liberation of Africa. If, on the other hand, as I have argued, Schuyler regards Belsidus and his organization as no better than (or just as bad as) a group of white fascists bent on establishing an empire for their own aggrandizement, then the depiction of Africa in the serials must be considered in a different light.

Rather than having any love for or loyalty toward Africa and Africans, Belsidus approaches both in a calculating and cynical way. Long before he launches his invasion of the continent, Belsidus relies on monumentalist and primitivist rhetoric and imagery to manipulate the black masses. Eventually he constructs hundreds of Temples of Love throughout the world to brainwash black people through drug-induced orgies and Third Reich–style propaganda spectacles. The Temple in Harlem is "a huge building closely resembling an Egyptian temple, and in the form of a truncated pyramid" (57). During the ceremony Slater attends, spotlights focus on the mechanized God of love, a "huge 50-foot statute of the nude Negro" (61). African music is then piped in: "evil, blood-stirring rhythms born in the steamy swamps of the Congo" (62). Eventually the goal of completely controlling the congregants' minds is achieved: "Gone was all restraint, gone all inhibitions as the throbbing drums and sensuous, pulsating music tore asunder and subjugated our conscious beings. The inner man, the subconscious mind, the primeval urges born in the Mesozoic ooze, completely controlled us, dominated us, motivated us" (62). Significantly, Schuyler equates the effects of this mass hypnosis with the phenomenon of "going native." Unlike *Slaves Today,* however, where to "go native" means to succumb to the corrupting influences of Africa, Reverend Binks's carefully choreographed stage show uses things African (Africanist and monumentalist) as props to induce a state of total mental, moral, and physical abandonment in the black masses so that they can be compelled to perform any act their leader wishes.

In detailing the Black Internationale's conquest of Africa, Schuyler offers his black readers a series of revenge fantasies that at first appear to right historical wrongs. As Hill and Rasmussen assert, it is no coincidence that Liberia serves as Belsidus's beachhead in Africa and that the invaders quickly overthrow the corrupt regime of Edwin Barclay, which Schuyler had frequently attacked in his journalism (Afterword, 271). Lacking the manpower and the weaponry to invade every African country, the Black Internationale establishes its base of operations in the Liberian hinterland, relying on its air power and the cells its has created, funded, and armed throughout the continent to defeat the colonial governments. Schuyler also uses the *Black Empire* novels to punish Italy fictively for its conquest of Ethiopia, ending the first serial with Ethiopia's liberation and the second with Italy's decisive defeat at the hands of the Black Empire, as Hill and Rasmussen point out (Afterword, 280–81). Particularly intriguing is Schuyler's account of the overthrow of the Belgians in the Congo:

> Not only did [the Congolese] in a few hours destroy what the Belgians had laboriously and cruelly erected in almost fifty years of colonial exploitation, but they slaughtered white men, women and children with great ferocity. You have no idea of the blood-chilling effect of the laconic report from the head of the Black Internationale cell there which read: "Belgium Congo belongs to us. No white person is alive." Later in the day we learned that in many of the principal cities the whites had been beheaded, their hands and feet cut off to be dried as charms, and their bodies thrown to crocodiles. The Belgium Congo was a shambles, indeed, but nothing else could be expected in view of the long series of Belgian atrocities. (129).

Slater's ambivalence is a key aspect of this passage. He seems to be falling back on Black Internationale propaganda to reassure himself that what he has just heard is good news—not only a victory for his organization but also comeuppance for the heartless colonials. Yet he cannot suppress his revulsion at the murder, the mutilation, and the waste. Once again Schuyler portrays people as having "gone native"; however, this time he leaves it unclear whether some corruption inherent to Africa, the manipulations of Belsidus's organization, or the savage lessons taught by the Belgian colonizers bear responsibility. In any event, Slater is clearly made uncomfortable by the lack of restraint shown by the Congolese, in part perhaps because it resembles the loss of control he himself experienced at the Church of Love ceremony.[19]

The most clichéd depiction of Africans in *Black Empire* occurs late in the second serial, by which time Schuyler's plot has broken down to such an extent that he seems to have been merely churning out one melodramatic installment after another. Slater, Givens, and two other Black Internationale officials are forced to crash land in the Sierra Leonean jungle, where they are surrounded by men with filed teeth who prove to be "cannibals." Just before they are to be stripped naked, crucified head down, set afire, and then eaten, a Black Empire squadron spots and rescues them. Responding to this episode, John A. Williams has observed, "I cannot say if these negative portraits [of Africans] were as potent to readers then as they may seem to many of us now, some fifty-odd years later, but I find them disturbing elements (somewhat like rooting for Tarzan in the movies instead of the indigenous people) in works that were seemingly designed to instill pride in African Americans of the time. And these elements reflected Schuyler's [elitist] allegiances precisely" (Foreword, xiii). Without question this stereotypical portrait of African cannibals is disturbing; however, because the serials strike me as profoundly anti-utopian, I am not convinced that Schuyler's aim was always to instill pride in his black readers or that this episode—or at least Williams's reading of it—accurately reflects his allegiances. Despite the fact that Schuyler sets the majority of *Black Empire* in Africa, very few scenes, unlike *Slaves Today,* actually involve African characters. Even in those instances when members of the Black Internationale do interact with indigenous people, there is little or no communion between Belsidus's officials and Africans. This lack of connection, which surfaces in Slater's horror at the news over the slaughter of the whites in the Congo, becomes particularly apparent in the episode with the cannibals. As an outside force equipped with sophisticated technology and bent on dominating the continent, the Black Internationale has more in common with the European colonial powers than the indigenous population. Because they have arrived in a commandeered French plane and many of the soldiers employed by the French are black, Slater and the others' assertions that they are friends, affiliated, as they tell the chief's interpreter, with "the great black chief whose brave armies have run the white men into the seas" (233), fail to convince the natives. In fact, the chief prepares the same fate for them as that endured by "[t]housands of French and British officials . . . during the conquest" of Africa organized by the Black Internationale (236). In keeping with a major theme in Schuyler's works, the cannibal episode—like the euthanasia program instituted by the Black Empire and the exploitation of the natives in *Slaves Today*—suggests that shared skin color does not guarantee fair treatment of the powerless by those in power.

Pan-African Resistance to Fascism in George Schuyler's "Revolt in Ethiopia"

"Revolt in Ethiopia: A Tale of Black Insurrection Against Italian Imperialism," published in the *Pittsburgh Courier* from July 1938 through January 1939, is one of two serials Schuyler wrote directly concerning the Ethiopian war and Italy's subsequent occupation. The other, "The Ethiopian Murder Mystery: A Story of Love and International Intrigue" (and the first half of *Ethiopian Stories*), began appearing in the newspaper the month the conflict started and concluded in February 1936. Unlike "Revolt in Ethiopia," set mostly in East and North Africa, "The Ethiopian Murder Mystery" takes place in New York City, primarily in Harlem, where an Ethiopian prince, Haile Destu, has been murdered. The combined talents of the inductive black police lieutenant Big Jim Williston and the ratiocinative black newspaperman, Roger Bates, are needed to solve the case. Bates eventually learns that the Ethiopian secret service has killed Destu in order to keep him from turning over the plans of a death ray, designed to turn the tide of the war for the Ethiopians, to a seductive white female spy working for the Italians.

Like his journalist counterpart Carl Slater in the *Black Empire* serials, Bates, who identifies himself as a "race man" and a supporter of Ethiopia, is taken aback by the boldness, ruthlessness, and single-mindedness of the Ethiopian spies, one of whom tells him, "We are secret agents. We come and go about the world without the ordinary formalities. We change our names as often as our shirts. We forge or steal passports as we need them. We are, Meester Bates, a law unto ourselves. Our only allegiance is to Ethiopia. Our only enduring enemy is stupidity" (122). However, in this serial, as in "Revolt in Ethiopia"—and in stark contrast to the *Black Empire* novels—the morality of the Ethiopian cause is presented without ambiguity. As the Ethiopian operative, Sadiu Mattchu, tells Bates, "This is war, my friend. . . . Ethiopia is fighting for her life. We cannot be squeamish. Italian bombs have killed thousands of defenseless women and children. What are the deaths of [Italian agents] compared to them?" (122).

Written under the pseudonym Rachel Call, a pen name Schuyler used frequently in the *Courier,* "Revolt in Ethiopia" was one of the last serials he wrote for the newspaper. Apart from the fact that the protagonists are black and the story is vigorously pro-Ethiopian, the novella closely resembles a conventional adventure tale and therefore lacks the ambiguity, complexity,

Meta Warrick Fuller (1877–1968) allegorizes Africa as a female figure rousing herself from a deep slumber and preparing to regain her past greatness in *The Awakening of Ethiopia*. Plaster full figure (bronze cast), ca. 1907–1910. Courtesy of the Arts and Artifacts Division, Schomburg Center for Research in Black Culture, The New York Public Library, Astor, Lenox and Tilden Foundations.

Above left, A widely published journalist during the nineteenth century, John E. Bruce (1856–1924) wrote a fascinating serial about an African detective, *The Black Sleuth,* co-founded the Negro Society for Historical Research in 1911, and held a high office in Marcus Garvey's Universal Negro Improvement Association. Date of photo unknown. Courtesy of the Prints and Photographs Division, Schomburg Center for Research in Black Culture, The New York Public Library, Astor, Lenox and Tilden Foundations. *Above right,* Influential and outspoken editor of Boston's *Colored American Magazine,* Pauline Hopkins (1859–1930) published four novels between 1900 and 1903, including *Of One Blood; Or, the Hidden Self,* parts of which are set in Nubia. From the *Colored American Magazine,* 1904.

The first opera by an African American to be performed by a professional cast, *Tom-Tom,* by Shirley Graham (1908–1977), was presented twice at Cleveland Stadium in the summer of 1932 before a combined audience of over twenty-five thousand as well as broadcast on NBC Radio. Courtesy of the Hatch-Billops Archives, New York.

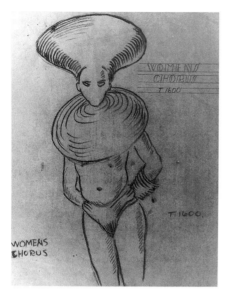

Above left, Drawing of a costume for the women's chorus for *Tom-Tom. Above right,* Noted baritone Jules Bledsoe as the Voodoo Man in *Tom-Tom. Below,* A scene from act 1 of *Tom-Tom.* All photos courtesy of the Hatch-Billops Archives, New York.

Langston Hughes (1902–1967) engaged with Africa throughout his long career in his poetry and in the first volume of his autobiography, *The Big Sea*. Date of photo unknown. Courtesy of the Prints and Photographs Division, Schomburg Center for Research in Black Culture, The New York Public Library, Astor, Lenox and Tilden Foundations.

Named poet laureate of Liberia in 1947, Melvin B. Tolson (1898–1966) wrote not only verse, most notably the *Libretto for the Republic of Liberia,* but also fiction and political commentary about Liberia, Ethiopia, and Africa generally. Date of photo unknown. Courtesy of the Prints and Photographs Division, Schomburg Center for Research in Black Culture, The New York Public Library, Astor, Lenox and Tilden Foundations.

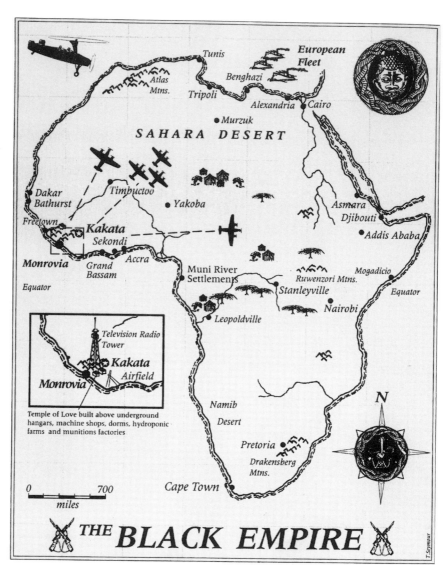

Map of the Black Empire, from George S. Schuyler's *Black Empire*. These novels depict a successful African American-led conspiracy to wrest Africa from the European colonial powers. Copyright © 1991 by Northeastern University Press and the Regents of the University of California. Reprinted with the permission of Northeastern University Press.

Using his own name as well as pseudonyms, George S. Schuyler (1895–1977) wrote more novels about Africa than any other African American writer in the first half of the twentieth century. Date of photo unknown. Courtesy of the Prints and Photographs Division, Schomburg Center for Research in Black Culture, The New York Public Library, Astor, Lenox and Tilden Foundations.

Cameron Mitchell as Charlie Morris and James Earl Jones as Tshembe Matoseh in Lorraine Hansberry's *Les Blancs,* Wednesday, October 21, 1970, at the Longacre Theatre, New York. Courtesy of the Theatre Collection of the Performing Arts Library of the New York Public Library.

and generic hybridity of the *Black Empire* novels. It features daring exploits, last-minute rescues, mysterious locations, and devilish villains, as well as a liberal amount of sex. As in earlier *Courier* serials, Schuyler emphasizes the importance of technology and, recalling *Slaves Today,* implicitly compares the cruelty of the Italian occupiers to nineteenth-century Southern slave owners. However, the major theme in "Revolt in Ethiopia" is the need for black American and Ethiopian (and thus by extension African) cooperation in resisting white oppression, whether it takes the form of Italian fascism, European colonialism, or American prejudice.

Traveling on a ship bound from France for North Africa as part of a world tour, wealthy black American playboy Dick Welland meets and quickly falls in love with the beautiful Princess Ettara Zunda, Haile Selassie's niece, who is on a dangerous mission to bring ancient treasure out of occupied Ethiopia to be used to buy arms for the underequipped resistance movement. Initially hesitant because Ettara's servant dies of stab wounds before his eyes, Dick soon agrees to help the princess. To evade the Italian agents on the ship, Dick hires a seaplane to take him, Ettara, and his servant, Bill Sifton, to Alexandria. Detained by customs officials because the Italians have planted heroin in their luggage, the trio are able to continue their adventure once Dick's references establish who he is and a fine is paid. Dick hires a plane to take them to Beni Shengui, a town near the Sudanese-Ethiopian border. After a brush with Italian planes, they meet up with the Ethiopian commander in the region, Dedjazmatch Yamrou, who flies them to Abra Destum, the sacred mountain where the Ethiopian treasure is held. Captured and assaulted by Italian soldiers, they are rescued by Ethiopian troops and led inside the mountain. After negotiating a series of passageways, Dick and Ettara appear before Bishop Truli Handem, keeper of both the treasure and the Ark of the Covenant and rumored to be two hundred years old. Ettara gives the bishop half of King Solomon's ring, entrusted to her by the emperor, and Handem presents them with a bag of precious stones. Contacting Yamrou by radio, the trio hope to be flown out of Ethiopia and eventually reach Europe. They are captured once more by the Italians only to escape again when Yamrou's plane and a large Ethiopian force liberates them. Quickly returning to Europe by air, the trio meet Ettara's father, Prince Dano Zunda, who immediately arranges to have the gems sold and to purchase rifles, machine guns, ammunition, and aircraft with the receipts. Their mission accomplished, Dick and Ettara marry.

Although "Revolt in Ethiopia" lacks the futuristic gadgetry of the *Black Empire* serials, Schuyler does emphasize the importance of technology in his final African novel. The whole point of bringing the treasure out of Ethiopia is to use it to buy modern weapons to dislodge the Italians. Schuyler shows that the Ethiopians can and will use sophisticated armaments effectively. Dick expresses surprise at seeing a telephone in isolated Abra Destum and is impressed by the Ethiopians' use of rifles equipped with silencers and telescopic sights. As in the earlier serials but still a year before the Nazis unleashed their blitzkrieg on Poland, two years prior to the Battle of Britain, and three years before the attack on Pearl Harbor, Schuyler presciently demonstrates how air power will transform modern warfare. In addition to portraying the destructive capabilities of aircraft, "Revolt in Ethiopia" emphasizes their speed: "Airplanes made such a difference. The same journey by any other available transportation would have taken weeks and weeks. Now it was merely a matter of hours. Who knew where they would be a week hence" (221).

In *Slaves Today* and the *Black Empire* serials, as I argue above, Schuyler targets black oppression of black people, the Americo-Liberians' exploitation of the native population and the fascism of Henry Belsidus's Black Internationale. In "Revolt in Ethiopia" the writer chooses a less controversial subject: the occupation of Ethiopia by Mussolini's fascist regime. To convey the cruelty and immorality of the Italians, Schuyler depicts them torturing, raping, and summarily executing Ethiopian prisoners. Once again signifying on the African American slave narrative, "Revolt in Ethiopia" contains a chapter reminiscent of *Slaves Today*'s extended comparison between Americo-Liberian brutality and sexual exploitation and that of Southern slaveholders. After the Italians take Dick, Ettara, and Bill prisoner soon after they alight on Abra Destum and strip them naked, Dick calls the fascist commander a swine for such treatment. In response, the Italian proceeds to whip the black American in a scene right out of antebellum black American literature: "The rifle sling rose again, and with an ominous whistle, bit deep into the flesh of Dick's back. The pain was excruciating but he only bit his lip to hold back his cries. Again and again the heavy strip of leather lashed Dick's back until it seemed that each time would be the last he could possibly stand. He was dizzy, numb with pain, aching in every muscle" (174). When Dick disavows any knowledge of the Solomonic ring, the commander turns to Ettara and is on the verge of raping her when he is shot dead by an Ethiopian. The criminality of the Italians is stressed once more when the fascists capture the trio and their escort of eight Ethiopian soldiers as they are fleeing from the sacred mountain. The Askari troops employed by the fascists immediately line up the Ethiopian soldiers and shoot them, which causes Dick to remark (in an echo of foreign correspondents' quips about the Italo-Ethiopian conflict), "Well . . . I see civilization has at last reached Ethiopia" (201).

In contrast to the ambivalence the Ethiopian elite at times demonstrated toward black people throughout the world, Ettara believes there is a racial kinship between herself and Dick and expects him to help her complete her assignment. A Howard graduate and eight-year resident in the United States, she is familiar with the character of the country and its people and uses this knowledge—and African American exceptionalist rhetoric—not only to flatter Dick (and Schuyler's readers) but to recruit him to her cause by suggesting that he has the qualifications necessary to outmaneuver the Italians: "You are an American, . . . and you have the dash and adventurousness of all Americans; that pioneering spirit that conquers, that spirit which has made our people in America the most progressive Negroes in the world" (135). At the same time, even though she admits she is attracted to Dick, she makes it clear that romance will not interfere with her mission. Motivated thus in part by his feelings for Ettara and in part by his desire "to see all colored people free" (134), Dick makes Ethiopia's cause his own.

In a memorable scene set inside Abra Destum that occurs halfway through the short novel, Schuyler conflates the classical Ethiopia (Nubia) celebrated by monumentalist writers with both ancient Abyssinia and modern Ethiopia in such a way that Dick experiences an overwhelming sense of racial continuity, kinship, and outrage. Beholding the glories of Ethiopia's past inside Abra Destum, the American believes he has been more than compensated for the perils he has already braved in fighting for the country's freedom and rededicates himself to the struggle: "It all moved Dick profoundly and made him feel rewarded for venturing on such a risky undertaking. Here was a Negro civilization older than any other except India and China; a civilization that had flourished before Greece and Rome, before Carthage, yes, before Egypt. Here were all the forms, the elaborate ritual, the culture that had made Ethiopia the admiration of the ancient world. Here it survived in spite of Mussolini, in spite of perfidious England, in spite of Ethiopia's desertion by the traitorous League of Nations. As the weird ancient music finally died and the priests fell back to their places, Dick wept unashamed. What a pity that this civilization should be destroyed by brutal Fascism. No, he resolved anew, it must not die; not if he could prevent it" (182).

Schuyler's emphasis on racial continuity in this passage and his use of ancient Ethiopian treasure generally in "Revolt in Ethiopia" recall Griggs's *Unfettered* and Hopkins's *Of One Blood,* first generation novels in which African American characters learn to their surprise that they are descended from African royalty and as a result come into the possession of great wealth. The links between "Revolt in Ethiopia" and *Of One Blood* are particularly striking. In both stories a black American man goes underground to behold ancient Ethiopian rituals still being practiced in the modern era, and at the end of each book the African American protagonist marries an Ethiopian woman of royal birth, thereby uniting their respective cultures. In addition, the theme of concealment plays a significant role in the two novels. During the course of Hopkins's work, which is subtitled *The Hidden Self,* Reuel Briggs discovers not only that he is a member of the Ethiopian royal family but that his wife and false "white" friend are his siblings. Using the motif of hiding in a more conventional manner, Schuyler portrays the Italians in three separate instances failing to find something the Ethiopian freedom fighters have hidden from them. Schuyler makes it clear that both the Ethiopians and the Italians need the wealth secreted in Abra Destum. Although the former have few weapons and almost no ammunition, the latter also need money. As Ettara explains to Dick, "the Italians are desperate. They are deeply in debt as a result of the Ethiopian disaster. No one will lend them any money because they can offer no security, nothing but boasting. The huge sum Menelik stored away would be more than enough for their purpose" (143). However, even though the Italians know the treasure is stored in Abra Destum, they have been unable to discover its secret entranceway, much less penetrate its defenses. Similarly, the Italians search Dick, Ettara, and Bill and their luggage but fail to uncover the Solomonic ring Ettara will present to Bishop Handem, which she has taped to her scalp. Captured once more after they have received the jewels, the trio trick the fascists yet again because Bill has hidden the gems in a large cake of soap, ensuring that these African natural resources will be used to finance an African freedom movement.

Thus, in contrast to *Unfettered* (where African treasure is used to improve the status of blacks in American society) and *Of One Blood* (in which ancient Ethiopian wealth remains underground until some unspecified future time when Africa and the diaspora will rise again), Schuyler's story depicts ancient African treasure being used for a modern African purpose: the liberation of Ethiopia from Italian fascism. Moreover, although Dick Welland is not directly descended from African kings, he nevertheless feels racial kinship with the Ethiopian freedom fighters, exhibiting none of the ambivalence so amply displayed by Dorlan Warthell and Reuel Briggs. Like so much of Schuyler's writing during the 1930s, "Revolt in Ethiopia" is anti-fascist and (in contrast to Griggs's and Hopkins's novels) anticolonial. Although *Slaves Today* and "Revolt in Ethiopia" fail to match the imaginative scope and exquisite ambiguity of the *Black Empire* novels, they address significant moments in the history of the two African countries best known to black Americans prior to World War II. Taken as a whole, Schuyler's African fiction makes him both the most prolific and the most important

African American novelist to write about Africa in the first half of the twentieth century.

As reflected in the texts of Hughes and Tolson written in 1935 and 1936, Ethiopianism became redirected toward the besieged East African country during the Italian invasion and explicitly anticolonial. However, in the wake of the Ethiopian defeat, these authors devoted their energy to analyzing the political and economic causes for the Italian takeover, with Hughes adopting an openly, and Tolson an implicitly, Marxian reading of the situation. Staunchly antifascist but also antitotalitarian rather than Marxist, Schuyler was likewise thoroughly familiar with the geopolitical and economic factors that cost Ethiopia her independence. In addition, more than any other black American writer to depict Africa in the first half of the twentieth century, he was acutely aware of the perils and the power of Ethiopianism. He employed monumentalist imagery and African American exceptionialism strategically to manipulate readers, disguising his anti-utopian intentions in the subtle, hybrid *Black Empire* serials and stirring up African American outrage over the Italian occupation in the more conventional "Revolt in Ethiopia."

5

The Promise of Africa-To-Be in Melvin Tolson's *Libretto for the Republic of Liberia*

I have the feeling that when we have come to terms with [Libretto for the Republic of Liberia and Harlem Gallery] by Melvin B. Tolson we shall be much closer to understanding the complex pattern of relations, in time and space, between America and Africa than we are at the moment.

GEORGE SHEPPERSON, *AFRICA IN AMERICAN HISTORY AND LITERATURE*

The story of Liberia is without beginning and without end. For here the past and present are but steps to the inspirational promise of the future.

CHARLES MORROW WILSON, *LIBERIA*

Melvin Tolson's humorous parody of Pope's cautionary couplet—"A little of the *Libretto* is a dangerous thing. / Drink deep or touch not the Liberian spring" (Tolson's journal; quoted in Farnsworth, 171)—pointedly comments on the content of as well as the critical response to the *Libretto for the Republic of Liberia* (1953), his eight-section, 770-line poem occasioned by the centennial of the West African nation's declaration of independence.[1] Written in an array of poetic styles, saturated with allusions to hundreds of works in a wide variety of languages, and accompanied by seventeen pages of notes, Tolson's poem cannot be taken lightly, nor was it intended to be. As the author reportedly told a bemused reader of the *Libretto,* "it took me six years to write it. Is it surprising that it takes more than one reading to understand it?" (quoted in Flasch, 81). The difficulty of Tolson's *Libretto* (as well as that of his next and last book of poetry, *Harlem Gallery* [1965])—specifically his use of modernist techniques most often associated with T.S. Eliot's *The Waste Land*—has been a key issue in Tolson scholarship. Both black and white critics have questioned the esoteric nature of Tolson's later poetry, which they believe alienates him from the black community.[2] Although his later style has had defenders since its debut in the early 1950s, only recently have critics begun to argue that Tolson's form in the *Libretto* suits both his subject matter (Liberia specifically and Africa more generally) and his political agenda of enabling his readers to see beyond both the tired clichés long used to describe the second largest continent and the present state of political and economic gridlock that keeps people throughout the world from realizing their true potential. Tolson's *Libretto* signifies on both modernist poetry and Africanist discourse, repeating and intertextually revising them with a black difference. More important, the poem diverges from much of the black American writing about Africa that precedes it by abandoning Ethiopianism's dependence on biblical authority, cyclical view of history, and African American exceptionalism in favor of historical research and the same kind of political and economic analysis found in his "Caviar and Cabbage" columns concerning the fate of Ethiopia in the late 1930s and early 1940s.

Aldon Nielsen argues that, far from an Uncle Tom mimicking modernism to gain access to the exclusive club of reactionary white poets, Tolson employed modernist techniques for revolutionary ends: "The poet [saw] his work as a guerilla strategy, but he did not see conservative Whites as his *only,* or even *primary,* audience. Nor did he see modernist poetics as no longer revolutionary. To the contrary, he came to see modernist poetics as having been already arrived at by African aesthetics, thus rendering the African-American tradition primary rather than merely imitative" (246, emphasis in original). As Nielsen notes, in lectures Tolson asserted that African proverbs and African American work songs, spirituals, and jazz provided a precedent for the "esoterica" or "double talk" of modernist poetry (247). In addition, Nielsen rightly asserts that Tolson's notes to the *Libretto,* rather than being pedantic or elitist, form an integral part of the poem because they document facts about Africa's past that had long been suppressed, denied, and/or ignored by white historians (253).

Despite his long poem about Liberia and frequent references to Africa elsewhere in his writings—particularly in *Rendezvous with America, Harlem Gallery,* and the unpublished "Dark Laughter"—Tolson's response to the continent, as George Shepperson remarks in the first epigraph to this chapter, has never been adequately assessed. His biographers tend to present his interest in Africa as coinciding with his appointment as the Poet Laureate of the Liberian Centennial and Peace Exposition in 1947, but Tolson wrote two unpublished novels about the continent many years before this: the no longer extant "Beyond the Zaretto" (1924), set on the Zaretto river, and "The Lion and the Jackal," discussed in the previous chapter (Flasch, 27;

Farnsworth, 32, 64, 68–69). Nielsen reports that Tolson not only amassed "hundreds of proverbs when preparing to write his *Libretto*" but that "[t]hroughout his career Tolson collected information about African culture, particularly information that belied the myth of an Africa without a history, or which unsettled myths of European primacy" (249). He was also a graduate of Lincoln University, an institution with a long history of contacts with the continent. As Tolson mentions in his notes to the poem, Lincoln was originally named in honor of Jehudi Ashmun, a white clergyman instrumental in the founding of Liberia (and a prominent figure in the *Libretto*), the school served as the site of an annual Lincoln-Liberian dinner, and it could count two ministers to the African republic among its graduates.[3]

Tolson's ambitious historiographic project in the *Libretto* revises and updates Ethiopianism. *The Hindered Hand, Of One Blood,* and *The Black Sleuth,* first generation African American novels about Africa, as well as much of the literature connected with Garveyism, evoke Ethiopianism without questioning any or most of its major tenets. To varying degrees, in contrast, the writers directly and indirectly associated with the New Negro Movement rejected Ethiopianism wholly or in part, thereby heeding Locke's call for direct contact and cooperation with Africans, scholarly inquiry into Africa's past and present conditions, and an end to paternalism. Downing in *The American Cavalryman,* Lubin in *The Promised Land* and Schuyler in *Slaves Today,* for example, largely or completely avoid Ethiopianist teleology, focusing upon contemporary Liberia in these novels. During the Ethiopian war and the Italian occupation, Schuyler in the *Black Empire* serials goes a step further, deliberately invoking Ethiopianism not to promote racial solidarity, as the turn-of-the-century authors do, but rather to expose the perils of race chauvinism epitomized by the Garvey movement. Tolson's *Libretto* represents a similar advance over earlier black American literature about Africa in terms of discourse awareness and manipulation. Although Tolson's emphasis on Africa's past glory and prediction of a bright future for the continent recalls the monumentalism and Ethiopianist teleology evident in Garvey's *Negro World* and turn-of-the-century black American fictional depictions of Africa, the resemblance ends there. Instead of relying on biblical prophecy, investing in a cyclical theory of races, and espousing an African American exceptionalism, the way earlier authors do, Tolson bases his argument in the *Libretto* on historical precedent. Put simply, the logic operating within the poem as a whole can be summarized as follows: if the idea of Liberia could enable early nineteenth-century Americans to find a way out of slavery and its attendant horrors and if the ideals of freedom and opportunity could enable the Black Pilgrims—in the face of disease, meager supplies, and native hostility—to create a nation that would not only stand for over a century as the sole black African republic but also aid the Allies in defeating Fascism, then this same idea can enable humankind to transcend its current economic, national, racial, and political divisions to usher in a new era of cooperation, equality, and prosperity.

There is a movement from the past to the present over the course of the first seven sections of the *Libretto* and then a movement from the present to the future in the final section. Although Tolson knew about the labor and ethnic problems in contemporary Liberia, even recommending Schuyler's *Slaves Today* to readers of his "Caviar and Cabbage" column (Farnsworth, 165), he chooses not to mention them in the poem, focusing instead on Liberia as the actualization of the idea of freedom. Tolson not only rewrites the history of West Africa, relying in part on Du Bois's *The World and Africa* (1947)—particularly in sections two ("Re") and five ("Sol")—but, by taking a long view of over 130 years of Liberian history that contrasts the tiny colony's inauspicious beginnings with the black republic's contributions to the Allied war effort, he also depicts present-day Liberia as the realization of a powerful dream of freedom and a better life in sections one ("Do"), three ("Mi"), five ("Sol"), and six ("La"). In section four ("Fa") and seven ("Ti"), however, Tolson shows how the current situation in the world, even though it represents an improvement over the brutalities and the iniquities of the past spawned by avarice and nationalism, nevertheless stifles human potential with its economic disparities, still-intact imperial apparatus, Cold War politics, and threat of nuclear annihilation. In the poem's eighth and final section ("Do"), Tolson portrays a future in which Africa has been liberated from Europe's control and leads humankind beyond the material and ideological barriers that have divided it to a technologically advanced world characterized by the synthesis of disparate elements.

The first six sections of the *Libretto* are brief, averaging less than fifty lines each, while the final two sections "Ti" and "Do" together make up over two-thirds of the poem. The initial section, "Do," effectively introduces many of the *Libretto*'s major themes and indicates its past-present-future trajectory. "Do" consists of seven eight-line stanzas, each beginning with the question "*Liberia?*" followed by three lines of definition by negation, the transitional fifth line "You are," and three concluding lines stating what Liberia is.[4] Thus, throughout "Do" Tolson contrasts the false descriptions of Liberia (and Africa generally) by past white writers and politicians with what he sees as its present reality. Moreover, through the reference to "Africa-To-Be" in line 16, Tolson adumbrates his poem's final section, also entitled "Do," in which Africa leads the world into a new age.

Beginning with Allen Tate in his preface to the *Libretto,* many critics have commented on the felicity of Tolson's image of Liberia early in the poem as "the quicksilver sparrow that slips / The [American] eagle's claw" (7–8).[5] The remainder of the initial stanza deserves recognition as well. Tolson asserts that, contrary to popular belief, Liberia has significance and therefore deserves more than brief mentions in fat encyclopedias of interest only to effete scholars: "No micro-footnote in a bunioned book / Homed by a pedant with a gelded look" (2–4). In fact, Liberia is a "ladder of survival dawn" (6), a powerful idea that justly merits a book-length poem because it can inspire people to climb out of their current dead-end existence. In the first six lines Tolson puns on the "foot" in "footnote" with the words "bunioned," "pedant," and "ladder," thereby contrasting a plodding, earth-bound approach to life with the high-flying and mercurial sparrow (Liberia) of the stanza's last two lines.

In the subsequent stanzas of "Do," Tolson rejects many of the images projected onto Africa by Africanist writers. It is not a "corpse," the "Dark Continent," a "Question Mark," a "caricature," a "charnel house," or a "waste land." Nor is Liberia, the protagonist of Tolson's poem, a thief ("Barabas"), a braggart ("Lemech"), a liar ("Ananias"), a clown ("merry-andrew"), or a swindler ("Breughel's cheat"). Instead, the black republic represents hope for the future ("The rope across the abyss" [15]), a welcome respite of harmonious diversity ("The Orient of Colors everywhere, / The oasis of Tahoua, the salt bar of Harrar, / To trekkers in saharas, in sierras, with Despair!" [22–24]), and Africa renascent and independent ("Black Lazarus risen from the White Man's grave, / Without a road to Downing Street" [38–39]). In the final stanza of "Do" Tolson deftly comments on the binarism that is symptomatic of not only the modern world but also Africanist discourse and that has so far characterized his poem, suggesting that the rest of the *Libretto* will indicate how dichotomies can be resolved and transcended: "You are / . . . Liberia and not Liberia, / A moment of the conscience of mankind!" (53, 55–56). Although he will return to such matters in the sections that immediately follow, Tolson here presents Liberia neither as a country located on the West Coast of Africa nor as a region with a history stretching back many centuries but rather as a temporal entity only, an opportunity that must be acted upon to ensure a quantum advancement of humankind.

Unlike "Do," where Tolson simply denies the validity of negative characterizations of Africa, in the second section of the *Libretto* he provides a detailed and well-documented refutation of assertions that Africa lacks history. "Re" comprises three parts and a coda. Each part concerns the social and intellectual achievements of the Songhai Empire in West Africa and consists of one two-line stanza—"The Good Gray Bard in Timbuktu chanted" followed by an African proverb—and two six-line stanzas. In his notes, Tolson translates the first proverb—"*Bron tron lo—eta ne a ne won oh gike!*" (58)—as follows: "The world is too large—that's why we do not hear everything." This "*eironeia* or mockery," as Tolson describes it in his notes, sardonically comments on Western ignorance about the greatness of Songhai, which flourished in the fifteenth and sixteenth centuries, and other African kingdoms. Long before Liberia's founding and even before "the Genoese [Columbus] diced west" (61), Songhai created a powerful empire from a diverse "quilt of tribes" and its "warriors and watermen" were able to keep the designing Portuguese at bay. In time, however, trade between Europe and West Africa intensified, mostly to the advantage of the white men, who secured "red ivory," "black pearls" (women), and "green gold" in exchange for "crucifixes," "Gewgaws," and "*pierres d'aigris.*" Although the proverb that begins the second part of "Re"—"*Wanawake wanazaa ovyo! Kazi yenu wazungu!*" ("The Women keep having children; it is the work of you white men" [72])—hints further at the eventual decline of Songhai, the two stanzas that follow celebrate its unprecedented achievements in health care, agriculture, and especially higher learning. Tolson states that the prestige of the University of Sankoré outstripped that of Oxford, attracting scholars from Africa, Asia, and Europe, who were welcomed with open arms. In the elegiac third section of "Re," the Whitmanesque Good Gray Bard's proverb, which cautions Africa to be vigilant because "Europe is an empty python hiding in the grass!" (86), initiates a plethora of animal imagery used to describe the European and Islamic outsiders responsible for Songhai's downfall. In describing "the white ants" who ate canoes, the "locust Portuguese," and the "leopard Saracen," Tolson deliberately reverses generations of white writing about Africa in which the continent is associated with animals, particularly those evocative of physical and moral corruption. Here alien forces are responsible for the "barren bones" of Songhai and the "weedy corridors of Sankoré" (98). The final two lines of "Re" return the reader to the present, in which "The Good Gray Bard chants no longer in Timbuktu" and "'maggots'" continue to grow "'fat on the yeas and nays of nut empires!'" (100).

Tolson's practice of juxtaposing the past and the present can be seen most clearly in the *Libretto*'s third section. "Mi" consists of six four-line stanzas written in blank verse. The first four and a half stanzas concern the American Colonization Society, an organization founded in 1816 for the purpose of finding a home for freed blacks, and the hardships that faced the first settlers to the ACS's colony in Liberia. "Mi" mentions a number of influential figures who were members of the ACS, from its founder, Robert Finley, to the abolitionist Charles Turner Torrey to pro-slavery Southerners, such as Henry Clay, Francis Scott Key, and Bushrod Washington (the nephew of George Washington and a Supreme Court justice). Harkening back to the bird imagery of the poem's first stanza, Tolson states that the efforts of the Society "eagled / The gospel for the wren Republic in Supreme Court chambers" (112–13). The ACS's funding of this back-to-Africa experiment not only "bought a balm for conscience" for its white supporters but also "verved / Black Pilgrim Fathers to Cape Mesurado, / Where sun and fever, brute and vulture, spelled / The idioms of their faith in whited bones" (115–18).

In the final six lines of "Mi," Tolson remarks that, given these humble beginnings, no one could have predicted Liberia's strategic role in the Second World War:

> No linguist of the Braille of prophecy ventured:
> *The rubber from Liberia shall arm*
>
> *Free peoples and her airport hinterlands*
> *Let loose the winging grapes of wrath upon*
> *The Desert Fox's cocained nietzcheans*
> *A goosestep from the Gateway of the East!* (119–24)

Here and elsewhere in the poem, Tolson's profound debt to Charles Morrow Wilson's *Liberia* is apparent. Tolson not only relies on Wilson's book for factual details but the poet's contrasting of the country's humble origins with its important recent contributions, the very fulcrum on which the central logic of the *Libretto* rests, derives from Wilson's *Liberia* as well. In "From the Eternal Jungle," Wilson's short opening chapter, he clearly attempts to establish the significance of Liberia and by extension his book, which was published in 1947, the centennial of the African republic. After outlining the region's ancient and more recent history and listing the highlights of the country's founding and its first hundred years' of existence, Wilson emphasizes Liberia's role in World War II in an extended passage: "Liberian Hevea groves provided a substantial part of the rubber so essential to the [Allied] fighting forces. Also, Liberia supplied several of the war's most important air bases. . . . Long-range bombers of the United States Air Force and the Navy Air Command and of the Royal Air Force (as many as 17,000 per month) received shelter, bombs, fuel, miscellaneous supplies and combat personnel at the great air bases of Liberia and from them proceeded to batter, harass, and paralyze Nazi supply lines and bases in North Africa and the Mediterranean, to help break the back of Rommel's Afrika Korps, and in time to spearhead the Mediterranean offensive" (5). In his note to line 122, Tolson states, "The airfields of Liberia sent 17,000 bombers a month against Rommel's *Afrika Korps*." Although he does not credit Wilson as the source of his information here, in his note to line 587 Tolson acknowledges his debt to Wilson for many of the Liberian references in the poem's final section. The influence of the historian's book can be seen in other sections of the poem. Just as Wilson's *Liberia* underscores the heroic roles played by Jehudi Ashmun and Elijah Johnson in the founding of the republic, so too Tolson concentrates on these men, making Johnson the central figure in "Sol" and Ashmun, the "Prophet" (an epithet also employed by Wilson), the focus of "La."

The shortest section of the *Libretto,* "Fa," composed of three ballad stanzas each succeeded by the single line "*in the interlude of peace,*" itself appears to function as a kind of interlude. Not only is fa the midpoint of the musical gamut and thus seemingly an appropriate place for a slight diversion from the main theme of the *Libretto,* but at least initially the content of Tolson's fourth section strikes one as distinctly different from the preceding sections. However, a closer inspection of "Fa" reveals that the section performs an important function within the overall structure of the poem. Building on the animal imagery of "Re," "Fa" describes three sated predators—a boa "gorged to the hinges of his jaws" (127), an unnamed raptor that "sags" upon a rock, and a tiger that "torpors in the grasses tan" (136). In a different context the refrain "*in the interlude of peace*" might recall the pious mysticism of T.S. Eliot's later poetry; however, that is not its function here. Discussing the *Libretto*'s relationship to other long modernist poems in an entry in his journal, Tolson declares that "[Hart Crane's] 'The Bridge' is a way out of the pessimism of 'The Waste Land'; the 'Libretto' is a vista out of the mysticism of 'The Four Quartets'" (quoted in Farnsworth, 171). Because "Mi" ends with a clear reference to World War II, this recurrent line in "Fa" refers to the immediate and, as the Korean War proved, short-lived peace that followed the Allied victory. Although other animals can relax for a time after a predator has found its prey, this period of calm is only temporary. For Liberia, frequently the target of English and French imperial designs in the past, "Fa" counsels continued vigilance despite the African republic's recent close cooperation with powerful Allied nations. For humankind generally, "Fa" warns that World War II, like its predecessor, was not the war to end all wars, but merely part of a series of conflicts that will not end until the economic, political, and racial barriers that divide people have been eliminated.[6]

The twenty-nine three-line stanzas of "Sol" connect the comparatively recent past of Liberia's founding with both the transatlantic slave trade and the ancient wisdom of the African griots. The first stanza establishes an American and a biblical context for Liberia's founding by linking the "Black

harmonious and technologically advanced future will eventually come to replace the fractionated present.

Despite the insights into the *Libretto* Robert Farnsworth provides in his biography of Tolson, in his reading of these final two sections I believe he puts far too much weight on a "Caviar and Cabbage" column in which Tolson outlines his "Ferris Wheel Theory of History" and a letter Tolson wrote to his publisher about the symbolism in his poem. In both the newspaper piece and the letter Tolson uses the images of the ferris wheel and the merry-go-round to represent the past and the future respectively. Initially, Tolson's use of these carnivalesque concepts in his 19 October 1940 *Washington Tribune* column appears to resemble the Ethiopianist teleology of earlier African American writing, particularly Hopkins's *Of One Blood:* "The history of man heretofore has been the history of the rise and fall of nations. I presume to call this the Ferris Wheel Theory of History. The vanity that makes a people think itself superior to another people is the vanity that leads to its defeat. Pride goeth before a great fall!" (quoted in Farnsworth, 157). However, Tolson rejects Ethiopianism's biblically inspired view of history, propounding his own politically and economically grounded reading of the fortunes of different peoples:

> There can be no democracy without economic equality. Thomas Jefferson said that when he wrote the Declaration of Independence. There can be no brotherhood of man without a brotherhood of dollars. I have another theory. It is based on economic and racial brotherhood. I presume to call this the Merry-Go-Round of History. On the merry-go-round all the seats are on the same level. Nobody goes up; therefore, nobody has to come down. That is democracy, as I see it. In a brotherhood, all the members are equal.
>
> Racial superiority and class superiority produced the hellish contraption called the Ferris Wheel of History. Democracy will produce the Merry-Go-Round of History. (Quoted in Farnsworth, 157–58)

Echoing this passage, which appeared thirteen years before the publication of the *Libretto,* Tolson informed his publisher that in the poem he uses "the Ferris Wheel of Tyranny and the Merry-go-round of democracy as . . . symbols, one for the past, the other for the future" (quoted in Farnsworth, 153). However, Tolson's letter clearly refers to an earlier version of the poem in which the ferris wheel and the merry-go-round appear in the eighth section and not in the seventh section as they do in the final version. Thus, what Tolson's letter to his publisher reveals is that very late in the composition of the *Libretto* the poet rearranged major sections and rethought the overall trajectory (and concomitant imagery) of the poem. As his note to line 619 unequivocally states, in the final version of the poem Tolson associates the merry-go-round with current conditions and uses various modes of transportation to represent the future: "the flux of men and things is set forth in symbols whose motions are vertical-circular, horizontal circular, and rectilinear. In spite of the diversity of phenomena, the underlying unity of the past is represented by the ferris wheel; the present by the merry-go-round; and the future by the automobile, the train, the ship, and the aeroplane." Although the equality inherent in the symbol of the merry-go-round stands as a clear advancement over the hierarchical ferris wheel, both images are circular and hence static. In the poem's final section, Tolson envisions a new age inspired by the idea of Liberia in which humankind moves in a vector toward the achievement of its full potential. By abandoning the circular imagery of not only the ferris wheel but also the merry-go-round in describing the Africa-To-Be in the published version of *Libretto*, Tolson distances himself even further than he does in his *Washington Tribune* column from the Ethiopianism that profoundly influenced black American writing about Africa in the first half of the twentieth century.

Running over two hundred lines in eleven parts that vary in size from six to thirty-five lines, "Ti" is almost as long as the previous six sections combined. Abandoning the more traditional meters and regularized stanzas of the *Libretto's* earlier sections, "Ti" (like the later *Harlem Gallery*) features free verse lines of varying lengths that are centered on the page rather than justified along the left hand margin.[7] Looking back to "Do," "Mi," "Sol," and "La," Tolson begins the first and shortest part of "Ti" by explicitly referring to Liberia's centennial: "O Calender of the Century, / red-letter the Republic's birth!" (255–56). Echoing "Fa," however, he suggests that there are forces at work that may undermine not only what the black republic has achieved but also the prospect for a brighter future it represents. The next seven parts discuss various forces that keep humankind from achieving unity, such as imperialism, racism, elitism in art, class and caste systems, and Cold War politics. In part three, for example, Tolson, echoing Blake's "The Tyger," asks Africa,

> What dread hand,
> to make tripartite, one august event,
> sundered Gondwanaland?
> What dread grasp crushed your biceps and
> back upon the rack

> chaos of chance and change
> fouled in Malebolgean isolation? (275–81)

Tolson regards the alienation of Africa in the modern era as false because cultures endlessly interpenetrate one another:

> Man's culture in barb and Arab lies;
> The Jordan flows into the Tiber,
> the Yangtze into the Thames,
> the Ganges into the Mississippi, the Niger
> into the Seine. (286–90)[8]

Although Tolson deems the current situation a modest advance over the past, it does not represent the new era of freedom and opportunity implicit in the idea of Liberia: "the case Caesarean, Lethean brew / nor instruments obstetrical at hand, / the midwife of the old disembowels the new" (399–401). Mired in the fractiousness of the past and lacking the necessary knowledge and technology, the present era cannot make humankind's bright future a reality.

The remainder of "Ti" offers two different ways of perceiving the present moment. Tolson makes clear the contrast between the current situation and the future in the ninth and tenth parts of "Ti." Referring to the new era as the *Höhere* (that which is higher), the poet provides an extensive list of the current practices that this future era "is beyond," including war, "*apartheid,*" despair, economic inequities, and imperialism. As the end of part ten emphasizes, such forces of conflict obscure the interdependent nature of the world in which we live: "O East, O West / on tenotomy bent, / Chang's tissue is / Eng's ligament" (457–60). Yet despite having stressed in the first ten parts of "Ti" that the current situation is only an intermediate step upon "the ladder of survival dawn," Tolson ends the penultimate section of the *Libretto* on a positive note by underscoring the progress that has been made so far. It is in the final stanza of "Ti" that the poet contrasts "the ferris wheel / of race, of caste, of class" (474–75) of the past with the "merry-go-round" of "Today."

The first of three major parts of "Do," the longest and last section of *Libretto,* acts as a kind of retort to the final stanza of "Ti." Lest humankind be tempted to rest contented with the progress it has made so far, the eleven six-line free verse stanzas lacking punctuation and capital letters that begin "Do" enumerate what is wrong with "the old she-fox today" (489). Nationalism, which Tolson calls "*blut und boden,*" continues to be a major force dividing peoples and delaying the advent of a global culture. Vain boasts, imperial designs, and the posturing of politicians still cause exploitation and war, only now the weaponry has become frighteningly sophisticated, as Tolson's reference to "today's baby boys" (atomic bombs) in line 547 points out. In the transitional second part of "Do," a single twenty-one line stanza that resembles those of "Ti," Tolson, adopting the perspective of "Tomorrow . . . O . . . Tomorrow," ironically uses the ubi sunt motif to look back on black figures of the past and the history of black-white relations. Once the "Africa-To-Be" has come into existence, there will be no need to ask "Where is" the glory of the African race—as so many Ethiopianist writers do—or to dwell upon the passing of the racial caste system of Johannesburg, the "witches' Sabbath of sleeping sickness" (564), or the notion of the white man's burden. Perhaps in an attempt to employ a radically different poetic style that complements the new age he describes, in the final part of "Do" Tolson turns to prose paragraphs, devoting one each to "The Futrafrique" (an automobile), "The United Nations Limited" (a train), "The Bula Matadi" (a ship), *Le Premier des Noirs* (an airplane), and "The Parliament of African Peoples" (a political body epitomizing the continent's communal approach to life that prefigures the Organization of African Unity but far exceeds it in terms of stature and effectiveness). Each mode of transportation travels through both space—toward the Parliament of African Peoples—and time—"toward Khopiru" (610), the Africa-To-Be foreshadowed in the first section of the poem. Reminiscent of Schuyler's *Black Empire*, Tolson envisions a technologically advanced Liberia and Africa that successfully competes with the rest of the world. In contrast to the regimentation, fascism, and global war that Schuyler depicts, however, in the last section of "Do" both Africa and the world generally are characterized by a progressive synthesis of diverse elements.

A product of an industrialized Liberia that features superhighways and subways, the Futurafrique travels past "Tubman University," a recreation of the University of Sankoré portrayed in "Re," attracting students "from seven times seven lands" (584).[9] On its journey to "the cosmopolis of Höhere" (628–29), the ebony automobile is flanked by models from the other continents, which attests to the global harmony that exists in the new era. Tolson further indicates the progress that has been made within the Africa-To-Be by describing it as "the bygone habitat of mumbo jumbo and blue tongue [catarrhal fever], of sasswood-bark jury [ordeal ceremonies] and tsetse fly, aeons and aeons before the Unhappie Wight of the Question Mark crossed the Al Sirat" (629–34). In the next three paragraphs the train, the ship, and the plane likewise traverse the African continent. Running both north and south and east and west, the United Nations Limited glimpses the diversity that is Africa; the Bula Matadi sails past Liberia and up the

Niger laden with goods from around the world;[10] and *Le Premier des Noirs,* named after Haiti's Toussaint, flies over West, Central, and East Africa. In the long final prose paragraph of the poem, Tolson depicts the Parliament of African Peoples as the culmination of the idea of the black republic through references to "Roberts Avenue, in Bunker Hill, Liberia" (696–97)[11] and "the Ashmun International House" (699–700), celebrating the Parliament's exemplary unity in diversity and its power to breathe synthesizing new life into the ideals of both Western democracy and Eastern Communism.

The first black American long poem devoted to Africa, the *Libretto for the Republic of Liberia* stands as a remarkable achievement. Rooting his argument in the African, American, and African American past, Tolson offers a political and economic analysis of the present moment and then looks beyond it to the Africa-To-Be without turning to the mysticism, circularity, exceptionalism, or nationalism of Ethiopianism. Moreover, by successfully integrating various poetic styles to form a coherent hybrid, in the *Libretto* Tolson provides his readers with an exemplification of the ideal of progressive synthesis he champions in the poem.

6

The Movement Away from Ethiopianism in African American Writing about Africa

What I am suggesting is that there is a quality of the mystic and the reactionary in our new version of history that troubles me. I don't believe it. Do we really have to go back to Shango and the university of Timbuktu to find some reason for going on with life? Is the far and misty past really helpful—or just a way to escape and transcend the awful reality of this day?

TONI MORRISON, "BEHIND THE MAKING OF *THE BLACK BOOK*"

And what is the result of decolonizing the spirit? It is as if one truly does possess a third eye, and this eye opens. One begins to see the world from one's own point of view; to interact with it out of one's own conscience and heart. One's own "pagan" Earth spirit. We begin to flow, again, with and into the Universe.

ALICE WALKER, *ANYTHING WE LOVE CAN BE SAVED*

By the second half of the twentieth century, Ethiopianism's influence had greatly diminished for a variety of reasons, even though some of its basic tenets have continued to figure in African American religious, cultural, and intellectual movements, such as the Nation of Islam, Black Judaism, Rastafarianism, the Black Arts Movement, and Afrocentrism.[1] A decline in religious faith generally and a lack of emphasis on Psalms 68:31 in sermons by African American preachers in particular stripped Ethiopianism of much of its spiritual power. As African independence movements grew after World War II, political and cultural movements on the continent began to influence black Americans significantly. For decades African Americans had regarded themselves as the vanguard of the black race, believing that their experiences in Western society qualified them to lead Africa and the people of the diaspora into a new era of freedom and accomplishment. However, as conditions in the United States failed to improve and Africans began to demand self-government, black Americans started to look to Africa for inspiration and guidance. African anticolonial struggles leading to the creation of dozens of independent African nations in the late 1950s and early to middle 1960s focused black American attention on contemporary political and economic conditions on the continent, diminished African American exceptionalism, and in many cases occasioned a wholesale reassessment of the relationship between black Americans and the people of Africa. African American literary artists who have written about the continent since mid-century have not only avoided invocations of Ethiopianism's cyclical view of races, with its emphasis on Africa's ancient past and destined bright future, but frequently adopted a skeptical or even hostile attitude toward organized religion—especially European, American, and in some cases African American missionary efforts in Africa. Although occasional expressions of African American exceptionalism and the use of binarism, image projection, and evolutionary language have not been uncommon, in general recent black American literature about Africa exhibits a greater awareness of both the problematic nature of Ethiopianism and the pernicious influence of Africanist discourse.

In the first half of the century, black American literary interest in Africa focused mainly on the continent's only independent states, Liberia and Ethiopia. Indeed, from 1900 to 1953 Liberia was the most frequently and consistently depicted African country; however, as independence movements spread throughout the continent, creating a New Africa, literary interest in Liberia almost completely dried up. More intense but of a briefer duration, African American identification with the country of Ethiopia, which reached its peak in the mid-1930s, quickly died in the aftermath the nation's defeat and occupation by the Italians in the late 1930s and early 1940s. Responding to the tumultuous changes taking place throughout the continent, black American writers since mid-century have portrayed a much wider range of countries, both real and imaginary, than their predecessors. One nation, however, has garnered more African American attention than any other—the West African republic of Ghana, which achieved its independence at the comparatively early date of 1957.

Since the mid-1950s, the New Africa has become a major theme in African American criticism and literature. Negritude, a term coined by the West Indian author Aimé Césaire in 1939 and elaborated by the Senegalese poet and President Léopold Senghor, had a strong influence on aesthetic theories during the 1960s and early 1970s, such as Maulana Karenga's cultural nationalism. Senghor openly acknowledged his movement's debt to New Negro writers, particularly Hughes, but also linked it to the turn-of-the-century anglophone African Personality movement.[2] Combining elements of Ethiopianism and Karenga's cultural nationalism, in the 1980s Molefi K. Asante elaborated a controversial philosophy challenging the traditional methods and assumptions of the study of Africa in works such as *The Afrocentric Idea* (1987).[3] African independence, Negritude, and Ethiopianist teleology are reflected in varying degrees in the poetry of the Black Arts Movement. In "Ka 'Ba," for example, Amiri Baraka describes black Americans as "beautiful people / with african imaginations" who "need magic" and "spells, to raise up / return, destroy, and create" (9–10, 20–22). The political significance of the New Africa and what this means to African Americans is a major theme of John A. Williams's novel *The Man Who Cried I Am* (1967).[4] A decade later Alex Haley's enormously popular *Roots* (1976) and the television miniseries based upon it contributed to a more positive black American attitude toward Africa by connecting a dignified African past to an equally dignified African American present. Apartheid in South Africa became a major issue for both black and white Americans in the 1970s and 1980s, and during these decades African American writers, occasionally choosing Africa as their subject, enjoyed an unprecedented popularity.

Reflecting the increased numbers of African American writers, journalists, field workers, and tourists visiting or temporarily settling in foreign countries, the postwar period has for the first time seen black American travel books produced on a consistent basis. Although the lands described since 1945 range from Asia to Russia to Cuba, Africa has been the most frequent subject for African American travel writers.[5] Eslanda Goode Robeson's *African Journey* (1945), journalist Era Bell Thompson's *Africa: Land of My Fathers* (1954), *Negro Digest/Black World* editor Hoyt Fuller's *Journey to Africa* (1971), Gwendolyn Brooks's "African Fragment" (from *Report from Part One* [1972]), and seasoned literary traveler Eddy L. Harris's *Native Stranger* (1992) describe the authors' experiences in two or more countries. Other works concern individual countries, such as Richard Wright's *Black Power*, Peace Corps volunteer Ed Smith's *Where to, Black Man* (1967), and Maya Angelou's *All God's Children Need Traveling Shoes* (1986)—each of which is about Ghana. Where many Ethiopianist writers were at best ambivalent about connections between African Americans and contemporary Africans, African American literary travelers search incessantly for communion with the people of the New Africa. Wright's *Black Power*, unquestionably the most significant of these travel accounts, Brooks's "African Fragment," and Angelou's *All God's Children* show their authors attempting but ultimately failing to escape completely the influence of Africanist discourse, which regards Africa either as a dream or a nightmare. Despite their awareness of the perils of echoing assessments made about

Africa and Africans by white authors, all of these writers end up reinforcing rather than escaping the dominant discourse. Each brings with him or her some romanticized notions about the continent; when Africa refuses to live up to their expectations, these authors become disillusioned with it and alienated from it.

A wide range of imaginative writers, including Williams, Haley, Frank Yerby, Lorraine Hansberry, Reginald McKnight, Charles Johnson, and Alice Walker have used Africa as the setting and Africans as major characters in their works. Hansberry sought to portray a contemporary African character authentically in *A Raisin in the Sun* (1959) and broke more new ground in her final play, *Les Blancs* (1973), attacking paternalistic white missionaries in Africa and actively rebutting Africanist depictions of the continent and its people. Walker—who reflects on her experiences as a student in Uganda in her first book of poems, *Once* (1968); questions the unqualified adoption of an African heritage by black Americans in "Everyday Use" (1973); depicts the imaginary African nation of Olinkaland in *The Color Purple* (1982), *The Temple of My Familiar* (1989), and *Possessing the Secret of Joy* (1992); and attacks female genital mutilation in Africa in several texts, especially *Possessing* and *Warrior Marks* (1993)—is not only the most popular, prolific, and controversial but arguably the most significant African American writer to engage Africa since Schuyler. Walker's prizewinning bestseller, *The Color Purple,* is, amongst many other things, a ringing condemnation of not only white and African American missionary efforts to convert Africans to Christianity but also Ethiopianism and the literary texts that invoke it. At the same time, however, by contrasting Celie's American success story with Nettie's debacle in Africa, the novel can be seen as perpetuating African American exceptionalism.

Attempting to Escape Prepossessions in *Black Power*

As a major novelist, a famous expatriate writer, and the author of three travel books, Richard Wright stands as the single most important African American literary traveler. In addition to *Black Power,* Wright wrote *The Color Curtain* (1955), an account of the Bandung Conference held in Indonesia in 1955 that brought together representatives from many African and Asian countries, and *Pagan Spain* (1957), based on three automobile trips he made throughout much of that country in 1954 and 1955. A resident of France for several years before he wrote his travel books, Wright believed that his experiences as an outsider first in the United States and later in Europe gave him special insight when he attempted to describe foreign countries; he also felt that his journeys to other lands helped him to maintain a certain detachment as a writer. As he explained to an interviewer in

1956, "I make many voyages to keep as close contact with contemporary man as possible. It is my way of avoiding the barrage of propaganda from all quarters and of exposing myself to reality first hand. This is what an artist should do as much as possible in order that his sensibilities can carry a rich burden of concrete reference" (Kinnamon and Fabre, 166). Many critics, however, have argued that Wright failed to achieve the objectivity he was striving for, frequently revealing his Western biases in his discussions of African and Asian countries.

One of the oldest of literary genres, travel literature remains one of the most amorphous. Mary B. Campbell defines the travel book—as opposed to a work of autobiography, fiction, or ethnography—as "a kind of witness: it is generically aimed at the truth. Neither power nor talent gives the travel writer his or her authority, which comes only and crucially from experience" (2–3). In other words, although literary travelers may exaggerate or even prevaricate, what matters is that they purport to be offering firsthand accounts of vistas actually beheld and events that really happened. Beyond this, travel writing requires that authors translate other places and people into language their readers can comprehend. As Mary Louise Pratt and other recent critics have noted, travel literature—the act of relating "them" and "theirs" to "us" and "ours"—implies a colonial situation; for this reason, the cultural tape measure has always been the most important piece of equipment in travel writers' suitcases or rucksacks. Moreover, far from guaranteeing objectivity and neutrality, failing to reflect upon their political position vis-à-vis both their subjects and their readers often places literary travelers in the imperialist camp. Given African Americans' marginalized status in their own country and the ongoing dilemma of whether to write for a black, white, or mixed audience, the considerable ambivalence that black American writers such as Wright have exhibited toward the whole project of travel writing is understandable.

The intentions behind *Black Power: A Record of Reactions in a Land of Pathos* distinguish its author from the white literary travelers who depicted Africa before him. Wright comes to Africa in an attempt to shed his Western frames of reference, in search of a race consciousness linking Africans and African Americans, and in the hope of accurately describing a continent undergoing radical political and economic changes. Nevertheless, in the final analysis, his book resembles the escapist travel books of the 1930s by authors such as Evelyn Waugh and Graham Greene.[6] Like some of his white predecessors, Wright questions Western assumptions but never succeeds in completely distancing himself from them. Binary oppositions, such as tribalism versus industrialism, and evolutionary language pervade *Black Power.* Moreover, instead of discovering connections between himself and

Africans, he finds himself alienated from them and cannot offer a coherent picture of the New Africa.

Although Wright wants to escape his Western frames of reference, he begins his trip by immersing himself in Africanist discourse, traveling to the Gold Coast by ship so he can read up on the colony's history. Sailing from Liverpool, which he notes was built up through the slave trade, he contemplates European contact with Africa since the fifteenth century. His analysis of English mercantilism leads him to formulate the following definition of a colony: "A vast geographic prison where the inmates were presumably sentenced for all time to suffer the exploitation of their human, agricultural, and mineral resources" (11). Wright claims that the British have "detribalized" the people of the Gold Coast without offering a viable alternative to their previous mode of living. Attacks such as these on colonial policies and attitudes occur throughout *Black Power*, eliciting protests from some English readers when the book was published. Although the sheer volume of these criticisms outweighs that to be found in previous travel books, Wright actually says little that has not been previously asserted by white authors.

On one topic in particular Wright differs from the vast majority of his predecessors, white and black, namely his incessant attacks on Western missionary activity in Africa. Describing himself as "areligious" and asserting, "I refuse to make a religion out of that which I do not know" (134, 21), Wright criticizes both indigenous religious beliefs motivated by fear and proselytization by Christian missionaries. He holds missionaries responsible for "slowly destroy[ing] the African's faith in his own religion and customs, thereby creating millions of psychologically detribalized Africans" (65), and for actively opposing Prime Minister Kwame Nkrumah's efforts to liberate the colony. Eschewing Ethiopianist teleology and monumentalism, Wright neither dwells on Africa's past glory nor predicts a bright future for the continent; nevertheless, he clearly believes Africans are in need of "redemption," a term he uses at least three times in the book. The ambivalent final paragraph of a speech Wright makes at a Convention People's Party rally suggests the extent to which he diverges from previous African American writing about Africa: "I am an American and therefore cannot participate in your political affairs. But I wish you victory in your bid for freedom! Ghana, show us the way! The only advice that I can give you is two thousand years old and was uttered by a Man Whose name is frequently used but Whose moral precepts millions choose to ignore. To a great and despoiled Africa, to an Africa awakening from its slumber, to an Africa burning with hope, I advise you: TAKE UP YOUR BED AND WALK!" (78). Reflecting a shift in black American thinking after mid-century, Wright avoids exceptionalism, refusing to envision himself in a leadership role vis-à-vis Africa and looking to the continent for guidance. At the same time, however, like many earlier African American writers, he considers Africa "despoiled" and barely conscious. Moreover, even though he roundly condemns missionary activity and attitudes, he invokes Christ's words to authorize his exhortation that Africans must rely on themselves to improve their conditions.

Commenting not only on the missionary impulse but the attraction and repulsion that Africa frequently has held for and elicited from outsiders generally, Wright in a remarkable passage indicates his consciousness of the distorting effects of the dominant discourse about the continent and accurately describes the process of Africanist image-making. However, he perpetuates this very cycle by coining a new image for Africa to do so: "Africa is a vast dingy mirror and what modern man sees in that mirror he hates and wants to destroy. He thinks, when looking into that mirror, that he is looking at black people who are inferior, but really, he is looking at himself and, unless he possesses a superb knowledge of himself, his first impulse to vindicate himself is to smash this horrible image of himself which his own soul projects upon this Africa" (158). This Africanist way of thinking that Wright has an awareness of is precisely what keeps him from establishing meaningful contacts with Africans. Vigorously trying but repeatedly failing to escape his Western assumptions, he often reminds himself of them or recognizes them in his initial reaction to an event. Wright cautions that "A Westerner must make an effort to banish the feeling that what he is observing in Africa is irrational, and, unless he is able to understand the underlying assumptions of the African's beliefs, the African will always seem a 'savage'" (117).

Yet Wright does not find his own prescription easy to follow. After witnessing a funeral procession featuring many partially clad Africans beating sticks together and firing muskets, Wright concedes he has understood none of it. Later, recalling white writers' excursions into the bush to "see how the natives really live" (and anticipating Brooks's desire for unmediated contact with Africans), Wright has an Accra taxi driver take him to the small fishing community of Lababi. There Wright suggests to an electrician he meets that a machine to make *fufu* should be invented. The people greet this suggestion with peals of laughter when they hear of it. Reflecting on the experience, Wright attempts to question his exceptionalist assumptions but in the process employs the tribalism-industrialism dichotomy, associating himself with the West and thus separate from the Africans: "I was assuming that these people had to be pulled out of this life, out of these conditions of poverty, had to be literate and eventually industrialized. But why? Was not the desire for that mostly on my part rather than on *theirs*? I was literate, Western, disinherited, and industrialized and I felt each day the pain and anxiety of it. Why then must I advocate the dragging of these people into my trap?" (147, emphasis in orginal). Wright views both alternatives as "dark": "The pathos of Africa would be doubled if, out of her dark past, her people were plunged into a dark future, a future that smacked of Chicago or Detroit" (226–7).

In his preface Wright says Akan society has "the most highly socially evolved native life of present-day Africa" (xiv). This example of evolutionary language illustrates Wright's inability to understand the assumptions behind "native life," an inability that evinces itself in a bewildering number of binary oppositions in Part Three of *Black Power*. In this section, Wright describes his journey to the regions of the Gold Coast containing the Akan people and the remnants of the kingdom of Ashanti, one of the strongest West African nations before the British subdued it in a series of fierce wars at the end of the nineteenth century. Previously, Wright had called tribal scarification he had seen in Accra "backward," but here he encounters a whole society whose customs are non-Western. Wright relies on Africanist oppositions to stress the difference between the Akan and Westerners, particularly in their thinking processes: "The tribal mind is sensuous: loving images, not concepts; personalities, not abstractions; movement, not form; dreams not reality" (264). Wright proceeds to claim that the Asante have no real history, no viable medicine, but do have a murderous conscience that assumes the guise of their ancestors haunting them.

Staunchly anticolonial and antimissionary, wary of exceptionalism, and partially conscious of Africanist discourse, Wright nevertheless fails both to escape his Western frames of reference and to establish meaningful connections with Africans. As a result, Wright cannot offer a coherent analysis of what he has observed in the Gold Coast or an accurate prediction of what lies ahead for Africa. This becomes clear at the conclusion of *Black Power* in a letter to Prime Minister Nkrumah, who was to become president of Ghana in 1957. Evolutionary language creeps in as Wright warns against the evils of tribalism and industrialization, but he can offer no third alternative. Because "African culture has not developed the personalities of the people to the degree that their egos are stout" and because Africans are "mentally incapable of grasping the workaday world," Wright counsels Nkrumah to "improvise" and "militarize" so as to "limit the burden of suffering to one generation." This "militarization of African life" will "atomize the fetish-ridden past" and "abolish the mystical and nonsensical family relations that freeze the African in his static degradation," serving "as a deliberate bridge to span the tribal and industrial ways of life" (348–9). But Wright's oppositional writing so completely argues against a middle ground between these societal extremes that his suggestion seems infeasible. It does not follow that the new society Wright hopes Nkrumah will fashion can avoid being tainted by these two "dark" alternatives that the author has thoroughly rejected.

Even more so than Wright, who writes about Africa on the eve of independence, Gwendolyn Brooks expects and actively looks for an immediate connection with postcolonial Africa. Not finding this, she goes through a dream-nightmare experience on her trip to East Africa described in a series of journal entries entitled "African Fragment." Writing soon after the completion of her journey, Brooks seems unaware of or unwilling to acknowledge just how disillusioning and alienating her visit to Kenya and Tanzania has been. Describing her first day in the continent, Brooks reveals the dream she has come looking for in Africa: "I want blacks—*right now*—to forge a black synthesis, a black union: so tight that each black may be relied on to protect, enjoy, listen to, and warmly curry his fellows" (91, emphasis in orginal). To accomplish this, Brooks wants to meet Africans, but, like Wright before her, she finds it difficult to do so. When she expresses this desire to Margaret Kenyatta, daughter of the Kenyan leader, Brooks learns that "these things must be arranged." She resolves not to visit Miss Kenyatta again because "I do not, on this trip, want a thoroughly official flavoring of my impressions. I want my impressions to be spontaneous" (96). However, Brooks's need to state her desire for spontaneity clearly indicates that she is not achieving it.

What Brooks actually experiences in East Africa is the nightmare of alienation: "I look at my brothers and sisters, and I am aware of both a warm joy and an inexpressible, irrepressible sadness. For these people, who resemble my 'relatives' [in the United States] are neatly separate from me" (88). She laments that she cannot speak their language, that Africans give scarcely a thought to "their stolen brothers and sisters," that as she takes pictures of Africans she is the "oddity." Not only does Brooks feel the separation between blacks in Africa and those in the United States, but the people in Kenya and Tanzania continually stress it: "THE AFRICANS! They insist on calling themselves Africans and their little traveling brothers and sisters 'Afro-Americans' no matter *how* much we want them to recognize our kinship" (130, emphasis in original). Thus, instead of establishing a connection with Africans, Brooks encounters a barrier; instead of meeting many African people, Brooks spends most of her time with and learns about Africa from African American expatriates; and instead of realizing her romantic dreams, Brooks experiences an Africa that disillusions and alienates her.

Describing her African journey immediately after completing it and relying on a journal format, Brooks implicitly uses a dream-that-becomes-a-nightmare pattern that recalls Africanist writing. Twenty years after her stay in Ghana, Maya Angelou offers another variation of the Africanist dream-nightmare opposition in *All God's Children Need Traveling Shoes.* Although the nightmare side of Africanist discourse frequently emerges in the book, Angelou constantly represses it, ultimately manufacturing the viable connection with Africa she has been unable to find. Like Wright and Brooks, Angelou experiences disillusionment and alienation in Africa. However, instead of stressing the nightmare side of Africanist discourse as her predecessors do, Angelou smothers these feelings, refuses to relinquish her romantic image of Africa, and opts for the dream side of Africanist discourse.[7]

In Ralph Ellison's *Invisible Man,* the protagonist comes to realize that there is always another trap waiting for African Americans upon escaping the snare in which they are currently enmeshed. Suspicious of previous depictions of Africa, black American travel writers go there to establish meaningful connections with Africans and bring back with them a more authentic account of the continent. Wright and Brooks succeed in overcoming their romantic presuppositions about Africa but in effect exchange one fantasy about the continent, that of a dream, for another, that of a nightmare. Repressing the disillusionment and alienation she experienced in the continent and unwilling to depict Africa as a bad dream, Angelou maintains her romantic image of Africa, thus aligning her work with other positively valorized versions of Africanist discourse. In contrast to white literary travelers, Wright comes to the Gold Coast to escape his Western frames of reference, to assess the effects of proselytization on the continent, to make connections with Africans, and to see if Africa can provide a new way of living for the rest of the world. Africanist discourse operating through the travel writing genre so colors his perception, however, that Wright instead retains his oppositional and evolutionary ways of thinking, experiences alienation, and can provide neither Nkrumah nor the reader with a coherent vision of the New Africa.

Lorraine Hansberry's Answer to *Heart of Darkness* in *Les Blancs*

To call a kid an African was an insult. It was calling him savage, uncivilized, naked, something to laugh at. A naked black savage with a spear and war paint. It was equivalent to ugliness. Everything distasteful and painful was associated with Africa. This came from school, from the movies, and from our own people who accepted this. In common talk, the term was always derogatory—"you are acting like a wild African!" This meant heathen, un-Christian. Most children absorbed this and acquired a deep shame of their African past. But I resented what I saw in the movies and I resented the teachers who couldn't give a more positive view. This too was mainly about our own American Negro past. We were very sensitive to such things as how the slavery issue was discussed, even in grade school. I resented all of it. I was very unique in that I extended this [resentment] to the African thing too. The others didn't do this, but I made the connection. . . . At the movies when one white man was holding off thousands of Africans with a gun, all the kids were with the hero, but I was with the Africans. When I was thirteen or fourteen I was more sophisticated. I had begun reading Carter Woodson. My brothers and I talked about Hannibal, we had passion, if not information, and we thought Africa was a great thing in the world.

LORRAINE HANSBERRY, 1960

The preceding quotation indicates that early in Lorraine Hansberry's life she recognized that the image of Africa dominating literature and popular culture was a distortion. Since her death in 1965, several literary and cultural critics have reached similar conclusions. Although Hansberry did not approach the subject theoretically, this Africanist means of portraying Africa these critics have described is precisely what she resented. In her early novel "All the Dark and Beautiful Warriors," in *A Raisin in the Sun,* and, most prominently, in *Les Blancs,* Hansberry attempts to rewrite the dominant image of Africa and Africans. Loosely based on her experiences at the University of Wisconsin, "All the Dark and Beautiful Warriors" depicts a well-spoken, intelligent African student, Monasse from Ethiopia, as does her smash Broadway debut with the Nigerian Asagai.[8] When *A Raisin in the Sun* was first performed, many in the audience regarded the scenes concerning Africa, particularly the one in which an intoxicated Walter leaps on a table and impersonates an African general, as comic relief from the tense scenes depicting the Younger family's struggle to move from the ghetto to an all-white neighborhood. Hansberry, however, took the African theme of her first play extremely seriously. In a 1959 interview with Studs Terkel, she claimed Asagai was her "favorite character," the one who makes "the statement of the play." According to Hansberry, audiences had never seen an African on stage without his "shoes around his neck and a bone in his nose or ears"; thus, she felt it would be "refreshing" to present Asagai as a "true intellectual" (". . . To Reclaim the African Past").[9] As important as the African theme is to *Raisin* and other texts, in *Les Blancs* Hansberry gives it its fullest treatment. In her final play—completed by her former husband and literary executor, Robert Nemiroff, after her death[10]—Hansberry intensifies her efforts to explode the dominant image of Africa by rewriting Joseph Conrad's *Heart of Darkness,* arguably the most influential (and imitated) white text about Africa. Where Wright links the missionary activity and attitudes to colonial exploitation but fails to account adequately for Africanist discourse, Hansberry connects all three in *Les Blancs.*

As the epigraph to this section indicates, at a young age the author was aware of and reading about the continent. Nemiroff reports that Hansberry "remembered vividly seeing newsreels of the Italian conquest of Ethiopia when she was five, and crying over them." (27). At nine she encountered Africa in the poetry of Countee Cullen, Waring Cuney, and, most importantly, Langston Hughes (Isaacs, "Five Writers," 334). Moreover, her uncle William Leo Hansberry, a noted African scholar, wrote a book about the image of Africa in classical authors, taught Nkrumah, Nnamdi Azikewe, and other African students at Howard University, and in 1962 had a college at Nsakka in Nigeria named after him in recognition of his contribution to African Studies (Nemiroff, 28). In addition to the work of Carter Woodson, Anne Cheney reports that Hansberry read Jomo Kenyatta's *Facing Mount Kenya,* Du Bois's *Black Folk Then and Now,* and other books on African culture before she went to the University of Wisconsin in 1948. While in Madison, she continued her reading and met African students.

Harold Isaacs makes much of the fact that Hansberry could not recall having heard about Marcus Garvey before she moved to New York in 1950 at the age of twenty ("Five Writers," 334). However, this strikes me as less of an "odd fact" than it does Isaacs. The middle-class Hansberry's knowledge of Africa was derived mainly from scholarly and literary rather than popular sources. Du Bois almost immediately dissociated himself from Garvey, whose popularity, though vast, was largely concentrated among lower-class blacks, and who was gradually relegated to obscurity in the United States after his deportation in 1927. In New York Hansberry took a year-long seminar on Africa with Du Bois, writing a research paper entitled "The Belgian Congo: A Preliminary Report on Its Land, Its History and Its People" (Nemiroff, 29). In 1951 she joined the staff of *Freedom* magazine, founded by Paul Robeson, writing three stories devoted to Africa during her five-year association with the Harlem-based publication. According to Nemiroff, during the 1950s Hansberry met many exchange students and exiles from African colonies. In 1961, two years after publishing *A Raisin in the Sun* and a year after starting *Les Blancs,* Hansberry wrote a letter to the editor of the *New York Times Magazine,* seeking forgiveness from Patrice Lumumba's widow for the actions of Dr. Ralph Bunche, whose "apologies" for demonstrations at the United Nations against the murder of the Congo's first and only democratically elected leader "shocked and outraged" African Americans ("Congolese Patriot," 4). Thus, beyond resenting distorted depictions of the continent from an early age, Hansberry studied Africa's history and knew its contemporary political realities.

In *Les Blancs,* American journalist Charlie Morris comes to the isolated hospital-cum-mission of the "saintly" Torvald Neilson, who for forty years has supposedly been assisting the Kwi tribe in the African colony of Zatembe. Morris makes the journey not only to write about this man "who to millions *is* Africa" (105, emphasis in original) but also to reawaken the spiritual side of himself. What he finds differs greatly from his expectations. The British colony is in a virtual state of war, with a Mau Mau-type native uprising generating such paranoia among the white settlers that even the mission itself turns into a battlefield. Most of the action surrounds Tshembe Matoseh, who has returned from England to attend his father's funeral. Despite his protestations of neutrality, Tshembe finds himself embroiled in the conflict. He and Morris engage in a series of conversations that force Tshembe to contemplate his allegiances and illustrate the inability of the basically sympathetic white American Morris to fathom the complexities and brutal realities of colonial race relations. Tshembe decides to join the rebellion after learning that his father had been its leader, but his hopes for a peaceful settlement quickly evaporate when the colonial government arrests a prominent African negotiator. The Reverend Neilson is killed in a native revolt, the country erupts in full-scale war complete with colonial aerial attacks on the African population, and Tshembe kills his own brother for betraying a member of the resistance to the police.

Although from this summary the relationship between *Les Blancs* and *Heart of Darkness* may seem remote, specific plot and setting details make the connection clear.[11] Charlie Morris is not only Mr. Charlie but also Charlie Marlow. Both men travel by riverboat in search of a legendary white figure deep in the African bush.[12] The colony's geography and history link it with the Belgian Congo, the setting of *Heart of Darkness.* Like the Congo, Zetembe is one fourth the size of the United States and its river leads into the Bremmer (rather than the Malebo, formerly the Stanley) Pool. Recalling the atrocities of King Leopold II's Congo Free State in the late nineteenth and early twentieth centuries, Tshembe refers to whites "chopping off the right hands of our young men by the hundred—by the tribe" in the early days of the colony (91). When the Belgians abruptly departed from the Congo in 1960 there were no African doctors; similarly, Morris learns that Zatembe has no native physicians. Furthermore, American planes carry out the air strikes on the African population in *Les Blancs,* just as United States aircraft were used to airlift Belgian troops to quell a rebellion following the ouster of Lumumba. More significant than either Morris' resemblance to Marlow or the links between the colony and the Congo, the Conradian theme of lying plays a major role in *Les Blancs*. Like Morris, the audience gradually realizes that the whole life of the missionary Neilson has been a lie. Rather than assisting the Africans, Neilson has actively supported the colonial government, refused to modernize his hospital, and denied treatment to his wife's closest African friend, Tshembe's mother, a married woman raped by a white settler, who consequently died giving birth to Tshembe's half brother Eric.

Hansberry has not merely written one more imitation of *Heart of Darkness,* a modernist obsession inspiring such diverse European, American, and West Indian artists as Andre Gide, T.S. Eliot, Louis-Ferdinand Celine, Graham Greene, V.S. Naipaul, and Francis Ford Coppola. Nearly every twentieth-century literary text by an outsider about Africa written before and most published since *Les Blancs* concern expatriates rather than Africans, typically assigning to the latter the roles of servants and criminals. Hansberry reverses this firmly established tradition by adopting a radically different focus, emphasis, and method.

First, her protagonist is not a Westerner but rather an educated African, Tshembe, around whom she constructs a *Hamlet*-like plot. While Morris serves an important function, drawing out the protagonist's beliefs and forcing him to confront his dilemma, he lacks Tshembe's stature and acumen. Even more significantly, Neilson, Hansberry's Kurtz figure, never appears on stage. She brilliantly conceives a way of making Neilson's presence, essential to the plot for the lie he represents, felt throughout the play without giving him speaking lines that might distract attention from Tshembe, the hero. In addition, Hansberry deliberately rewrites Conrad's negative portrayal of women. In *Heart of Darkness,* the doubled female characters, the African woman Marlow observes beckoning Kurtz to stay (and with whom the latter has apparently committed unspeakable acts) and the white women Marlow visits (and lies to) on his return to Europe, Kurtz's Intended, represent corruption and falsehood respectively. Through her mysterious character, the Woman, who appears to Tshembe at strategic moments in the play, Hansberry creates a female figure who symbolizes pride, truth, and strength to her African protagonist and her audience.

Second, in *Heart of Darkness* and the numerous texts it has inspired, which in *White on Black* I designate as composing the expatriate (or "going native") tradition, Africa represents a corrupt environment that causes the outside protagonist—whether Kurtz, Greene's Scobie (in *The Heart of the Matter*), or Naipaul's Salim (in *A Bend in the River*)—to decay physically, morally, or mentally. Hansberry reverses this, too. Neilson has not, as a result of exposure to the physical corruption of Africa, betrayed the colonial mission by seducing or raping Tshembe's mother as the play initially hints, Morris erroneously supposes, and the expatriate tradition would dictate.[13] Instead, Neilson's corruption, the thing that makes his life a lie, is his Africanist attitude. An extreme example of the paternalism that Hansberry chided Jean Genet and Norman Mailer for in a 1961 *Village Voice* article, the missionary regards Africans as radically other.[14] So long as they act like children, he cares for them, but when the Africans petition for independence, he becomes angry. Likewise, we learn that when syncretism presented itself in the flesh and blood form of Tshembe's soon-to-be-born half-brother, Neilson refused to countenance the possibility, praying for both the child and the mother to die. As the Reverend's wife acknowledges, "Eric was the living denial of everything he [Neilson] stood for: the testament to three centuries of rape and self-acquittal" (125).

Hansberry not only reassigns the blame for the falsehood and corruption of Africa to colonialism and Africanist thinking but shows that this is only the first step. As Tshembe tells Morris, merely exposing colonialist sentiments as a lie (as Conrad does in *Heart of Darkness*) is not enough because such falsehoods kill people: "I am not merely saying that a device is a device, but that it also has consequences: once invented it takes on a life, a reality of its own. So, in one century, men invoke the device of religion to cloak their conquests. In another, race. Now, in both cases you and I may recognize the fraudulence of the device, but the fact remains that a man who has a sword run through him because he refuses to be a Moslem or Christian—or who is shot in Zatembe or Mississippi because he is black— is suffering the utter *reality* of the device. And it is pointless to pretend that it doesn't *exist*—merely because it is a *lie!*" (92, emphasis in original). Here Hansberry anticipates one of Chinua Achebe's major objections to *Heart of Darkness* in his influential and controversial essay "An Image of Africa" (1977). Achebe condemns *Heart of Darkness,* a text that has become a standard in undergraduate literature classes, because it perpetuates a distorted image of Africa, a lie that, he contends, echoing Tshembe's sentiments quoted above, has very real and at times fatal consequences. Although Achebe's goal in writing his essay was not to revitalize critical debate about the novel and change the way it is taught, these are precisely the effects that it has produced. Over a decade before "An Image of Africa," Hansberry in *Les Blancs* deliberately set out to alter how people think about Africa and how it is depicted by radically revising *Heart of Darkness*.

Lastly, Hansberry, similar to Tolson in the *Libretto,* attempts to use African methods to tell an African story. In addition to calling for authentic

African drums that are *"distinct, erratic and varied statements of mood and intent"* rather than *"'movie drums'"* (41), she employs what she describes as the *"tradition of oral folk art"* (95) at a strategic juncture in her play. In act 2, scene 2, Peter, a docile servant at the mission who is actually a leader in the revolutionary movement where he goes by the name of Ntali, relates the tale of Modingo to convince Tshembe to join the resistance. Modingo was a wise hyena who lived between the other hyenas and the elephants. When the elephants clamor for more room because of their size, the hyenas, who were there first, seek Modingo's advice. As he ponders the problem, the elephants force the hyenas off of their land. According to Ntali, this "bitter joke" played upon the hyenas while they "reasoned" explains their "terrible laughter" (95).[15] As Cheney has noted, Hansberry adapted this tale from one she reported on in a December 1952 *Freedom* article entitled "Kenya's Kikuyu: A Peaceful People Wage Struggle Against the British." Like Modingo, Tshembe has been deliberating how his people should respond to the demands of the white men. Recited by Ntali near the midpoint of the play, this folk tale convinces Tshembe to take action; moreover, the cry of a hyena that can be heard at key moments in the play underscores the significance of this orally transmitted fable. Additionally, in her portrayal of Ntali, the revolutionary who uses subservience and a pidgin English spoken by no other character in the play to disguise his true allegiances, Hansberry may once again be signifying on Conrad, who in *Heart of Darkness* allows his African characters only two isolated utterances: the cannibalistic "Catch 'im . . . catch 'im. Give 'im to us. . . . Eat 'im!" (42) and the haunting, ungrammatical pronouncement "Mistah Kurtz—he dead" (69).

By rewriting perhaps the most influential text ever written about Africa in order to explode the standard, distorted image of the continent, Hansberry in *Les Blancs* implicitly rejects Ethiopianism. Despite a heightened awareness of the ways in which language has been used to subjugate black people, since mid-century several African American authors, particularly travel writers such as Wright, Brooks, and Angelou, have succumbed to the pervasive influence of Africanist discourse. In an effort to change the image of the continent pervading literature and popular culture, which she had resented since she was a child, Hansberry updates and revises Conrad's *Heart of Darkness*. In doing so, she shifts the focus, emphasis, and methods of outside writing about the continent, making an educated African her protagonist (and thereby avoiding the exceptionalism characteristic of black American Ethiopianism), using oral tradition to tell an African story, and designating colonialism, the missionary enterprise, and Africanist thinking as the sources for corruption and killing in Africa.

The End of Ethiopianism in *The Color Purple*

Alice Walker's *The Color Purple* does not direct its attention to contemporary Africa, as Wright's *Black Power* and Hansberry's *Les Blancs* do; rather, the book investigates political, racial, sexual, and spiritual colonization that occurred in both America and Africa in the first half of the twentieth century. Unlike Wright and Hansberry, whose targets are white missionaries in Africa, Walker makes African American missionaries, who journey to West Africa to convert people to Christianity, major characters in her novel. Samuel, Corrine, and Nettie cross the Atlantic inspired by Ethiopianism, hoping to effect the glorious future it foretells. The failure of their efforts, which they themselves come to repudiate, serves as a condemnation of not only nineteenth- and early twentieth-century missionary endeavors in Africa inspired by Ethiopianism but by extension the Ethiopianist impulse that dominated African American literary depictions of Africa into the 1950s.

Walker's most popular book intermixes a series of letters written by Celie to God and to her sister Nettie and a series of letters from Nettie to Celie.[16] While Celie remains at home, ultimately triumphing over the racist and sexist forces that oppress her, Nettie journeys to Africa with her fellow missionaries Samuel and Corrine only to have her high hopes of converting Africans to Christianity frustrated by a combination of native indifference and colonial brutality. Walker produces a sensitive, historically grounded but thoroughly condemnatory portrayal of the African American missionary impulse in regards to Africa. She attacks not only black Americans' eager, uncritical acceptance of an orthodox, patriarchal Christianity that alienates them from themselves but also the paternalism at the base of missionary efforts to civilize and proselytize the people of Africa. In doing so, Walker finds it necessary to grapple with Ethiopianism.[17]

In over thirty years as a published author, Walker has frequently attacked Christianity. An early story, "The Diary of an African Nun," for example, asserts the incompatibility of Roman Catholic religious service and the worldview, needs, and desires of an African woman. The author's portrayal of black American missionaries in *The Color Purple*, published in 1982, likewise reflects her still-evolving critique of traditional white religion. This critique, which she has continued to develop in subsequent writings, has been most fully expressed in her important 1995 essay with the absurdly long but revealing title "The Only Reason You Want to Go to Heaven Is That You Have Been Driven Out of Your Mind (Off Your Land and Out of Your Lover's Arms): Clear Seeing Inherited Religions and Reclaiming the Pagan Self." "In it," as she explains in the introduction to *Anything We Love Can Be Saved* (1996), "I explore my awareness, beginning in childhood of the patriarchal Christianity into which I was born; as well as my realization, over time, that my most cherished, instinctual, natural self, the pagan self, was in danger of dying from its oppression by an ideology that had been forced on my ancestors, under threat of punishment or death, and was, for the most part, alien to me." Coining a phrase in "The Only Reason" that concisely expresses the connection between her religious and political agendas, Walker states the need for people to "decolonize their spirits" (4), an act of empowerment that will enable them to embrace rather than fear the earth.

To provide an example of this decolonization, she quotes in full a letter from *The Color Purple* (199–204) in which Celie, whom Walker calls "the confused Christian," describes to Nettie her conversation with Shug about religion, which eventually leads to Celie's conversion to her friend's "pagan" theology. Shug explains that she has rejected Christianity and "the white folks' white bible" in favor of a set of pantheistic beliefs. Unlike Celie, who imagines God as a big white man with a long beard and thus completely disconnected from herself, Shug declares that God links people to their surroundings and doesn't look like anything: "It ain't a picture show. It ain't something you can look at apart from anything else, including yourself. I believe God is everything, say Shug. Everything that is or ever was or ever will be. And when you can feel that, and be happy to feel that, you've found it" (quoted in "Only Reason," 7–8). Although she was not aware of it when she wrote *The Color Purple,* Walker later came to realize that Shug is echoing the words "spoken, millennia ago, by Isis, ancient Goddess of Africa, who, as an African, can be said to be a spiritual mother of us all" ("Only Reason," 3–4). Considering herself a "born-again pagan" (*Same River,* 25), Walker asserts that the earth is actually paradise but patriarchal religion has kept many people from recognizing this. Women know this instinctually, claims Walker, but organized religion has consistently denied them a voice. Speaking of her devoutly religious mother, Walker notes the irony in the fact that "the very woman out of whose body I came, whose pillowy arms still held me, willingly indoctrinated me away from herself and the earth from which both of us received sustenance, and toward a frightful, jealous, cruel, murderous 'God' of another race and tribe of people, and expected me to forget the very breasts that had fed me and that I still leaned against. But such is the power of centuries-old indoctrination" ("Only Reason," 20). According to Walker, not being able to worship their own God, a God that loves them, has had profoundly alienating effects on African Americans: "We have been beggars at the table of a religion that sanctioned our destruction. Our own religions denied, forgotten; our own connections to All Creation something of which we are ashamed. I maintain that we are empty, lonely, without our pagan-heathen ancestors" ("Only Reason," 25).

Because of her negative assessment of black Americans' adoption of traditional, patriarchal Christianity, Walker regards as particularly sad and bitterly ironic the efforts of African American missionaries to carry the process of indoctrination to Africa. As a kind of coda to her essay "The Only Reason," Walker prints a photograph of a West African woman garbed only in plant fronds who is leaning against a rain forest tree. The caption reads in part, "She is beautiful, self-sufficient, elegantly dressed, and serene, and the God/Goddess of Nature, which surrounds her and of which she is part, has obviously earned her complete trust. Only to enslave her spirit and body to the will of others need another God, foreign to her experience of Creation, be introduced" (27). In *The Color Purple,* Samuel, Corrine, and Nettie gradually come to realize that they have unintentionally abetted the British colonizers in subjugating the roofleaf-worshipping Olinka, who exist largely in harmony with nature. As Lauren Berlant remarks, these characters come to realize that "what passed for racial identification across borders and historical differences was really a system of cultural hegemony disguised as support and uplift" (848).

Furthermore, Walker uses her missionary characters in the novel to engage profoundly with Ethiopianism. Samuel, Corrine, and Nettie cross the Atlantic inspired by Ethiopianism, hoping to bring about the glorious future it foretells. The failure of their efforts, which they themselves come to renounce, serves as a condemnation of not only those nineteenth- and early twentieth-century missionary endeavors in Africa inspired by Ethiopianism but by extension the Ethiopianist impulse that dominated African American literary depictions of Africa in the first half of the twentieth century. Displaying a keen sense of history, Walker recognizes the firm grasp Ethiopianism held on the African American imagination for over 150 years and the urgent need to break free from it. In short, she thematizes—one might even say resurrects—Ethiopianism in *The Color Purple* in order to bury it.

In her letters to Celie, Nellie charts her attempt to educate herself about Africa. Shocked at how "*ignorant*" she is, Nettie admits, "I never dreamed of going to Africa! I never even thought about it as a real place" (138, 137, emphasis in original). Soon, however, she begins to read all of Samuel and Corrine's books about the continent (including the work of J.A. Rogers), which she hopes will prepare her for what she will encounter in Africa. From early on, however, her (mis)education about the continent is colored by Ethiopianism, Africanist discourse, and white imperialism. Recalling the send-off she and her fellow missionaries received from their church, Nettie enthusiastically states, "Everyone has such high hopes for what can be done in Africa. Over the pulpit is a saying: *Ethiopia Shall Stretch Forth Her Hands to God.* Think what it means that Ethiopia is Africa!" (140). Significantly, Nettie's enthusiastic declaration indicates that she travels to the continent with a fully formed idea of what she will encounter—the Africa of Ethiopianist texts. Stopping at white missionary societies in New York and London, Nettie, Samuel, and Corrine are constantly reminded that most of the missionaries who have preceded them have been white rather than persons of color and that Africa's riches have frequently been plundered by outsiders claiming to be acting in the interest of Africans. Refusing to allow this to dampen their resolve, Samuel justifies their endeavor by relying on Ethiopianism's exceptionalist assumptions that Africans need civilizing and that black Americans like themselves are the most qualified to undertake this mission: "[He] reminded us that there is one big advantage we have. We are not white. We are not Europeans. We are black like the Africans themselves. And that we and the Africans will be working for a common goal: the uplift of black people everywhere" (143).

What these African American missionaries find as soon as they reach Olinkaland, however, is a pagan culture in which the people worship the roofleaf they use to cover their round huts. Joseph tells Samuel, Corrine, and Nettie the story, containing an implicit anti-imperialist moral, behind the celebration of the roofleaf that figures so prominently in the welcoming ceremony held in their honor, and then declares, "The white missionary before you would not let us have this ceremony. . . . But the Olinka like it very much. We know a roofleaf is not Jesus Christ, but in its own humble way, is it not God?" (160). Thus, from the very start, the new missionaries must decide whether to follow in the footsteps of their white predecessor and deny the people their traditional religious beliefs and practices. There are other hints from the beginning of Nettie's more than twenty-year sojourn among the Olinka of Christianity's irrelevance in West Africa. She is disturbed to note how "[e]ven the picture of Christ which generally looks good anywhere looks peculiar" in the round, roofleaf-covered hut she loves so much (165). Nevertheless, Nettie remains committed to her faith and missionary enterprise, allowing Christianity to so structure her life that for many years she writes to Celie (who for decades does not receive her letters and cannot write back) only at Christmas and Easter.

Their own exceptionalist attitudes coupled with Olinkan indifference gradually undermine the plans Samuel, Corrine, and Nettie have for Olinkaland and even destroy Corrine's emotional and physical health, eventually taking her life. However, it is colonial greed and brutality that causes Samuel and Nettie finally to abandon their careers as missionaries in Africa.

Samuel does not outlaw the celebration of the roofleaf—although he inter-venes to prevent the killing of wives accused of witchcraft and infidelity—but its destruction is later accomplished by the British, who strip the land for a rubber plantation. Armed road builders level the Olinka's church, school, and huts. When the chief goes to the coast to complain, he learns that "the whole territory, including the Olinka's village, now belongs to a rubber manufacturer" (175), and in time the Olinka are forced to relocate to parched land. Beyond all of this physical hardship, Olinkan spirituality receives a devastating blow. A dejected Nettie informs Celie that "the most horrible thing to happen had to do with the roofleaf, which, as I must have written you, the people worship as a God and which they use to cover their huts. Well, on the barren strip of ground the planters erected workers' bar-racks. . . . But, because the Olinka swore they would never live in a dwell-ing not covered by their God, Roofleaf, the builders left these barracks uncovered. Then they proceeded to plow under the Olinka village and ev-erything else for miles around. Including every last stalk of roofleaf" (233). When a journey to their bishop in London to protest what is happening in Olinkaland achieves nothing, Samuel angrily declares that, if they are to remain in Africa, their sole course of action is join the resistance movement and urge the Olinka to do so as well (238).

Looking back on his life, Samuel comes to regard his efforts among the Olinka as a total failure. He tells Nettie, "It all seems so improbable. . . . Here I am, an aging man whose dreams of helping people have been just that, dreams. How Corrine and I as children would have laughed at ourselves. TWENTY YEARS A FOOL OF THE WEST, OR MOUTH AND ROOFLEAF DISEASE: A TREATISE ON FUTILITY IN THE TROPICS, Etc., Etc. We failed so utterly." (241–42). Samuel and Nettie do not give up their com-mitment to religion, but they begin to move away from patriarchal Chris-tianity and open themselves up to African spirituality. Nettie tells Celie in a late letter that echoes Shug's beliefs, "God is different to us now, after all these years in Africa. More spirit than before, and more internal. Most people think he has to look like something or someone—a roofleaf or Christ—but we don't. And not being tied to what God looks like, frees us" (264). In *The Temple of My Familiar*, Celie's biological daughter Olivia concisely sums up her adoptive father's years in Olinkaland: "My father, Samuel, was a mis-sionary also, but by the time we returned to America he had since lost his faith; not in the spiritual teachings of Jesus, the prophet and human being, but in Christianity as the religion of conquest and domination" (146). Samuel and Nettie's renunciation of their goal to convert Africans to Christianity also amounts to an implicit rejection of the Ethiopianist rhetoric that in-spired them to undertake their mission.

It is at the point in the story where Samuel experiences profound disillusionment about his missionary efforts that he recalls meeting W.E.B. Du Bois in Atlanta before he and Corrine were married. His Aunt Althea and Corrine's Aunt Theodosia had been missionaries in the Belgian Congo, and, although Samuel and Corrine regarded them as comical figures, they nevertheless followed in their footsteps. "We made fun of them, but were riveted by their adventures, and on the ladies' telling of them," recalls Samuel, adding in a statement cognizant of his earlier Africanist and exceptionalist assumptions, "And of course the prevailing popular view of Africans at that time contributed to our feeling of amusement. Not only were Africans savages, they were bumbling, inept savages, rather like their bumbling, inept brethren at home. But we carefully, not to say studiously, avoided this very apparent connection" (240). At a gathering hosted by Corrine's aunt, after listening impatiently as she proudly tells the story of having received a medal for "service as an exemplary missionary" from King Leopold of Belgium, Du Bois—identified as "a young Harvard scholar named Edward. DuBoyce was his last name. . . . or perhaps his name was Bill"—asks Theodosia, "do you realize King Leopold cut the hands off workers who, in the opinion of his plantation overseers, did not fulfill their rubber quota? Rather than cherish that medal, Madame, you should regard it as a symbol of your unwitting complicity with this despot who worked to death and brutalized and eventually exterminated thousands and thousands of African peoples" (242–43). The father of Pan-Africanism who became an ardent critic of colonialism, Du Bois chides not only Theodosia but through this memory Samuel as well for participating in colonialism. However, for many years Du Bois, like Theodosia and Samuel, espoused Ethiopianism, which, as Walker shows, likewise contributed to the European exploitation of Africa. Thus, within the context of Walker's anti-Ethiopianist novel, Edward DuBoyce's charge of "unwitting complicity" redounds to a certain extent upon his own head. Thus, by including Du Bois, the author of *The Souls of Black Folk* in her novel, Walker directs her implicit criticism of Ethiopianism all the way back to the most influential early literary figure to endorse it.

As incisive and historically significant as Walker's portrayal of African American missionaries and her attack on Ethiopianism are, she may not completely escape being implicated by her own critique. Joining the chorus of critics who have expressed reservations about the African scenes of *The Color Purple* and their relationship to the rest of the novel, I must acknowledge that Walker's decision to use Nettie's eventual disillusionment with the continent to highlight the magnitude of Celie's achievements at home raises serious questions.[18] As Berlant puts it, "instead of infusing the African side of the compound term [African American] with the positive historical identification usually denied in the American context, the last half of the novel returns 'Africa' to the space of disappointment and insufficiency, finally overwhelmed by the power of 'America' to give form to the utopian impulse" (851).[19] Just as Sutton Griggs relied on Africa in *Unfettered* and *The Hindered Hand* eighty years earlier to solve the American problem of his novels (see chapter 2), Walker can be seen as perpetuating a form of African American exceptionalism through the contrast between Nettie's failure as a missionary in Africa and Celie's success with her business venture Folkspants, Unlimited and her construction of a mutually supportive community around her in America.

Reflecting a shift away from Ethiopianist teleology, monumentalism, and exceptionalism, Wright in *Black Power* initiates a new era of black American writing about Africa by journeying to and focusing his attention on contemporary Africa on the eve of independence rather than dwelling on the continent's past glory or its biblically foretold bright future. Although the alienation he experiences in the Gold Coast and his conventional use of travel writing cause him to revert to Africanist gestures, particularly in his depictions of and statements about African tribal life, Wright roundly condemns the missionaries who greatly facilitated Europe's domination of the continent and attempts—but fails—to provide a coherent analysis of colonialism and the long-term effects it will have on postcolonial Africa. Like Wright, Hansberry in *Les Blancs* concentrates on the struggle for independence in contemporary Africa, eschews exceptionalism, and is sharply critical of the missionary enterprise. She goes much further than Wright, however, directly taking on Africanist discourse by rewriting one of its most influential texts, making the falsehood at the heart of the missionary impulse on the continent a central theme, and, like Tolson before her, using African methods to tell and African story. Setting *The Color Purple* in Africa and the American South in the first half of the twentieth century, Walker exposes the alienating effects of patriarchal Christianity on African Americans, compassionately but thoroughly condemns black American missionaries who in ignorance sought to export this alienation to Africa and thereby abetted colonial rule, and targets religious, cultural, and political uses of Ethiopianism, which she regards as contributing to the political and spiritual colonization of black people. Beyond this, the novel implicitly critiques the Ethiopianist literature that dominated black American writing about Africa into the 1950s, even though the contrasts between Africa and America that structure the book may themselves reveal the lingering effects of black American exceptionalism.

Notes

1. Historical and Theoretical Introduction to African American Writing about Africa

1. Throughout this book I will be using the terms African American and black American interchangeably. In addition, America and the United States will be used synonymously unless stipulated otherwise.

2. Versions of the Stolen Legacy can be found in addresses by Prince Hall, George Lawrence, and William Hamilton in the late 1700s and early 1800s; in several articles appearing in the American Colonization Society's *African Repository and Colonial Journal* and in *Freedom's Journal* in the 1820s; and in African American speeches and writings from the middle to late nineteenth century and beyond. For more on the early examples, see Porter, *Early Negro Writing*, and Hinks, chapter 3.

3. Here I am echoing the objections of August Meier, Wilson Moses, and others. Moses, for example, asserts, "Lefkowitz's book has served only to obscure definitions further; it is ahistorical, presentist, synchronic, and absolutely devoid of any of the methods of serious cultural or intellectual history" (*Afrotopia*, 9).

4. In this most recent book, Moses somewhat anachronistically uses "Afrocentric," a term of comparatively recent coinage and associated with considerable controversy, to characterize the Ethiopianist works of nineteenth- and early twentieth-century African American writers. Despite my problem with this choice of words, I find *Afrotopia* especially valuable because Moses, displaying a keen historical sensibility, repeatedly acknowledges and accounts for the undeniable contradictions of much Ethiopianist writing without condemning the authors who produced them for failing to be consistent.

5. For general discussions of Ethiopianism, see Drake; James Wesley Johnson; Eric J. Sundquist, *To Wake*, 551–63, and the introduction to *The Oxford W.E.B. Du Bois Reader*, 22–26; and Moses' *The Golden Age, The Wings of Ethiopia, Alexander Crummell: A Study of Civilization and Discontent*, as well as his Introduction to *Classical Black Nationalism*. For information on the political dimension of Ethiopianism in colonial Africa, see Shepperson and Price's *Independent African*, Shepperson's "Ethiopianism," as well as his "Notes."

6. As will be discussed in the following chapter, the detailed description of the ancient underground city of Telassar and the emphasis on a glorious Ethiopian past in Pauline Hopkins's serial *Of One Blood* make the novel's approach to

Africa a monumentalist one. In contrast, by largely eschewing references to antiquity and focusing on contemporary Africa, John E. Bruce in *The Black Sleuth* produces a less monumentalist novel.

7. For information on African American missionaries in Africa, see Jacobs's *Black Americans and the Missionary Movement in Africa,* Walter L. Williams, and Chirenje

8. For information on the Congress on Africa, see Bowen, and Fierce, 25–30.

9. For information on African American interest in Ethiopia at the turn of the century, see Weisbord.

10. For links between Garvey's theology and Ethiopianism, see Potter.

11. The United States occupied Haiti from 1915 to 1934; in the late 1920s and early 1930s, as will be discussed in chapter 3, the Fernando Po scandal crippled the Liberian government.

12. Information on the Pan-African Conference and the Pan-African Congresses has appeared in a variety of works, including Esedebe, Geiss, Hamedoe, Legum, Mathurin, Padmore, and Walters (chapter 20).

13. For a critique of *The Signifying Monkey* that identifies Gates's "nostalgia for tradition" (137) as the aporia in his argument, see Adell.

14. For an excellent theoretical introduction to and historical overview of Africanist discourse, see Christopher Miller's *Blank Darkness.*

15. According to Gates, Phillis Wheatley critically signifies on Milton and Pope's poetry and Kant and Hume's aesthetic theories, the slave narrators not only recast such sentimental figures as the noble Negro of texts like Aphra Behn's *Oronooko* and the "Dying Negro" of the English Romantic poets but also reconfigure the sentimental and the picaresque novel, and the authors associated with the Harlem Renaissance rewrite turn-of-the-century anti-Negro propaganda. The process does not work in only one direction, however, for Gates regards the plantation novel as a counterdiscourse to the slave narrative. Nor do black texts only signify on white ones and vice versa. Gates describes Zora Neale Hurston's *Their Eyes Were Watching God* as a "double-voiced" novel that interfuses African American oral tradition and the free indirect discourse used by European authors such as Flaubert and Woolf; similarly, he reads Ishmael Reed's *Mumbo Jumbo* as a complex revision of both white and black texts.

16. The George W. Ellis African Collection, an extensive array of ethnological specimens that Ellis sent to the Smithsonian Institution after his return to the United States in 1910, is now part of the Fisk University Museum of Art in Nashville (Fleming and Logan, 211; Wardlaw, 65). For biographical information on Ellis, see Fleming and Logan.

17. Other problematic and/or comic elements of the novel include Eva's hairbreadth escape from deadly leopard men on the back of an ostrich fitted with a saddle, Eva and Lucretia's dance in the moon temple "to the tune of Ta ra ra bum deah" (79), and, late in the novel, the mention of the First World War, the first reference to a specific historical event in the narrative, which under-

mines the plausibility of the early portions of the book and complicates a combined British, American, and German hunting and exploring expedition traversing the African continent by Zeppelin that figures prominently in the final chapters.

2. Double-Consciousness, Ethiopianism, and Africa

An earlier version of part of this chapter appeared in Robert Latham and Robert A. Collins, *Modes of the Fantastic: Selected Essays from the Twelfth International Conference on the Fantastic in the Arts* (Westwood, Conn.: Greenwood, 1995).

1. I have in mind the following well-known passage:

> After the Egyptian and the Indian, the Greek and Roman, the Teuton and the Mongolian, the Negro is a sort of seventh son, born with a veil, and gifted with second sight in this American world,—a world which yields him no true self-consciousness, but only lets him see himself through the revelation of the other world. It is a peculiar sensation, this double-consciousness, this sense of always looking at one's self through the eyes of others, of measuring one's soul by the tape of a world that looks on in amused contempt and pity. One ever feels this twoness,—an American, a Negro; two souls, two thoughts, two unreconciled strivings; two warring ideals in one dark body, whose dogged strength alone keeps it from being torn asunder.
>
> The history of the American Negro is the history of this strife,— this longing to attain self-conscious manhood, to merge his double self into a better and truer self. In this merging he wishes neither of the older selves to be lost. He would not Africanize America, for America has too much to teach the world and Africa. He would not bleach his Negro soul in a flood of white Americanism, for he knows that Negro blood has a message for the world. He simply wishes to make it possible for a man to be both a Negro and an American, without being cursed and spit upon by his fellows, without having the doors of Opportunity closed roughly in his face. (102)

2. For readings of Du Bois's changing use of the word "race," see Appiah, 28–46, and Sundquist, *To Wake,* 461–63.

3. Although recently critics such as Eric Sundquist have asserted that Du Bois means African or Africanity when he uses the word "Negro" in *Souls,* it must be stressed that Du Bois, who subscribed to African American exceptionalism for much of his life, deliberately refrains at times from explicitly depicting or discussing Africa in this text which was primarily designed to articulate the value of African American cultural experience.

4. It is also worth noting that in the double-consciousness passage Du Bois

anticipated by almost thirty years—and transcended—the famous debate that appeared in the *Nation* between George Schuyler and Langston Hughes over whether black American artists should pursue a specifically black aesthetic. See Schuyler's "The Negro-Art Hokum" and Hughes's "The Negro Artist and the Racial Mountain" (which are discussed in the introduction to chapter 3).

5. Moses' statement overlooks the efforts of Pauline Hopkins, who not only published four novels between 1900 and 1903 but solicited, published, and promoted the work of other African American writers in her capacity as editor of the *Colored American Magazine.*

6. For biographical information on Griggs, see Rampersad's "Griggs." For readings of Griggs's novels and assessments of his significance, see Bone, 33–35; Elder, 69–103; Gloster, 56–67; Moses, *The Golden Age,* 170–193, and *The Wings of Ethiopia,* chap. 13.

7. Although "unfettered" no doubt refers in part to the condition black Americans will enjoy once "Dorlan's Plan" has been implemented, it also describes both Morlene's release from her unhappy marriage to Harry Dalton and the one word message Morlene is to write in her telegram to Dorlan if she agrees to marry him after reading his "Plan." In the later novel, as Moses has observed, "the hindered hand," refers in part to the effect that American racial policies have had on the "hand" which, according to the Psalms passage (and Griggs's epigraph), Ethiopia is endeavoring to stretch forth to God (*The Golden Age,* 172).

8. Kwame Anthony Appiah defines racialism as the view "that there are heritable characteristics, possessed by members of our species, which allow us to divide them into a small set of races, in such a way that all members of these races share certain traits and tendencies with each other that they do not share with members of any other race" (13).

9. It is worth noting that in *The Negro* (1915) and "What Is Civilization" (1926) W.E.B. Du Bois, no doubt repeating assertions found in standard historical works about Africa, makes somewhat similar claims about the Africa's geographical isolation and "African laziness." Another possible source for these assertions by Griggs and Du Bois may be Frederick Douglass's "The Claims of the Negro Ethnologically Considered."

10. Diop's most important book is *The African Origin of Civilization;* Asante has written and edited a number of books, including *The Afrocentric Idea;* Van Sertima is the editor of the *Journal of African Civilizations;* Bernal has published two of the projected four volumes of *Black Athena.*

11. See Rensberger; Bruce Williams, "The Lost Pharoahs of Nubia"; and Wilford. For a dissenting view, see Adams. For Williams's response to Adams, see "Forbears of Menes in Nubia: Myth or Reality?"

12. Discussions of Hopkins's editorial responsibilities and the role politics played in the purchase and the subsequent demise of the *Colored American Magazine* can be found in Braithwaite; Du Bois, "The Colored Magazine in America"; Johnson and Johnson; and Meier, "Booker T. Washington."

13. For biographical information on Hopkins, see Shockley, Porter, McKay, and Campbell. The most extensive readings of Hopkins's works to date can be found in Carby, *Reconstructing;* Tate, *Domestic Allegories;* and Gruesser, *The Unruly Voice.*

14. The presence of such elements as reincarnation, telepathy, an underground African civilization, and female continuity in *Of One Blood* recalls H. Rider Haggard's *She* (1887). According to Sandra Gilbert, Haggard's novel was immensely popular, particularly among male readers, because it is a fantasy rife with Victorian fears about female power. Although in general Hopkins's work is more concerned about racial than gender politics in *Of One Blood,* she is certainly signifying on *She* in her novel. For discussions of the role that gender issues play in *Of One Blood,* see Kassanoff, "'Fate'"; and Schrager, "Pauline Hopkins."

15. As is frequently the case in Hopkins's texts, her choice of Dianthe Lusk as the name for the major female character in *Of One Blood* is historically significant. This was the name of John Brown's first wife, who married Brown at nineteen in 1821 and died soon after giving birth to their seventh child in 1832. Like Hopkins's character, the historical Lusk was a singer and suffered from an inherited mental condition. Two further connections are even more intriguing. First, just as the historical Lusk traced her ancestry back to the famous Adams family of Massachusetts (Villard, 19), Hopkins's character adopts the name Felice Adams after an accident robs her of her memory. Second, like Reuel Briggs, who at various times in the novel has visions of Dianthe, John Brown "always felt [his deceased first wife's] influence near him and in 1859, a few months before his execution, he told his oldest son John, while on the road and lying in bed together in the morning, that he had dreamed of Dianthe Lusk during the night" (quoted in Boyer, 123–24).

16. Although I cannot say how, where, or even whether Hopkins may have encountered the following historical source for the subterranean city of Telassar, in her discussion of Meroe in *A Tropical Dependency* (1906) Lady Lugard reports that in 1886 Zebehr Pasha told her

> the history of his ephemeral empire in the Bahr-el-Ghazal. It was that, having occasion to act as the military ally of a certain native king Tekkima . . . he was informed that he had to fight against magicians, who habitually came out of the earth, fought, and disappeared. A careful system of scouting disclosed to him the fact that they came from under ground, and when, after cutting off their retreat and conquering them, he insisted on being shown their place of habitation, he found it to be deeply buried in the sand, a wonderful system of temples "far finer," to use the words in which he described it, "than modern eyes have seen in the mosques of Cairo and Constantinople." It was, he said, such work of massive stone as was done only by the great races of old. Through this underground city of stone there ran

a stream, and by the stream his native antagonists lived in common straw native huts. "Were your people, then," he asked them, "a nation of stonecutters?" And they said, "Oh, no! This is not the work of our forefathers, but our forefathers found it here, and we have lived for many generations in these huts." (225)

17. Du Bois himself acknowledged to Harold Isaacs, "I did not myself become actively interested in Africa until 1908 or 1910. Franz Boas really influenced me to begin studying this subject and I began really to get into it only after 1915" (quoted in Moses, *Afrotopia*, 11).

18. Responding to the conflicting impulses in Hopkins and other Ethiopianist writers, Moses accurately remarks that "The contradictions in the thinking of literate nineteenth-century African Americans reflected the complexity of the situation they encountered. People like Hopkins felt obliged to strive toward authenticity as apostles for an African point of view, but they also hoped to see African people benefit from the progressive Victorian culture that surrounded them" (*Afrotopia*, 84).

19. For an excellent discussion of the case and its relationship to late nineteenth-century American literature, see Sundquist, "Mark Twain and Homer Plessy." For a discussion of the relationship between this case and *Of One Blood,* see Kassanoff.

20. Although there is no proof that Hopkins read Griggs's *Unfettered,* which was published the same year that *Of One Blood* began running in the *Colored American Magazine,* it is quite possible that the mark which identifies Dorlan Warthell's African ancestry inspired Hopkins's use of the lotus lily birthmark in her novel. In any event, both writers raise the possibility of a direct blood link to past African glory, which may have caused their readers to rethink their attitude toward their ancestral home.

21. Eric Sundquist remarks that "one can be certain that Hopkins's intent was less to promote back-to-Africa philosophy than to draw from it a popularized basis for black pride and, more important, a theoretically complex way to understand African American double-consciousness. Africanity, according to *Of One Blood,* can be awakened in the individual pysche, just as it can be awakened in the political dimension of national consciousness: it exists 'behind the Veil' of racist historiography and evolutionary social theory, but also behind the veil of [African Americans'] ignorance about their African past, in some cases even their slave past." (*To Wake,* 573).

22. This paternalism recalls Dorlan Warthell's attitude toward Africa in Griggs's *Unfettered* and contrasts with the experiences of Sadipe Okekenu, the main character in John E. Bruce's *The Black Sleuth,* which I will discuss in the next section. Sadipe, a Yoruba who spends time in America and England acting as a kind of "spy in enemy country," learns the ways of the white man presumably in order to assist his people when he returns home.

23. As early as 1844 in *Light and Truth: Collected from the Bible and Ancient and Modern History, Containing the Universal History of the Colored and the Indian Race, from the Creation of the World to the Present Time,* a work published in Boston, the black writer Robert Benjamin Lewis asserted that the Fall of humankind occurred in Ethiopia: "Adam and his posterity settled on the river Gihon, that went out of the Garden of Eden, and compassed the whole land (or country) of Ethiopia; and they tilled the ground, from which Adam was taken." Lewis also described Adam and Eve as black people: "The word *Adam* is derived as follows: Adam, Adamah, Adami, Admah—which means *earthy.* The earth is a rich, dark substance and from it our first parents were taken. Now if we admit . . . Bible Dictionaries are correct in their explanations of the meanings of the terms, then the deduction must be that Ethiopia (Gen. 2:13) was *black,* and the first people were Ethiopians, or blacks" (quoted in McCarthy, 138, emphasis in original).

24. In fact, Nubia was Christian from the sixth through the fifteenth centuries, making it one of the longest-lasting African Christian kingdoms (Wilford, C10). For a thoroughly revisionary, African-centered account of the origins and development of the Christian religion exhibiting neither Hopkins's faithfulness to scriptural sources nor her concerns about offending devout readers, see Ishmael Reed's *Mumbo Jumbo* (1972), esp. 161–187.

25. This discussion of *Of One Blood* originated during an NEH Summer Seminar on the Problem of Race in American and Afro-American Literature, 1860–1930, at the University of California, Berkeley in 1990.

26. For information on Bruce's life and career, see Bullock, 78; Crowder, "John E. Bruce"; Ferris, *An African Abroad,* 80–86; Fierce, 50–54; Peter Gilbert; Gruesser, "Bruce"; Kaiser; Meier, *Negro Thought,* 262–63; and Bruce's "John Edward Bruce: Three Documents." For Bruce's role in the Garvey movement, see Martin's *Literary Garveyism* and *Race First* and Stein, *World of Marcus Garvey.*

27. Precisely dating *The Black Sleuth* presents serious challenges. The only copy I know of is in Bruce's papers at the New York Public Library's Schomburg Center for Research in Black Culture. The novel originally appeared in the Philadelphia-based *McGirt's Magazine,* a publication whose highest estimated circulation, according to Walter Daniel, was 1,500. Penelope Bullock reports that publication of *McGirt's* began in 1903 (probably in August) and the magazine ran monthly until August 1908. A new series began in 1909 when the journal came out on a quarterly basis, and then it ceased publication. Dating *The Black Sleuth* is difficult for two reasons. First, according to Bullock, only seventeen issues of *McGirt's* are extant, and these are scattered among various libraries. Second, the pages of the novel from *McGirt's* in the Bruce papers do not indicate the issue in which they appeared, with two exceptions. *The Black Sleuth* runs seventeen chapters and appeared in seventeen installments, but these are not identical—the first installment contained chapters 1 and 2, and the last chapter is split between the final two installments. The pages from *McGirt's* in the Bruce papers contain corrections and some marginal notes (including chapter num-

bers in two cases), presumably by Bruce. The first page of the thirteenth installment has the words "Sept 1908" and "Chap XIV" written on it. The fifteenth
installment has the notes "XVI" (presumably the chapter number) and what
appears to be "Janu Feb Mar" (probably referring to the January/February/March
1909 issue of *McGirt's*) written at the top of the first page. Working backward
and forward from these notes (and assuming that the serial appeared in every
issue of *McGirt's* that was published during the time that it ran), I estimate that
The Black Sleuth began in September 1907 and ended with the July/August/Sep-
tember issue of 1909. These calculations were partially confirmed by the librarians at Atlanta University, who stated that the final issue of *McGirt's* (October/
November/December 1909), the only extant copy of which is owned by Atlanta,
does not contain an installment of *The Black Sleuth*. However, if my dating of the
serial is correct, there must have been two additional issues of the magazine in
1908 that Bullock does not list—September 1908 and either an October, November, or December, or an October/November/December 1908 issue. Because
of the uncertainty in dating the serial and for the sake of convenience, I have
chosen to number each separate page of *McGirt's* on which *The Black Sleuth*
appears in the Bruce papers—there are sixty-four pages total—and list these
numbers in parenthesis when referring to the novel.

28. It is possible that Bruce intended the serial to continue for many more
chapters, but the imminent demise of *McGirt's* prevented this. However, if this is
so, it is odd that Bruce did not attempt to wrap the novel up in the final issue of
periodical, October/November/December 1909.

29. There are some interesting parallels between the fictional Bradshawe
and a notorious thief by the name of Adam Worth (1844–1901), whom the
Pinkerton detective agency described as "the most remarkable, most successful
and most dangerous professional criminal known to modern times" (quoted in
MacIntyre, "Disappearing," 30). Born in the United States, Worth settled in London and coordinated a crime syndicate extending from Europe to Asia Minor to
South Africa. Worth served as the model for Conan Doyle's Professor Moriarty.
For more on Worth, see MacIntyre's "Disappearing" and *Napoleon*; see also Horan,
280–320.

30. Bruce's use of an expanded frame of reference recalls Frederick
Douglass's *My Bondage and My Freedom* and Harriet Jacobs's *Incidents in the Life
of a Slave Girl* in which these slave narrators describe their journeys to England
in order to contrast the comparative lack of racial prejudice there with conditions in the United States. Bruce significantly expands this technique by setting
his novel in Africa as well as Great Britain and America.

31. The reference is to Moses da Rocha of Lagos, with whom Bruce corresponded.

32. Later Bruce anticipates the phrasing of T.S. Eliot's indictment of morally bankrupt whites (e.g. Kurtz from Joseph Conrad's *Heart of Darkness*) in
"The Hollow Men" when Mojola, speaking of his English teacher and the mis-

sionary zeal of this man's congregation in London, states that "the hollowness of their professions of brotherhood was to me so transparent I determined that I would, on the first opportunity that presented itself, return to my own country" (6).

33. Here Bruce may be slyly alluding to the Skinner Expedition to Abyssinia, a target of one of his most staunchly anticolonial and anti-imperial essays—"The Dusky Kings of Africa and the Islands of the Sea."

34. Sadipe's argument in this passage parallels that of Bruce's article "The Stronger Nations vs. the Weaker Nations."

35. A clear expression of this idea can be found in Du Bois's "The Conservation of Races," a speech he made to the American Negro Academy (of which both he and Bruce were members) in 1897.

3. The New Negro and Africa

An earlier version of part of this chapter appeared in *The Journal of African Travel-Writing* 7 (October/November 1999): 45–56.

1. Tony Martin's *African Fundamentalism: A Literary and Cultural Anthology of Garvey's Harlem Renaissance* amply documents Garveyism extensive use of Ethiopianism. See, for example, Arnold J. Ford's "O Africa, My Native Land" (1920): "I now arise with solemn mind, / The haven of thy shores to find, / Grievous and heavy is my load, / And dark and dreary is the road; / Stretch forth thine hands to me— / Stretch forth thine hands to me" (202)—and John E. Bruce's lengthy essay, "On Negro Poetry" (1923), which concludes with the following paragraph: "This is not quite the Negro's day in literature. He is dead now but he is soon to arise with healing in his wings. Rejuvenated, disenthralled, redeemed, he will stand in the full stature of a man and will ably fulfill the promise that Ethiopia shall suddenly stretch forth her hands unto God and then princes shall come out of Egypt. For out of Egypt have I called my son. We are coming and the Father of us all will bless and prosper the race that gave hospitality and protection to the Son of Righteousness, if it will only believe in itself and be itself" (63–64).

2. As Moses notes, New Negro writers evince ambivalence about not only civilization but also savagery, frequently promoting and romanticizing both (*Afrotopia*, 211). For a useful discussion of the attractions and perils primitivism held for these authors, see Chinitz.

3. Both James B. Barnes and Johnny Washington have noted inconsistencies and inaccuracies in Locke's assertions about the relationship between African and black American art and culture, although they differ as to the causes. Barnes states that Locke's "limited exposure to the African reality and his failure to observe African music and dance affected his judgment" (107). In contrast, Washington claims that Locke's inconsistencies, particularly on the question of whether Africans and black Americans have a common race psychology, "stem ... from the paradoxical conditions engendered by slavery under which blacks lived. . . . Whites attempted to force Black Americans during slavery to abandon their Afri-

can culture and also attempted to prevent them from being fully integrated into American culture. People cannot live in the absence of culture. . . . While remaining on the periphery of American culture, African-Americans created their own folkways which played a key role in the formation of American culture" (196).

4. For a discussion of Du Bois, Padmore, and George Schuyler's response to the Liberian scandal, see Hooker.

5. A new version of *In Dahomey,* with book by Shauneille Perry, was produced at Karamu House in 1990 and published in Woodie King's *The National Black Drama Anthology* (1995). A recently restored version of the original *In Dahomey* was published in the updated version of *Black Theatre USA: Plays by African Americans, 1847 to Today,* edited by James V. Hatch and Ted Shine (1996).

6. Shirley Graham was neither the first African American to write an opera nor the first African American to write an opera depicting Africa. These distinctions belong to Harry Lawrence Freeman, a Cleveland native whose works include *The Martyr* (1893), *Zuluki* (1898), *An African Kraal* (1903), and the tetralogy *Zululand* (1932–1947) (Brawley, "A Composer"; Hatch and Abdullah).

7. Dean may also be the "bitter, black American who whispered how an army of the Soudan might someday cross the Alps" that Du Bois recalled encountering at the 1900 Pan-African Conference in "The Immortal Child," his eulogy to Samuel Coleridge-Taylor in *Darkwater* (581).

8. In his introduction Shepperson relies heavily on Burger's thesis and praises his pioneering research. Drawing liberally on Dean's diaries and notebooks at the DuSable Museum of African American History in Chicago, Burger not only provides dates for some of the events mentioned in Dean's book but also recounts the author's life after the period covered in *The Pedro Gorino.* He describes Dean's activities in Liberia between 1909 and 1914, his two periods in Chicago (1914–1920 and 1927–1935), his unsuccessful efforts in the 1920s to purchase a ship to conduct trade between California and Liberia, his founding of a nautical college for blacks in Alameda, California, in 1924, his lectures on Africa and black history, and his efforts to establish black agricultural communities in Washington state in the 1930s. In 1998, I was able to confirm some of Burger's assertions about Dean's activities in California in the early 1920s. The 1924 Oakland City Directory includes a "Dean, Harry," with the occupation of "mstr mar" (presumably master mariner), residing at 1530 Lincoln Avenue in Alameda (624). In addition, "Capt. Harry Dean" published two articles in the *San Francisco Chronicle* in 1923—"Liberian Development Possibilities" and "Ship Deal Discrimination Charge." In the former, which is accompanied by a portrait of Dean, he claims the "wonderful country" of Liberia holds the key to the "Solution of the Negro Problem" and mentions his nautical school.

9. There are at least two discrepancies between the American and British editions of Dean's book. In the American edition, Book I is entitled "I Go to Sea at the Age of Twelve." Interestingly, there is also a negative comment about Cecil Rhodes that appears only in the American edition. After describing Rhodes's

giant cement crypt in Matabeleland, Dean remarks, "Thus his body might never be removed from the country he had conquered, and his iron spirit might continue to subdue the Ethiopian race even after he was gone. This was the last grandiose gesture of an African conqueror whose cruelty was only equaled by that of Henry the Navigator" (*The Pedro Gorino,* 202). Dean's autobiography was also published in Berlin in 1929, but I have not been able to consult this edition.

10. North's claims about Dean's travels around and within Africa closely resemble those in the undated three-page "Biography" by and about Dean in Dean's papers. The 1989 Pluto Press reissue of the British version of the book does not contain North's preface, which provides information about Dean and the composition of the book. Quotations from Dean's autobiography are taken from the reprint of the British edition unless indicated otherwise.

11. Dean was not the only descendant of Paul Cuffe—if this was in fact the case as I discuss below—to write a biography of his ancestor. Henry Noble Sherwood reports that "Horatio P. Howard, a great grandson of Captain Cuffe, wrote a short biography of his grandsire [in 1913] and erected a monument in his memory [in Westport, Massachusetts in 1913]" (225). Howard also established the Captain Paul Cuffe Scholarships at Tuskegee (226).

12. In an anonymous essay about Paul Cuffe's grave in the New Bedford Public Library's Paul Cuffe Collection entitled "Uncle John's Burying Place" that probably dates from the 1970s, Dean is described as "a man who claims descent, and I think must have looked into the Cuffe papers and then let his truly inspired imagination flow freely." Although the library's record of researchers who have used the Cuffe Collection does not go back as far as the 1920s, the glass plates with Cuffe's letters in Dean's papers indicate that at some point he must have had access to the Cuffe papers. Moreover, his inclusion in *The Pedro Gorino* of a story concerning the origins of Paul Cuffe's father that has been refuted by Cuffe's biographers suggests that he may have contacted Cuffe's descendants and/or their neighbors in the New Bedford area at the time he consulted the library's Cuffe materials. Dean's account in his first chapter of a young boy named Said Kafu who nursed the Scottish pirate McKinnon Paige back to health and accompanied him to Massachusetts, where they took the names of Cuffe and Slocum respectively, closely resembles the "family tradition" about Paul Cuffe's father that was repeated in a 1930 *Boston Globe* article entitled "The Story of Paul Cuffee," which briefly mentions Dean's book. I am grateful to Paul Cyr of the New Bedford Free Public Library for bringing both "Uncle John's Burying Place" and "The Story of Paul Cuffee" to my attention.

13. Dean dates the letter from "John Cuffee" January 13, 1818. The actual date was exactly one year earlier (Thomas, 157).

14. Paul Cuffe discusses his repudiation of his "son John Cuffe" in a 1 March 1817 letter to James Forten (quoted in Harris, 249). This letter was written in response to a 25 January 1817 letter by Forten in which Forten mentions the impostor.

15. This is a possibility that Lamont Thomas suggested to me in a 24 May 1993 phone conversation.

16. John S. Burger told me in a 10 June 1993 phone conversation that he did not recall Celestine T. Fulchon, a member of Dean's family with some knowledge of its genealogy, being able to verify Dean's claim that he was descended from Paul Cuffe.

17. Although Dean cannot be held responsible for any inaccuracies in his uncle's story and its veracity is of course less important than its effect on Dean, the tale of the *Full Moon* is hard to verify. A Dutch man-of-war commanded by a Captain Jope did land the first black people in the English colonies near Jamestown in August of 1619; however, Wesley Frank Craven states that a letter by John Rolfe, the source of all later accounts of the episode, including that of John Smith, "clearly indicates that the Negroes had been acquired in the West Indies and such a conclusion is reinforced by unmistakable evidence of . . . [the] number of the Spanish names among the few Negroes listed by name in the census of 1625" (81). Rolfe does not mention the name of the Dutch vessel. In his Notes to *The Libretto for the Republic of Liberia* (which is discussed in chapter 5), Melvin Tolson states that the name of the ship that landed near Jamestown was the *Jesus*. See also Bennett, 29–30.

18. The story is well known in Norway, and thus it is quite possible that Dean may have purchased a ship named after this girl. I am grateful to Styrk Fjose for this information.

19. Throughout his book Dean puts the word "negro" in quotation marks. North explains in his preface to *The Pedro Gorino* that "Captain Dean feels that the word 'negro' is of false derivation, undescriptive, and in every way unfit for the position it fills in our language. He claims there is no 'negro' race, only many African races" (*The Pedro Gorino,* xii).

20. For a recent discussion of Dean's missionary work in South Africa, see James T. Campbell, 201.

21. I have in mind the long first paragraph of the second chapter of Conrad's novel, which concludes: "The sea of the past was an incomparably beautiful mistress, with inscrutable face, with cruel and promising eyes. The sea of to-day is a used-up drudge, wrinkled and defaced by the churned-up wakes of brutal propellers, robbed of the enslaving charm of its vastness, stripped of its beauty, of its mystery and of its promise" (*An Outcast of the Islands,* 25).

22. In a 28 July 1994 conversation in his office at Princeton University, Arnold Rampersad wholeheartedly concurred with the reading of this passage that I present here.

23. Hughes's sexual preference may have played a role in the disgust he registers in recounting this incident. Rampersad reports that Hughes had his first homosexual experience during his stint on the *West Heseltine* (*Life,* 77).

24. A brief notice in the *Crisis,* one of only two contemporary reviews of Downing's novel I have been able to locate, saw no conflict between the book's

polemical and melodramatic aspects, praising it as "an excellent and frank exposition of Liberia's problems, done in the form of romance" (15 [1918]: 186).

25. For biographical information about Downing, see Contee. In a short essay entitled "An African Novel," appearing in the *Negro World* in 1920, William Ferris reports that "Mr. Henry Downing of New York City is writing *Songhay: An African Tale,* the scene of which is laid on the soil of Africa. It pictures the civilization of Timbucktu and the Songhay people during the Middle Ages. The tale hinges around 'The Sacred Jar,' which was given to Mohamed Askia and handed down by him to his descendants. It sustained the same relation to the Songhay people that the Ark of the Covenant did to the Children of Israel. The story tells of the plans of the Emperor of Morocco to obtain the Sacred Jar" (26). Despite this detailed description, *Songhay: An African Tale* apparently was never published.

26. Gilbert Lubin's novel *The Promised Land* (1930), discussed in the next section, may be indebted to Downing's *Liberia and Her People*. Not only do certain statements Lubin makes about the republic echo assertions to be found in Downing's book, but the novel acts on the earlier writer's prediction that African American immigration to Liberia would succeed in turning the country around.

27. In a review appearing in the *Journal of Negro History,* Ida Gibbs Hunt objected to the novel's generally unsympathetic depiction of Africans and African customs: "It is written from a white man's point of view and shows a tendency to regard the white man's civilization as the only true standard" (444).

28. Dale's phrasing here closely resembles a passage in Downing's "Liberia" recounting the "pathetic" story of the Americo-Liberians: "After a few years under the care of incompetent nurses, they were weaned and expected to walk at once. They were encouraged to establish a Government, Republican in form. . . . Even the most able of men, assisted by wealth and experience, would have found this task exceedingly difficult to accomplish" (299).

29. Downing, who in 1902 appealed to Booker T. Washington to send some of his recent graduates to Africa to help develop cotton fields (Contee, 188), advocated the development of an "industrial educational institution similar to Tuskegee or Hampton" in Liberia to serve all of Africa, and sought to generate African American investment in the republic, declaring that it "offers a wonderful field for self-development well worth seeking" (*Liberia and Her People,* 13, 20).

30. Without intervention such as Dale's, Downing believed Liberia's prospects were grim: "if no more effective means be used to perpetuate the State's independence, she will be divided between her strong neighbors—America retaining Monrovia as a coaling station" ("Liberia," 300).

31. Downing dedicated *The American Cavalryman* to Joel and Arthur Spingarn. Even though Downing was living in London when he wrote and published the novel, Hugh Gloster sees this as an indication of "the growing influence of the National Association for the Advancement of Colored People upon Negro Writers" (95).

32. Interestingly, despite the novel's apparent disapproval of mixed-race relationships, Downing's second wife was an Irish woman named Margarita Doyle, whom he married in 1894 and moved to London with the following year (Contee, 188).

33. In *White Man's Grave* (1994), for example, Richard Dooling invents a printed Sierra Leonean Krio designed to capture the sound of the spoken language as well as convey its logic, complexity, and beauty.

34. This discussion continues on the book's back cover. Although Lubin or his editor acknowledges that the ease with which the emigration plan is effected "constitutes the 'visionary' part of the tale, the part that has not yet come true," that "[s]imilar efforts have been made before . . . that have not had the hoped for success," and that "it is doubtful if any wholesale emigration from this country is likely to take place," the assertion is made that "there seems no good reason why Liberia should not eventually become all that this author pictures it, as a place of refuge for the Negro." This description of Liberia as a "place of refuge" for African Americans recalls Ensal Ellwood's statements about the republic at the conclusion of Griggs's *The Hindered Hand*.

35. According to Sundiata, "In 1930 Liberia's Americo-Liberian population was, perhaps exaggeratedly, estimated at between 10,000 and 12,000" (7). He also cites the country's "laterite soils" as a factor responsible for slowing the development of agricultural products for export (3). These statements contradict not only *The Promised Land*'s assertions but also those found in Henry F. Downing's *Liberia and Her People* (1925), which may have inspired Lubin's novel. Downing lists 25,000 as the Americo-Liberian population and declares that the country's "soil is exceedingly rich and very responsive" (10, 20).

36. The negative reaction to Jesse Jackson's suggestion that the West begin paying back the great debt it owes people of African descent for the slave trade is worth noting here.

37. Garvey's failure to secure a beachhead in the black republic with its open immigration policy proved fatal to his ambitious plans for the continent. According to Arnold Hughes, "With the collapse of the Liberian Colonisation Scheme, on which Garvey had pinned so much hope for gaining a foothold in Africa—even intending moving the UNIA headquarters to Monrovia and holding the 1924 World Convention there—UNIA support in Africa ebbed. Pockets of organized Garveyism survived, notably in South Africa, and admiration for Garvey's vision and sacrifice never disappeared; but any prospect of establishing a significant and concrete foothold in Africa vanished with the Liberian venture" (109–10).

38. For information on opposition to emigration, see Moses, *The Golden Age*, 34–39, and Sundiata, 3.

39. Prince elaborates Wesley's Fortunate Fall argument in the fourth chapter when he tells the members of Congress, "we were not ready for [Liberia] sixty years ago. If the newly enfranchised slaves had gone at that time there

would have been danger of their reverting to barbarism; so you have kept us here and gradually prepared us for our final departure" (35).

40. For information on the origins of the term "going native," see Watt, 145. For an extended analysis of the "going native" or expatriate theme in white literature about Africa, see Gruesser, *White on Black*.

41. Schuyler's passage anticipates V.S. Naipaul's assertion in "The Crocodiles of Yamousouskro" that those who come to convert Africa to the modern world are often converted to Africa's "night" or "magic" world. In this travel piece about the Ivory Coast and in his fictional works about the continent, Naipaul relies heavily on the "going native" theme. See Gruesser, *White on Black,* chap. 3.

4. The African American Literary Response to the Ethiopian Crisis

An earlier version of part of this chapter appeared in *African American Review* 27 (winter 1993): 679–86.

1. Du Bois's ambivalence toward European colonialism at the turn of the century is evident in his discussion of British rule in Africa in "The Present Outlook for the Dark Races of Mankind" (1900).

2. Assigning a precise date to "The Lion and the Jackal" presents a serious challenge. Although Joy Flasch claims that Tolson wrote it in 1935 (27), in her chronology of his life she claims he finished the novel in 1939 (16). The 105 typewritten pages of the manuscript in Tolson's papers, however, do not amount to a complete story. Further complicating matters, the folder containing it in Tolson's papers at the Library of Congress bears the description "Novel: *The Lion and the Jackal* C. 1945." I suspect that the 1935 date is correct and that the rapidity of the Ethiopian defeat took Tolson by surprise and caused him to abandon the manuscript. I am grateful to Aldon Nielsen for providing me with a copy of this novel.

3. The exiled emperor declared, "I have come myself to testify against the crime perpetrated against my people . . . and to give Europe warning of the doom that awaits it if it bows down before the *fait accompli*" (quoted in Davis, 596).

4. For information on Garvey's reactions to the Italo-Ethiopian War and criticism of Haile Selassie, see Lewis, 168–75.

5. William Scott here elaborates an assertion first made by Harold Isaacs in *The New World of Negro Americans* (1963): "Nowadays . . . Ethiopia does not figure prominently in the new shape of Negro interest in Africa" (153).

6. For information on Robinson and Julian, see William Scott, 69–95, and Weisbord.

7. For a discussion of the numerous references to the Ethiopian war in *Rendezvous,* see Doreski, 82–83.

8. Tolson's assertion that capitalism was responsible for the defeat of Ethiopia is repeated in another "Caviar and Cabbage" column entitled "Frankenstein and the Monster," which appeared in 1940.

9. Schuyler had a penchant for such names, at least in his satirical works. In *Black No More,* for example, he lampooned Du Bois and Garvey respectively through the characters of Dr. Shakespeare Agamemnon Beard and Santop Licorice. Likewise, his rather artless unpublished novel, "Uno Me, Pal!" (You know me, pal), set on an island in the Indian Ocean known as the Rektum Republic, features such figures as Hung Far Low, Cecil Percival Olden-Faggot, Dorothy Outhouse, Bertha Buttox, and Dr. Omi Gosch.

10. "The Black Internationale: Story of Black Genius Against the World" ran in the *Pittsburgh Courier* from 21 November 1936 to 3 July 1937. "Black Empire: An Imaginative Story of a Great New Civilization in Modern Africa" ran in the *Courier* from 2 October 1937 to 16 April 1938.

11. In addition to foretelling the widespread development of these technologies, Schuyler also predicts the women's liberation movement and the global dominance of the English language.

12. In her illustration of the extent to which Schuyler's newspaper writings, particularly from early in his career, conflict with the claims he makes about himself and his beliefs in *Black and Conservative* (1966), Ann Rayson anticipates Gates's reading of the writer in "A Fragmented Man." Speaking of Schuyler's pose in his autobiography, Rayson claims: "beneath this objective, unemotional, and unreasonably extroverted self-portrayal certainly exists a divided self" (106).

13. Almost thirty years later and by then a confirmed red-baiter, Schuyler would nevertheless have this to say about the militant essay: "In view of what has happened in the world since World War II, I think the most significant article I wrote during the entire period was in *The Crisis* for August, 1938, on 'The Rise of the Black Internationale.' It was the leading article in that issue and a lengthy one, which predicted much that has happened in the developing color conflict, including the worldwide liberation of the colored peoples from white rule, which I referred to as the White Internationale. This was exactly a year before the Nazi invasion of Poland. It was a factual summary and an analysis which led logically to the inevitability of World War II and the awakening of the nonwhite people everywhere" (*Black and Conservative,* 248).

14. The similarities between Cranfield in "Strange Valley" and Dr. Henry Belsidus in the *Black Empire* novels are striking, but the differences between them are notable, too. Although Cranfield demands strict discipline from his men, he is a much more attractive and less ruthless mastermind than Belsidus.

15. Hill and Rasmussen seem relatively untroubled by the Black Internationale's fascism, viewing Belsidus's methods as consistent with those of other successful schemers in Schuyler's *Courier* fiction and with the revenge fantasies against white oppression that Schuyler occasionally included in his *Courier* editorials and columns. The editors' analysis of what might be called the Black Internationale's crimes against humanity at times evinces a rather startling detachment. For example, of Belsidus's successful effort to cripple Great Britain's infrastructure by luring fifteen thousand civilian "Master Technicians" to a Lon-

don production of the *Congo Ballet* and gassing them to death, Hill and Rasmussen remark, "What exquisite irony that a product of superior black chemistry should be used to wipe out England's finest technicians as they savor a tranquil African ballet!" ("Afterword," 304).

16. John Reilly reads Schuyler's *Black No More* as a "black anti-utopia" that anticipates William Melvin Kelley's *A Different Drummer.*

17. In his introduction to Schuyler's *Ethiopian Stories,* published three years after *Black Empire,* Robert Hill seems to have modified some of his ideas about Schuyler. In the later work, Hill rightly emphasizes Schuyler's antifascism: "Notwithstanding Schuyler's anticommunism . . . , which arose out of what he saw as the American Communist party's opportunistic takeover of the Scottsboro Boys' case, his writing during this period formed a significant contribution to the literature of 1930s American antifascism, rivaled among African-American writers perhaps only by that of Langston Hughes. Like the broader African-American contribution to the worldwide movement against fascism, this aspect of Schuyler's work still needs to be properly assessed" (38). Moreover, Hill ultimately portrays Schuyler as a gadfly and a moralist: "Schuyler's caustic wit, haughty independence of spirit, whimsical singularity, and contemptuous rejection of convention were expressions of his lifelong struggle with the problem of radical self-sufficiency, dictated by Cynic precepts governing the training of the mind and body. It was for this reason that he was always keen to expose the moral laxity of conventional American beliefs held by blacks and whites about each other and themselves" (40).

18. Immediately following this comment, Max indicates that, despite his present position and white skin, he has not forgotten that he is playing a role, telling Bunny, "I know I'm a darky and I'm always on the alert" (147). This ability to remember who he really is underneath the mask is the key to Max's survival in race-crazy America, an ability Schuyler himself possessed during the 1920s and 1930s. By the 1950s, however, he had apparently forgotten Max's important insight. Unable or unwilling to stop playing his longest and last role— George Schuyler the anti-Communist—late in his career he became, as Gates aptly describes him, "a gadfly trapped in amber" ("Fragmented," 43).

19. This passage is also fascinating because of the way it resonates with Joseph Conrad's *Heart of Darkness,* not only one of the earliest and certainly the most famous narrative about "going native" but also a work that has been variously interpreted as a denunciation of European colonialism and a portrait of the innate depravity of Africa.

5. The Promise of Africa-To-Be in Melvin Tolson's *Libretto for the Republic of Liberia*

1. The original—"A little learning is a dangerous thing; / Drink deep or taste not the Pierian spring"—appears in Part II of *An Essay on Criticism,* lines 215–16.

2. Tolson was stung by such criticism and specifically addressed it in a letter to the editor of the Baltimore *Afro-American* and in *Harlem Gallery* (Flasch, 96–97; Farnsworth, 166–68, 170). For a discussion of the critical reception of Tolson, see Berube.

3. Lincoln University was also the alma mater of at least two Africans who played key roles in liberating their countries from colonial rule: Nnamdi Azikiwe, the first president of Nigeria, whom Tolson quotes in his notes, and Kwame Nkrumah, the first prime minister and later the president of Ghana.

4. The question and answer structure of "Do" recalls the last two stanzas of the title poem of Tolson's *Rendezvous with America,* which begin with the question "America?"

5. The 1953 Twayne edition of the *Libretto* has no page numbers for either the poem or the notes. I provide the line numbers of passages quoted from the poem in parenthesis.

6. It is possible that in "Fa" Tolson is also subtly referring to war, particularly the Allied air power that was the subject of the preceding section's final stanza, through his use of the words "corsair," to describe the rock upon which the raptor sags, and "typhoon," to describe the tiger. The Corsair was a fighter plane built for the United States Navy during World War II. The Typhoon was a ground attack aircraft used by the British in the same conflict.

7. Although the poem's opening section consists of seven six-line stanzas, the lines within the stanzas are of varying lengths and are centered on the page. Thus, through its form as well as its content, the *Libretto*'s first "Do" anticipates "Ti" and the second "Do."

8. Tolson's position here contrasts starkly with Griggs's dubious statements about Africa's isolation in the appendix to *The Hindered Hand* (discussed in chapter 2). Tolson may have had Langston Hughes's early poem "The Negro Speaks of Rivers," which Hughes dedicated to Du Bois, in mind in these lines.

9. The school is named for William V. Tubman, who served as president of Liberia from 1944 to 1971.

10. *Bula Matadi,* which means breaker of rocks, was the name given to Henry Morgan Stanley whose 1874–1877 expedition through the Congo opened up the region for colonization by Leopold II of Belgium. Stanley brought a portable boat, the *Lady Alice,* with him on his journey through Central Africa, using it to sail down the Congo River.

11. The reference is to Joseph Jenkins Roberts, the last governor of the colony of Liberia and the republic's first president.

6. The Movement Away from Ethiopianism in African American Writing about Africa

Earlier versions of parts of this chapter appeared in *Black American Literature Forum* 24, no. 1 (spring 1990): 5–20; and *American Drama* 1, no. 2 (spring 1992): 1–14.

1. On Ethiopianism's influence on Black Judaism and the Nation of Islam, see Shapiro. On the influence of Ethiopianism on Rastafarianism, see Horace Campbell. Addressing this subject in a recent review, Landeg White observed that "[t]hough the term itself has largely dropped out of use since the Sixties, 'Ethiopia' as an idea remains a powerful force behind the British Rastafarian movement which, for all its lack of interest in post-revolutionary Ethiopia, remains the most powerful expression of Afrocentrism in Britain. It is a good example of myth overtaking and suppressing reality" (7).

2. See Senghor's "Negritude: A Humanism of the Twentieth Century," a speech he presented at the first Festival of African Arts in Dakar in 1966. In yet another cross-cultural interaction, the African Personality movement associated with Edward Blyden and Majola Agbebi in turn influenced the African American journalist, historian, and novelist John E. Bruce, who became a key figure in the UNIA (see chapter 2). See also Hughes's "The Twenties," where he claims, "Had the word *negritude* been in use in Harlem in the twenties, Cullen, as well as McKay, Johnson, Toomer, and I, might have been called poets of *negritude*" (32).

3. As noted in chapter 1, the best-known critique of Asante's movement has been Mary Lefkowitz's superficial *Not Out of Africa,* a book that fails to place Afrocentrism in the larger context of African American history and literature.

4. Williams's 1987 novel *Jacob's Ladder,* which echoes *The Man Who Cried I Am* in somewhat muted tones, is also worth noting. The time of each book is roughly the same, and Williams even resurrects the protagonist of his earlier novel, Max Reddick, to write a 1978 newspaper story about the facts behind the 1966 coup that closes the later book. Like *The Color Purple,* which is discussed below, *Jacob's Ladder* thematizes African American missionary involvement in Africa.

5. The story of African American travel literature about Africa is the story of black American writers' struggle with both their romantic preconceptions about Africa and the pervasiveness of Africanist discourse. As discussed in chapter 3, Hughes, Du Bois, and Schuyler visited the continent in the 1920s and early 1930s—and Robert Campbell's *A Pilgrimage to My Motherland* was published much earlier (1860)—but for the most part African American travel books about Africa did not appear until after mid-century.

6. For a discussion of Greene and Waugh's *entre les guerres* travel books about Africa, see *White on Black,* chapter 2.

7. For a thorough analysis of Angelou and a more detailed reading of Brooks, as well as a discussion of William Gardner Smith's description of his sojourn in Ghana during the early 1960s in *Return to Black America* (1970), see Gruesser, "Afro-American Travel Writing and Africanist Discourse."

8. The main character of the novel, Candace, is presumably named for the ancient Ethiopian warrior queen. This supposition is supported by the fact that the preceding section in *To Be Young, Gifted and Black,* concerning Hansberry's high school years, bears the title "Queen of the Ethiopes" (67–71). In addition,

Robert Nemiroff reports that in early drafts of *Les Blancs* the name of the African protagonist was Candace (31).

9. In his study of Hansberry's dramatic works, Steven Carter reports that she had also researched and projected a work on the ancient Egypt of Aknaton, also known as Amenhotep IV, who ruled from 1375–1357 B.C. and is credited with reforming Egyptian religion (184).

10. For a description of his role in preparing the final version of *Les Blancs,* see Nemiroff, 34–35.

11. In fact, the most extended comparison of *Les Blancs* with another literary work to date has been Carter's elaboration of the connections between Hansberry's play and *Hamlet,* in which Tshembe resembles the indecisive Danish prince, Major Rice functions as a Claudius figure, the Woman beckons the protagonist to act in a manner reminiscent of the Ghost of Hamlet's father, and Charlie Morris will presumably tell the world of Tshembe's struggle as Horatio does for Hamlet (102–8).

12. In addition to Marlow, it should be noted that in his nationality and profession Morris resembles Henry Morgan Stanley, the man who "found" the "saintly" Livingstone and who opened up the Congo for exploitation by King Leopold II of Belgium.

13. Carter asserts that Hansberry modeled Neilson on Albert Schweitzer, particularly John Gunther's portrayal of the Nobel Peace Prize winner in *Inside Africa* (114–15).

14. Hansberry, in fact, chose *Les Blancs* as her title in order to respond pointedly to Genet's play *The Blacks.*

15. Carter discusses the origin and Hansberry's use of this folk tale at length in his chapter on *Les Blancs* (106–9). He also notes another use of African oral tradition in *Les Blancs:* uttering a war cry in act 2, scene 6, the resistance leader Ngago becomes a "poet-warrior invoking the soul of his people" (108).

16. *The Color Purple* is widely considered to be the first African American epistolary novel, one of the oldest novelistic traditions in the English language.

17. Several critics, including Kimberly Chambers, Lori Kelly, and Diane Scholl, have written about religion in *The Color Purple.* However, no one to my knowledge has discussed the novel in connection with Ethiopianism.

18. In reference to Celie's American success story, which she regards as a conservative element in an otherwise revolutionary novel, Linda Kauffman states, "Celie's progress from victimization to success as a pantsmaker and businesswoman could be seen as a black feminist version of the Horatio Alger myth" (206–7).

19. In a controversial early essay that is highly critical of Walker's book, Trudier Harris describes Nettie's letters to Celie as "really extraneous to the central concerns of the novel," linking them to "the whaling chapters in *Moby Dick*— there more for the exhibition of a certain kind of knowledge than for the good of the work" (157). Using Northrop Frye's archetypal approach to literature, Molly

Hite links the African scenes of *The Color Purple* to the "green world" of romance generally and Shakespeare's *A Winter's Tale* in particular. In a muted echo of Berlant, Hite asserts, "The function of the 'Africa' section is clearly to provide analogies and contrasts to the dominant action," which takes place in the United States (113).

Works Cited

Achebe, Chinua. "An Image of Africa: Racism in Conrad's *Heart of Darkness*." In Joseph Conrad, *Heart of Darkness,* 3rd ed., edited by Robert Kimbrough. New York: Norton, 1988.

Adams, William Y. "Doubts about the 'Lost Pharoahs.'" *Journal of Near Eastern Studies* 44 (1985): 185–92.

Adas, Michael. *Machines as the Measure of Men: Science, Technology, and Ideologies of Western Dominance.* Ithaca: Cornell Univ. Press, 1989.

Adell, Sandra. *Double-Consciousness/Double Bind: Theoretical Issues in Twentieth-Century Black Literature.* Urbana: Univ. of Illinois Press, 1994.

Angelou, Maya. *All God's Children Need Traveling Shoes.* New York: Random House, 1986.

Appiah, Kwame Anthony. *In My Father's House: Africa in the Philosophy of Culture.* New York: Oxford Univ. Press, 1992.

Asante, Molefi K. *The Afrocentric Idea.* Philadelphia: Temple Univ. Press, 1987.

Asante, S.K.B. *Pan-African Protest: West Africa and the Italo-Ethiopian Crisis, 1934–1941.* London: Longman, 1977.

Azikiwe, Nnamdi. "Liberia: Slave or Free." In *Negro: An Anthology,* edited by Nancy Cunard. 1934. Reprint, New York: Frederick Unger, 1970.

Baraka, Amiri. "Ka 'Ba." In *New Black Voices,* edited by Abraham Chapman, 208. New York: NAL, 1972.

Barnes, James B. "Alain Locke and the Sense of the African Legacy." In *Alain Locke: Reflections on a Modern Renaissance Man,* edited by Russell J. Linnemann. Baton Rouge: Louisiana State Univ. Press, 1982.

Bell, Derrick. "The Afrolantica Awakening." *Faces from the Bottom of the Well: The Permanence of Racism.* New York: Basic Books, 1992.

Bennett, Lerone, Jr. *Before the Mayflower: A History of Black America.* 1961. Reprint, Chicago: Johnson, 1969.

Berlant, Lauren. "Race, Gender, and Nation in *The Color Purple*." *Critical Inquiry* 14 (Summer 1988): 831–59.

Bernal, Martin. *Black Athena: The Afroasiatic Roots of Classical Civilization.* 2 vols. New Brunswick: Rutgers Univ. Press, 1987, 1991.

Berube, Michael. *Marginal Forces/Cultural Centers: Tolson, Pynchon, and the Politics of the Canon.* Ithaca, N.Y.: Cornell Univ. Press, 1992.

Blyden, Edward Wilmot. "The Call of Providence to the Descendants of Africa in

America." In *Classical Black Nationalism: From the American Revolution to Marcus Garvey,* edited by Wilson J. Moses. New York: New York Univ. Press, 1996.

Bone, Robert. *The Negro Novel in America.* New Haven: Yale Univ. Press, 1965.

Bowen, J.W.E., ed. *Africa and the American Negro.* Atlanta: Gammon Theological Seminary, 1896.

Boyer, Richard O. *The Legend of John Brown: A Biography and a History.* New York: Knopf, 1973.

Braithwaite, William Stanley. "Negro America's First Magazine." *Negro Digest* 6 (Dec. 1947): 21–27.

Brawley, Benjamin. "A Composer of Fourteen Operas." *Southern Workman* 62 (July 1933): 311–15.

———. *A Social History of the Negro in America.* 1921. Reprint, Chicago: Johnson, 1968.

Brooks, Gwendolyn. *Report from Part One.* Detroit: Broadside, 1972.

Brown, William Wells. *The Black Man, His Antecedents, His Genius, and His Achievements.* 2nd ed. New York: Thomas Hamilton, 1863.

———. *The Rising Son; Or, the Antecedents and Advancement of the Colored Race.* Boston: A.G. Brown, 1882.

Bruce, Dickson D., Jr. "Ancient Africa and the Early Black American Historians." *American Quarterly* 36 (winter 1984): 684–99.

Bruce, John E. *The Black Sleuth.* 1907–1909. John E. Bruce Collection. Reel 3. Schomburg Center for Research in Black Culture, New York.

———. "Dusky Kings of Africa and the Islands of the Sea." *Voice of the Negro* 2 (August 1905): 573–75.

———. "John Edward Bruce: Three Documents." In *Afro-American Writers before the Harlem Renaissance.* Vol. 50 of *Dictionary of Literary Biography.* Edited by Trudier Harris and Thadious M. Davis. Detroit: Gale, 1986.

———. "The Negro in Poetry." In *African Fundamentalism: A Literary and Cultural Anthology of Garvey's Harlem Renaissance,* edited by Tony Martin. Dover, Mass.: Majority Press, 1991.

———. "The Stronger Nations vs. the Weaker Nations." *Voice of the Negro* 2 (April 1905): 256–57.

Bruce, Richard. *Sahdji: An African Ballet.* In *Plays of Negro Life: A Source Book of Native American Drama,* edited by Alain Locke and Montgomery Gregory. 1927. Reprint, Westport, Conn.: Negro Universities Press, 1970.

Bullock, Penelope. *The Afro-American Periodical Press, 1838–1909.* Baton Rouge: Louisiana State Univ. Press, 1981.

Buni, Andrew. *Robert L. Vann of the "Pittsburgh Courier": Politics and Black Journalism.* Pittsburgh: Univ. of Pittsburgh Press, 1974.

Burger, John S. "An Introduction to Harry Dean Pan-Negro-Nationalist." Master's thesis, Roosevelt University, 1973.

Burroughs, Edgar Rice. *Tarzan of the Apes.* 1912. Reprint, New York: Ballantine, 1977.

Butler, Jon. *Awash in the Sea of Faith: Christianizing the American People*. Cambridge, Mass.: Harvard Univ. Press, 1990.

Campbell, Horace. *Rasta and Resistance: From Marcus Garvey to Walter Rodney*. Trenton, N.J.: Africa World Press, 1987.

Campbell, Jane. "Pauline Elizabeth Hopkins." In *Afro-American Writers before the Harlem Renaissance*. Vol. 50 of *Dictionary of Literary Biography*. Edited by Trudier Harris. Detroit; Gale Research, 1986.

Campbell, Mary B. *The Witness and the Other World: Exotic European Travel Writing, 400–1600*. Ithaca, N.Y.: Cornell Univ. Press, 1988.

Carby, Hazel. Introduction to *The Magazine Novels of Pauline Hopkins,* by Pauline E. Hopkins. New York: Oxford Univ. Press, 1988.

———. *Reconstructing Womanhood: The Emergence of the Afro-American Woman Novelist*. New York: Oxford Univ. Press, 1987.

Casely Hayford, J.E. *Ethiopia Unbound: Studies in Race Emancipation*. 2d ed. 1911. Reprint, London: Cass, 1969.

Chambers, Kimberly R. "Right on Time: History and Religion in Alice Walker's *The Color Purple*." *College Literature Association Journal* 31.1 (Sept. 1987): 44–62.

Child, Lydia Maria. *An Appeal in Favor of That Class of Americans Called Africans*. 1833. Reprint, New York: Arno Press, 1968.

Chinitz, David. "Rejuvenation through Joy: Langston Hughes, Primitivism, and Jazz." *American Literary History* 9.1 (spring 1997): 60–78.

Chirenje, J. Mutero. *Ethiopianism and Afro-Americans in Southern Africa, 1883–1916*. Baton Rouge: Louisiana State Univ. Press, 1987.

Churchill, Winston. *My African Journey*. 1909. In *The Collected Works*. Vol. 1. Centenary Limited Edition. London: Library of Imperial History, 1973.

Conrad, Joseph. *An Outcast of the Islands/Almayer's Folly*. London: Collins, 1955.

———. *Heart of Darkness*. 3rd ed. Edited by Robert Kimbrough. New York: Norton, 1988.

Contee, Clarence G., Sr. "Downing, Henry F[rancis]." In *Dictionary of Negro Biography,* edited by Rayford W. Logan and Michael R. Winston. New York: Norton, 1989.

Cook, Will Marion. *In Dahomey: A Negro Musical Comedy*. London: Keith, Prowse, 1902.

Craven, Wesley Frank. *White, Red, and Black: The Seventeenth Century Virginian*. Charlottesville: Univ. of Virginia Press, 1971.

Crowder, Ralph. "John Edward Bruce: Pioneer Black Nationalist." *Afro-Americans in New York Life and History* 2.2 (July 1978): 47–66.

———. "Street Scholars: Self-Trained Black Historians." *Black Collegian* 9.3 (Jan./Feb. 1979): 8+.

Daniel, Walter C. *Black Journals of the United States*. Westport, Conn.: Greenwood Press, 1982.

Davis, Kenneth S. *FDR: The New Deal Years, 1933–1937: A History*. New York: Random House, 1986.

Dean, Harry. "Biography [of Dean]." Harry Dean Collection. DuSable Museum of African American History, Chicago.

———. "Liberian Development Possibilities." *San Francisco Chronicle,* 8 July 1923.

———. *The Pedro Gorino: The Adventures of a Negro Sea-Captain in Africa and on the Seven Seas in His Attempts to Found an Ethiopian Empire.* Boston: Houghton Mifflin, 1929.

———. "Ship Deal Discrimination Charge." *San Francisco Chronicle,* 28 December 1923.

———. *Umbala: The Adventures of a Negro Sea Captain in Africa and on the Seven Seas in His Attempts to Found an Ethiopian Empire.* 1929. Reprint, London: Pluto, 1989.

Delany, Martin. *Blake; or, The Huts of America.* Edited by Floyd J. Miller. Boston: Beacon Press, 1970.

Del Boca, Angelo. *The Ethiopian War 1935–1941.* Translated by P.D. Cummins. Chicago: Univ. of Chicago Press, 1969.

Diop, Cheikh Anta. *The African Origin of Civilization.* Translated by Mercer Cook. New York: L. Hill, 1974.

Dooling, Richard. *White Man's Grave.* New York: Farrar, Straus and Giroux, 1994.

Doreski, C.K. *Writing America Black: Race Rhetoric in the Public Sphere.* New York: Cambridge Univ. Press, 1998.

Douglass, Frederick. "The Claims of the Negro Ethnologically Considered." In *The Frederick Douglass Papers,* edited by John Blassingame et al. Vol 2. New Haven: Yale Univ. Press, 1982.

———. "The Heroic Slave." Vol. 5 of *The Life and Writings of Frederick Douglass.* Edited by Philip S. Foner. New York: International Publishers, 1975.

———. *My Bondage and My Freedom.* 1855. Reprint, New York: Dover, 1969.

Downing, Henry F. *The American Cavalryman: A Liberian Romance.* 1917. Reprint, College Park, Md.: McGrath, 1969.

———. "Liberia." *African Times and Orient Review* 1 (April 1913): 288–300.

———. *Liberia and Her People.* N.p.: Henry Francis Downing, 1925.

Drake, St. Clair. *The Redemption of Africa and Black Religion.* Chicago: Third World, 1970.

Du Bois, W.E.B. "American Negroes and Africa's Rise to Freedom." In *The World and Africa.* 1947. Reprint, Millwood, N.Y.: Kraus-Thomson Organization, 1976.

———. "The Colored Magazine in America." *The Crisis* 3 (Nov. 1912): 33–35.

———. "The Conservation of Races." In *Pamphlets and Leaflets by W.E.B. Du Bois,* edited by Herbert Aptheker. White Plains, N.Y.: Kraus-Thomson, 1986.

———. *Dark Princess: A Romance.* 1928. Reprint, Millwood, N.Y.: Kraus-Thomson, 1974.

———. *Darkwater: Voices from within the Veil.* In *The Oxford W.E.B. Du Bois Reader,* edited by Eric J. Sundquist. New York: Oxford Univ. Press, 1996.

———. "The Drama Among Black Folk." In *An ABC of Color*. Berlin: Seven Seas, 1963.

———. *The Negro*. 1915. Reprint, Millwood, N.Y.: Kraus-Thomson, 1975.

———. "The Negro in Literature." *The Crisis* 36 (November 1929): 376.

———. *The People of Peoples and Their Gifts to Men*. 1913. In *Creative Writings by W.E.B. Du Bois: A Pageant, Poems, Short Stories, and Playlets,* edited by Herbert Aptheker. White Plains, N.Y.: Kraus-Thomson, 1985.

———. "The Present Outlook for the Dark Races of Mankind." In *The Oxford W.E.B. Du Bois Reader,* edited by Eric J. Sundquist. New York: Oxford Univ. Press, 1996.

———. "'The Star of Ethiopia': A Pageant." 1915. In *Pamphlets and Leaflets by W.E.B. Du Bois,* edited by Herbert Aptheker. White Plains, N.Y.: Kraus-Thomson, 1986.

———. *The Souls of Black Folk*. 1903. In *The Oxford W.E.B. Du Bois Reader,* edited by Eric J. Sundquist. New York: Oxford Univ. Press, 1996.

———. "What Is Civilization." 1926. In *The Oxford W.E.B. Du Bois Reader,* edited by Eric J. Sundquist. New York: Oxford Univ. Press, 1996.

Dunbar, Paul Laurence. *The Complete Poems of Paul Laurence Dunbar.* New York: Dodd, 1944.

Duncan, Thelma Myrtle. *The Death Dance: An African Play.* In *Plays of Negro Life,* edited by Alain Locke and Montgomery Gregory. Westport, Conn.: Negro Univ. Press, 1970.

"Editorial and Publisher's Announcements." *Colored American Magazine* 6 (May/June 1903): 466–67.

Elder, Arlene. *The "Hindered Hand": Cultural Implications of Early African-American Fiction.* Westport, Conn.: Greenwood Press, 1978.

Ellis, George W. *The Leopard's Claw.* New York: International Authors' Association, 1917.

———. *Negro Culture in West Africa*. 1914. Reprint, New York: Johnson, 1970.

Equiano, Olaudah. *Equiano's Travels: His Autobiography: The Interesting Narrative of the Life of Olaudah Equiano or Gustavus Vassa the African.* 1789. Edited by Paul Edwards. London: Heinemann, 1967.

Esedebe, P. Olisanwuche. *Pan-Africanism: The Idea and Movement, 1776–1991.* 2d. ed. Washington, D.C.: Howard Univ. Press, 1994.

Farnsworth, Robert M. *Melvin B. Tolson, 1898–1966: Plain Talk and Poetic Prophecy.* Columbia: Univ. of Missouri Press, 1984.

Ferris, William H. *The African Abroad, or His Evolution in Western Civilization.* Vol. 2. 1913. Reprint, New York: Johnson, 1968.

———. "An African Novel." In *African Fundamentalism: A Literary and Cultural Anthology of Garvey's Harlem Renaissance,* edited by Tony Martin. Dover, Mass.: Majority Press, 1991.

Fierce, Milfred C. *The Pan-African Idea in the United States 1900–1919.* New York: Garland, 1993.

Flasch, Joy. *Melvin B. Tolson*. New York: Twayne, 1972.

Fleming, John E., and Rayford W. Logan. "Ellis, George Washington." In *Dictionary of Negro Biography*, edited by Rayford W. Logan and Michael R. Winston. New York: Norton, 1989.

Ford, Arnold J. "O Africa, My Native Land!" In *African Fundamentalism: A Literary and Cultural Anthology of Garvey's Harlem Renaissance*, edited by Tony Martin. Dover, Mass.: Majority Press, 1991.

Fredrickson, George M. *Black Liberation: A Comparative History of Black Ideologies in the United States and South Africa*. New York: Oxford Univ. Press, 1995.

Fuller, Hoyt W. *Journey to Africa*. Chicago: Third World Press, 1971.

Gaither, Edmund Barry. "Heritage Reclaimed: An Historical Perspective and Chronology." In *Black Art: Ancestral Legacy: The African Impulse in African-American Art*, edited by Robert V. Rozelle, Alvia Wardlaw, and Maureen A. McKenna. New York: Dallas Museum of Art/Harry N. Abrams, 1989.

Gaines, Kevin K. *Uplifting the Race: Black Leadership, Politics, and Culture in the Twentieth Century*. Chapel Hill: Univ. of North Carolina Press, 1996.

Gann, L.H. "Menelik II, Emperor of Ethiopia." In *New Grolier Multimedia Encyclopedia*, 1993 ed.

Garvey, Marcus. "African Fundamentalism." 1924. In *African Fundamentalism: A Literary and Cultural Anthology of Garvey's Harlem Renaissance*, edited by Tony Martin. Dover, Mass.: Majority Press, 1991.

Gates, Henry Louis, Jr. *Figures in Black: Words, Signs, and the "Racial" Self*. 1987. Reprint, New York: Oxford Univ. Press, 1989.

———. "A Fragmented Man: George Schuyler and the Claims of Race." *New York Times Book Review*, 20 Sept. 1992: 31+.

———. *The Signifying Monkey: A Theory of Afro-American Literary Criticism*. New York: Oxford Univ. Press, 1988.

Geiss, Imanuel. *The Pan-African Movement: A History of Pan-Africanism in America, Europe and Africa*. Translated by Ann Keep. New York: Africana, 1974.

Gilbert, Peter, ed. *The Selected Writings of John Edward Bruce: Militant Black Journalist*. New York: Arno Press, 1971.

Gilbert, Sandra M. "Rider Haggard's Heart of Darkness." In *Coordinates: Placing Science Fiction and Fantasy*, edited by George E. Slusser, Eric S. Rabkin, and Robert Scholes. Carbondale: Southern Illinois Univ. Press, 1983.

Gilroy, Paul. *The Black Atlantic: Modernity and Double Consciousness*. Cambridge, Mass.: Harvard Univ. Press, 1993.

Gloster, Hugh M. Introduction to *Imperium in Imperio*, by Sutton E. Griggs. 1899. Reprint, New York: Arno Press, 1969.

———. *Negro Voices in American Fiction*. New York: Russell & Russell, 1965.

Graham, Shirley. "Black Man's Music." *The Crisis* 40 (August 1933): 178–79.

———. *Tom-Tom*. 1932. In *The Roots of African American Drama: An Anthology of Early Plays, 1858–1938*, edited by Leo Hamalian and James V. Hatch. Detroit: Wayne State Univ. Press, 1991.

———. Music for *Tom-Tom*. Jules Bledsoe Collection. Schomburg Center for Research in Black Culture, New York.

Greene, Graham. *The Heart of the Matter*. 1948. Reprint, New York: Penguin, 1978.

Griggs, Sutton E. *The Hindered Hand: or The Reign of the Repressionist*. 3rd ed. 1905. Reprint, New York: AMS, 1969.

———. *Unfettered. A Novel*. 1902. Reprint, New York: AMS, 1971.

Gruesser, John Cullen. "Afro-American Travel Literature and Africanist Discourse." *Black American Literature Forum* 24 (spring 1990): 5–20.

———. "Bruce, John E." In *The Oxford Companion to African American Literature*, edited by William L. Andrews, Trudier Harris, and Frances Smith Foster. New York: Oxford Univ. Press, 1997.

———. *White on Black: Contemporary Literature about Africa*. Urbana: Univ. of Illinois Press, 1992.

———, ed. *The Unruly Voice: Rediscovering Pauline Elizabeth Hopkins*. Urbana: Univ. of Illinois Press, 1996.

Guinn, Dorothy C. *Out of the Dark*. In *Plays and Pageants from the Life of the Negro*, edited by Willis Richardson. Washington, D.C.: Associate Publishers, 1930.

Gunner, Frances. *The Light of the Women*. In *Plays and Pageants from the Life of the Negro*, edited by Willis Richardson. Washington, D.C.: Associate Publishers, 1930.

Haggard, H. Rider. *She*. 1887. Reprint, London: Collins, 1957.

"Haile Selassie, Emperor of Ethiopia." In *New Grolier Multimedia Encyclopedia*, 1993 ed.

Haley, Alex. *Roots*. New York: Dell, 1977.

Hamedoe, S.E.F.C.C. "The First Pan-African Conference of the World." *Colored American Magazine*, Sept. 1900, 223–31.

Hansberry, Lorraine. "All the Dark and Beautiful Warriors." In *To Be Young, Gifted and Black*, edited by Robert Nemiroff, 75–85. New York: NAL, 1969.

———. "Congolese Patriot." *New York Times Magazine*, 26 March 1961, 4.

———. "Genet, Mailer and the New Paternalism." *Village Voice*, 10 June 1961, 28–33.

———. "Kenya's Kikuyu: A Peaceful People Wage Struggle Against the British." *Freedom*, Dec. 1952, 3.

———. *Les Blancs*. 1973. In *The Collected Last Plays*, edited by Robert Nemiroff. New York: NAL, 1983.

———. ". . . To Reclaim the African Past." In *Lorraine Hansberry Speaks Out: Art and the Black Revolution*, edited by Robert Nemiroff. Caedmon, TC 1352, 1972.

———. *A Raisin in the Sun*. 1959. Reprint, New York: NAL, 1966.

———. *To Be Young, Gifted and Black*. Edited by Robert Nemiroff. New York: NAL, 1969.

Harlan, Louis. "Booker T. Washington and the White Man's Burden." In *Black Brotherhood: Afro-Americans and Africa,* edited by Okon Edet Uya. Lexington, Mass.: Heath, 1971.

Harris, Eddy L. *Native Stranger: A Black American's Journey into the Heart of Africa.* New York: Simon and Schuster, 1992.

Harris, Joseph E. *African-American Reactions to War in Ethiopia, 1936–1941.* Baton Rouge: Louisiana State Univ. Press, 1994.

Harris, Sheldon H. *Paul Cuffe: Black Americans and the African Return.* New York: Simon and Schuster, 1972.

Harris, Trudier. "On *The Color Purple,* Stereotypes, and Silence." *Black American Literature Forum* 18 (winter 1984): 155–61.

Hatch, James V., and Omanii Abdullah. *Black Playwrights, 1823–1977: An Annotated Bibliography of Plays.* New York: Bowker, 1977.

Hatch, James V., and Ted Shine, ed. *Black Theatre USA: Plays by African Americans, 1847 to Today.* New York: Free Press, 1996.

Hill, Robert A. Introduction to *Ethiopian Stories,* by George S. Schuyler. Northeastern Univ. Press, 1994.

Hill, Robert A., and R. Kent Rasmussen, ed. Afterword to *Black Empire,* by George S. Schuyler. Boston: Northeastern Univ. Press, 1991.

———. "Editorial Statement" to *Black Empire,* by George S. Schuyler. Boston: Northeastern Univ. Press, 1991.

Hinks, Peter P. *To Awaken My Afflicted Brethen: David Walker and the Problem of Antebellum Slave Resistance.* University Park, Pa.: Pennsylvania State Univ. Press, 1997.

Hite, Molly. *The Other Side of the Story: Structures and Strategies of Contemporary Feminist Narrative.* Ithaca: Cornell Univ. Press, 1989.

Hooker, James. *The Impact of African History on Afro-Americans, 1930–45.* Buffalo, N.Y.: Council on International Studies, SUNY Buffalo, 1971.

Hopkins, Pauline E. *Of One Blood; Or, the Hidden Self.* In *The Magazine Novels of Pauline Elizabeth Hopkins.* New York: Oxford Univ. Press, 1988.

———. *A Primer of Facts Pertaining to the Early Greatness of the African Race and the Possibility of Restoration by Its Descendants.* Cambridge, Mass.: P.E. Hopkins, 1905.

Horan, James D. *The Pinkertons: The Detective Dynasty That Made History.* New York: Crown, 1967.

Huggins, Nathan Irvin, ed. *Voices from the Harlem Renaissance.* New York: Oxford Univ. Press, 1976.

Hughes, Arnold. "Africa and the Garvey Movement in the Interwar Years." In *Garvey: Africa, Europe, the Americas,* edited by Rupert Lewis and Maureen Warner-Lewis. Trenton, N.J.: Africa World Press, 1994.

Hughes, Langston. "Ballad of Ethiopia." *Afro-American,* 28 September 1935, 3.

———. *The Big Sea: An Autobiography.* 1940. Reprint, New York: Hill and Wang, 1963.

————. *The Collected Poems of Langston Hughes*. Edited by Arnold Rampersad and David Roessel. New York: Knopf, 1994.

————. "The Negro Artist and the Racial Mountain." In *Voices from the Harlem Renaissance*, edited by Nathan Irvin Huggins. New York: Oxford Univ. Press, 1976.

————. "The Twenties: Harlem and Its Negritude." *Langston Hughes Review* 4 (spring 1985): 29–36.

————. "V-J Night in Harlem." In *Langston Hughes and the Chicago Defender: Essays on Race, Politics, and Culture, 1942–62*, edited by Chistopher C. De Santis. Urbana: Univ. of Illinois Press, 1995.

Hunt, Ida Gibbs. Review of *The American Cavalryman*, by Henry F. Downing. *Journal of Negro History* 3 (1918): 444–45.

Isaacs, Harold. "Five Writers and Their African Ancestors." *Phylon* 21 (1960): 243–65, 317–36.

————. *The New World of the Negro Americans*. New York: Day, 1963.

Jacobs, Harriet A. *Incidents in the Life of a Slave Girl*. 1861. Edited by Jean Fagan Yellin. Cambridge, Mass.: Harvard Univ. Press, 1987.

Jacobs, Sylvia M. "Pan-African Consciousness among Afro-Americans." In *Black Studies: Theory, Method and Cultural Perspective*, edited by Talmadge Anderson. Pullman: Washington State Univ. Press, 1990.

————, ed. *Black Americans and the Missionary Movement in Africa*. Westport, Conn.: Greenwood Press, 1982.

Johnson, Abby Arthur, and Ronald M. Johnson. *Propaganda and Aesthetics: The Literary Politics of Afro-American Magazines in the Twentieth Century*. Amherst: Univ. of Massachusetts Press, 1979.

Johnson, Charles. *Middle Passage*. New York: Atheneum, 1990.

Johnson, James Weldon. "The Dilemma of the Negro Writer." *American Mercury* 15 (December 1928): 477–81.

Johnson, James Wesley. "Ethiopianism." Vol. 2 of *The African American Encyclopedia*. Edited by Michael W. Williams. New York: Marshall Cavendish, 1993.

Kaiser, Ernest. "Bruce, John Edward." In *Dictionary of Negro Biography*, edited by Rayford W. Logan and Michael R. Winston. New York: Norton, 1989.

Kassanoff, Jennie. "'Fate has linked us together': Blood, Gender and the Politics of Representation in Pauline Hopkins' *Of One Blood*." In *The Unruly Voice*, edited by John Cullen Gruesser. Urbana: Univ. of Illinois Press, 1996.

Kauffman, Linda S. *Special Delivery: Epistolary Modes in Modern Fiction*. Chicago: Univ. of Chicago Press, 1992.

Kelley, William Melvin. *A Different Drummer*. Garden City, N.Y.: Anchor, 1969.

Kelly, Lori Duin. "Theology and Androgyny: The Role of Religion in *The Color Purple*." *Notes on Contemporary Literature* 18.2 (March 1988): 7–8.

Kieh, George Klay, Jr. *Dependency and the Foreign Policy of a Small Power: The Liberian Case*. San Francisco: Mellen Research Univ. Press, 1992.

King, Woodie, Jr., ed. *The National Black Drama Anthology: Eleven Plays from America's Leading African-American Theaters.* New York: Applause, 1995.

Kinnamon, Keneth, and Michel Fabre. *Conversations with Richard Wright.* Jackson: Univ. of Mississippi Press, 1993.

Lefkowitz, Mary. *Not Out of Africa: How Afrocentrism Became an Excuse to Teach Myth as History.* New York: Basic Books, 1996.

Legum, Colin. *Pan-Africanism: A Short Political Guide.* Rev. ed. New York: Praeger, 1965.

Lewis, Rupert. *Marcus Garvey: Anti-Colonial Champion.* Trenton, N.J.: Africa World Press, 1988.

Locke, Alain. "Apropos of Africa." In *Apropos of Africa: Sentiments of Negro American Leaders on Africa from the 1800s to the 1950s,* edited by Adelaide Cromwell Hill and Martin Kilson. London: Cass, 1969.

————. "The Legacy of Ancestral Arts." In *The New Negro,* edited by Alain Locke. 1925. Reprint, New York: Arno Press, 1968.

————. "The Negro in American Culture." In *Black Voices,* edited by Abraham Chapman. New York: NAL, 1968.

————. "Negro Youth Speaks." In *The New Negro,* edited by Alain Locke. 1925. Reprint, New York: Arno Press, 1968.

————. "The New Negro." In *The New Negro,* edited by Alain Locke. 1925. Reprint, New York: Arno Press, 1968.

————, ed. *The New Negro: an Interpretation.* 1925. New York: Arno Press, 1968.

Locke, Alain, and Montgomery Gregory, eds. *Plays of Negro Life: A Source Book of Native American Drama.* 1927. Reprint, Westport, Conn.: Negro Universities Press, 1970.

Logan, Rayford W., and Michael R. Winston. *Dictionary of Negro Biography.* New York: Norton, 1989.

Lubin, Gilbert. *The Promised Land.* Boston: Christopher, 1930.

Lugard, Flora Louisa Shaw. *A Tropical Dependency.* 1906. Reprint, New York: Barnes and Noble, 1965.

Lynch, Hollis R. *Edward Wilmot Blyden: Pan-Negro Patriot, 1832–1912.* London: Oxford Univ. Press, 1967.

MacIntyre, Ben. "The Disappearing Duchess." *New York Times Magazine,* 31 July 1994, 30–31.

————. *The Napoleon of Crime: The Life and Times of Adam Worth, Master Thief.* New York: Farrar, Straus and Giroux, 1997.

Martin, Tony. *Literary Garveyism: Garvey, Black Arts, and the Harlem Renaissance.* Dover, Mass.: Majority Press, 1983.

————. *Race First: The Ideological and Organizational Struggles of Marcus Garvey and the Universal Negro Improvement Association.* Westport, Conn.: Greenwood Press, 1976.

————, ed. *African Fundamentalism: A Literary and Cultural Anthology of Garvey's Harlem Renaissance.* Dover, Mass.: Majority Press, 1991.

Mathurin, Owen Charles. *Henry Sylvester Williams and the Origins of the Pan-African Movement, 1869–1911.* Westport, Conn.: Greenwood Press, 1976.

McCann, James C. "Ethiopia." In *New Grolier Multimedia Encyclopedia,* 1993 ed.

McCarthy, Michael. *Dark Continent: Africa as Seen by Americans.* Westport, Conn.: Greenwood Press, 1983.

McCoo, Edward J. *Ethiopia at the Bar of Justice.* In *Plays and Pageants from the Life of the Negro,* edited by Willis Richardson. Washington, D.C.: Associated Publishers, 1930.

McKay, Nellie. Introduction to *The Unruly Voice: Rediscovering Pauline Elizabeth Hopkins,* edited by John Cullen Gruesser. Urbana: Univ. of Illinois Press, 1996.

McKnight, Reginald. *I Get on the Bus: A Novel.* Boston: Little, Brown, 1990.

Meier, August. "Booker T. Washington and the Negro Press." *Journal of Negro History* 38 (Jan. 1953): 67–90.

———. *Negro Thought in America, 1880–1915.* 2d ed. Ann Arbor: Univ. of Michigan Press, 1988.

Miller, Christopher L. *Blank Darkness: Africanist Discourse in French.* Chicago: Univ. of Chicago Press, 1985.

Miller, May. *Samory.* In *Negro History in Thirteen Plays,* edited by Willis Richardson and May Miller. Washington, D.C.: Associated Publishers, 1935.

Morrison, Toni. "The Making of the *Black Book.*" *Black World* (Feb. 1974): 86–90.

Moses, Wilson J. *Afrotopia: The Roots of African American Popular History.* New York: Cambridge Univ. Press, 1998.

———. *Alexander Crummell: A Study of Civilization and Discontent.* New York: Oxford Univ. Press, 1989.

———. *The Golden Age of Black Nationalism, 1850–1925.* New York: Oxford Univ. Press, 1988.

———. "More Stately Mansions: New Negro Movements and Langston Hughes' Literary Theory." *Langston Hughes Review* 4 (spring 1985): 40–46.

———. *The Wings of Ethiopia: Studies in African-American Life and Letters.* Ames: Iowa State Univ. Press, 1990.

———, ed. *Classical Black Nationalism: From the American Revolution to Marcus Garvey.* New York: New York Univ. Press, 1996.

Mudimbe, V.Y. *The Invention of Africa: Gnosis, Philosophy, and the Order of Knowledge.* Bloomington: Indiana Univ. Press, 1988.

"Music." *The Crisis* 39 (August 1932): 258.

Naipaul, V.S. *A Bend in the River.* New York: Vintage, 1980.

———. "The Crocodiles of Yamoussoukro." *Finding the Center.* New York: Vintage, 1986.

Nielsen, Aldon L. "Melvin B. Tolson and the Deterritorialization of Modernism." *African American Review* 26 (summer 1992): 241–255.

North, Sterling. Preface to *The Pedro Gorino,* by Harry Dean. Boston: Houghton Mifflin, 1929.

———. Letter to Dr. Robert I. Rotberg. 5 June 1965. Harry Dean Collection. DuSable Museum of African American History, Chicago.

Oakland, Berkeley, Alameda City Directory. Oakland: Post-Husted, 1924.

Padmore, George. *Pan-Africanism or Communism? The Coming Struggle for Africa.* New York: Roy Publishers, 1956.

Peplow, Michael W. *George S. Schuyler.* Boston: Twayne, 1980.

Perkins, Kathy A. "Shirley Graham." In *Afro-American Writers, 1940–1955.* Vol. 76 of *Dictionary of Literary Biography.* Edited by Trudier Harris and Thadious M. Davis. Detroit: Gale Research, 1988.

———. "The Unknown Career of Shirley Graham." *Freedomways* 25.1 (1985): 6–17.

Potter, Philip. "The Religious Thought of Marcus Garvey." In *Garvey: His Work and Impact,* edited by Rupert Lewis and Patrick Bryan. Trenton, N.J.: Africa World Press, 1991.

Porter, Dorothy. "Hopkins, Pauline Elizabeth." In *Dictionary of Negro Biography,* edited by Rayford W. Logan and Michael R. Winston. New York: Norton, 1989.

Porter, Dorothy, ed. *Early Negro Writing, 1760–1837.* Boston: Beacon Press, 1971.

Pratt, Mary Louise. *Imperial Eyes: Travel Writing and Transculturation.* New York: Routledge, 1992.

Raboteau, Albert J. *A Fire in the Bones: Reflections on African-American Religious History.* Boston: Beacon Press, 1995.

Rampersad, Arnold. *The Art and Imagination of W.E.B. Du Bois.* Cambridge, Mass.: Harvard Univ. Press, 1976.

———. "Griggs, Sutton E[lbert]." In Dictionary of Negro Biography, edited by Rayford W. Logan and Michael R. Winston. New York: Norton, 1989.

———. *The Life of Langston Hughes.* Vol 1. New York: Oxford Univ. Press, 1986.

Rayson, Ann. "George Schuyler: Paradox Among 'Assimilationist' Writers." *Black American Literature Forum* 12 (1978): 102–6.

Reed, Ishmael. *Mumbo Jumbo.* 1972. Reprint, New York: Atheneum, 1988.

Reed, Ishmael, and Steve Cannon. "George S. Schuyler, Writer." In *Shrovetide in Old New Orleans,* by Ishamel Reed. Garden City, N.Y.: Doubleday, 1978.

Reilly, John M. "The Black Anti-Utopia." *Black American Literature Forum* 12 (1978): 107–9.

Rensberger, Boyce. "Ancient Nubian Artifacts Yield Evidence of Early Monarchy." *New York Times,* 1 March 1979, A1, A16.

Richardson, Willis. *The Black Horseman.* In *Plays and Pageants from the Life of the Negro,* edited by Willis Richardson. Washington, D.C.: Associated Publishers, 1930.

———. *In Menelik's Court.* In *Negro History in Thirteen Plays,* edited by Willis Richardson and May Miller. Washington, D.C.: Associated Publishers, 1935.

————, ed. *Plays and Pageants from the Life of the Negro.* Washington, D.C.: Associated Publishers, 1930.

Richardson, Willis, and May Miller, eds. *Negro History in Thirteen Plays.* Washington, D.C.: Associated Publishers, 1935.

Riis, Thomas L. *Just before Jazz: Black Musical Theater in New York, 1890–1915.* Washington: Smithsonian Institution, 1989.

Rinehart, Robert. "Historical Setting." In *Liberia: A Country Study,* edited by Harold D. Nelson. Washington, D.C.: GPO, 1985.

Robeson, Eslanda Goode. *African Journey.* New York: John Day, 1945.

Rozelle, Robert V., Alvia Wardlaw, and Maureen A. McKenna, eds. *Black Art: Ancestral Legacy: The African Impulse in African-American Art.* New York: Dallas Museum of Art/Harry N. Abrams, 1989.

Scholl, Diane Gabrielsen. "With Ears to Hear and Eyes to See: Alice Walker's Parable *The Color Purple.*" *Christianity and Literature* 40 (spring 1991): 255–66.

Schrager, Cynthia D. "Pauline Hopkins and William James: The New Psychology and the Politics of Race." In *The Unruly Voice,* edited by John Cullen Gruesser. Urbana: Univ. of Illinois Press, 1996.

Schuyler, George S. *Black and Conservative: The Autobiography of George S. Schuyler.* New Rochelle, N.Y.: Arlington House, 1966.

————. *Black Empire.* Edited by Robert A. Hill and R. Kent Rasmussen. Boston: Northeastern Univ. Press, 1991.

————. *Black No More: Being an Account of the Strange and Wonderful Workings of Scenes in the Land of the Free, A.D. 1933–1940.* 1931. Reprint, College Park, Md.: McGrath, 1969.

————. *Ethiopian Stories.* Edited by Robert A. Hill. Boston: Northeastern Univ. Press, 1994.

————. "The Negro-Art Hokum." 1926. In *Voices from the Harlem Renaissance,* edited by Nathan Irvin Huggins. New York: Oxford Univ. Press, 1976.

————. "Our Greatest Gift to America." In *Ebony and Topaz,* edited by Charles S. Johnson. 1927. Reprint, Freeport, N.Y.: Books for Libraries Press, 1971.

————. "The Rise of the Black Internationale." In *Black Empire,* by George S. Schuyler. Boston: Northeastern Univ. Press, 1991.

————. *Slaves Today: A Story of Liberia.* 1931. Reprint, College Park, Md.: McGrath, 1969.

————. "Strange Valley." *Pittsburgh Courier,* 18 Aug. to 10 Nov. 1934, sec. 2: 1.

————. "Uno Me, Pal!" George Schuyler Collection. Schomburg Center for Research in Black Culture, New York.

————. "Views and Reviews." *Pittsburgh Courier,* 1 July 1933, sec. 1, 10.

Schwab, Peter, ed. *Ethiopia and Haile Selassie.* New York: Facts on File, 1972.

Scott, Freda L. "*The Star of Ethiopia:* A Contribution Toward the Development of Black Drama and Theater in the Harlem Renaissance." In *Harlem Renaissance: Revaluations,* edited by Amritjit Singh, William S. Shiver, and Stanley Brodwin. New York: Garland, 1989.

Scott, William R. *The Sons of Sheba's Race: African-Americans and the Italo-Ethiopian War, 1935–1941.* Bloomington: Indiana Univ. Press, 1993.

Sears, E.H. "The African Race." *The Christian Examiner and Religious Miscellany* 41 (July 1846): 33–48.

Senghor, Leopold. "Negritude: A Humanism of the Twentieth Century." In *Colonial Discourse and Postcolonial Theory: A Reader,* edited by Patrick Williams and Laura Chrisman. New York: Columbia Univ. Press, 1994.

Shapiro, Deanne. "Factors in the Development of Black Judaism." In *The Black Experience in Religion,* edited by C. Eric Lincoln. Garden City, N.Y.: Anchor Press, 1974.

Shepperson, George. *Africa in American History and Literature.* London: British Academy, 1981.

———. "Ethiopianism and African Nationalism." *Phylon* 1.1 (1953): 9–18.

———. Introduction to *Umbala,* by Harry Dean. London: Pluto, 1989.

———. "Notes on Negro American Influences on the Emergence of African Nationalism." *Journal of African History* 1 (1960): 299–312.

Shepperson, George and Thomas Price. *Independent African: John Chilembwe and the Origins, Setting, and Significance of the Nyosaland Native Rising of 1915.* Edinburgh: Univ. of Edinburgh Press, 1958.

Sherwood, Henry Noble. "Paul Cuffe." *Journal of Negro History* 8 (April 1923): 153–229.

Shockley, Ann Allen. "Pauline Elizabeth Hopkins: A Biographical Excursion into Obscurity." *Phylon* 33 (spring 1972): 22–26.

Smith, Ed. *Where to, Black Man.* Chicago: Quadrangle, 1967.

Smith, William Gardner. *Return to Black America.* Engelwood Cliffs, N.J.: Prentice Hall, 1970.

Stein, Judith. *The World of Marcus Garvey: Race and Class in Modern Society.* Baton Rouge: Louisiana State Univ. Press, 1986.

Stewart, Maria W. "An Address Delivered at the African Masonic Hall in Boston, Feb. 27, 1833." In *Early Negro Writing, 1760–1837,* edited by Dorothy Porter. Boston: Beacon, 1971.

"The Story of Paul Cuffee." *New Bedford Sunday Standard,* 5 January 1930.

Sundiata, I.K. *Black Scandal: America and the Liberian Labor Crisis, 1929–1936.* Philadelphia: Institute for the Study of Human Issues, 1980.

Sundquist, Eric J. "Mark Twain and Homer Plessy." *Representations* 6 (fall 1988): 102–128.

———. *To Wake the Nations: Race in the Making of American Literature.* Cambridge: Harvard Univ. Press, 1993.

———, ed. *The Oxford W.E.B. Du Bois Reader.* New York: Oxford Univ. Press, 1996.

Tate, Claudia. *Domestic Allegories of Political Desire: The Black Heroine's Text at the Turn of the Century.* New York: Oxford Univ. Press, 1992.

Thomas, Lamont D. *Paul Cuffe: Black Entrepreneur and Pan-Africanist.* Urbana: Univ. of Illinois Press, 1988.

Thompson, Era Bell. *Africa: Land of My Fathers*. Garden City, N.Y.: Doubleday, 1954

Thompson, Robert Farris. *Flash of the Spirit: African and Afro-American Art and Philosophy*. New York: Random House, 1983.

Tolson, Melvin B. *Caviar and Cabbage: Selected Columns by Melvin B. Tolson from the Washington Tribune, 1937–1944*, edited by Robert M. Farnsworth. Columbia: Univ. of Missouri Press, 1982.

———. "Dark Laughter." Melvin B. Tolson Papers. The Library of Congress, Washington, D.C.

———. "Drama: 'The Tragedy of Ethiopia,' May 28, 1938." In *Caviar and Cabbage: Selected Columns by Melvin B. Tolson from the Washington Tribune, 1937–1944*, edited by Robert M. Farnsworth. Columbia: Univ. of Missouri Press, 1982.

———. "Frankenstein and the Monster, May 25, 1940." In *Caviar and Cabbage: Selected Columns by Melvin B. Tolson from the Washington Tribune, 1937–1944*, edited by Robert M. Farnsworth. Columbia: Univ. of Missouri Press, 1982.

———. *Harlem Gallery: Book I, The Curator*. New York: Twayne, 1965.

———. *Libretto for the Republic of Liberia*. New York: Twayne, 1953.

———. "The Lion and the Jackal." Melvin B. Tolson Papers. Library of Congress, Washington, D.C.

———. *Rendezvous with America*. New York: Dodd, Mead, 1944.

Turner, Henry McNeal. "The American Negro and the Fatherland." In *Africa and the American Negro*, edited by J.W.E. Bowen. Atlanta: Gammon Theological Seminary, 1896.

Turner, John W. "Historical Setting." In *Ethiopia: A Country Study*, edited by Thomas P. Ofcansky and LaVerle Berry. Washington, D.C.: Library of Congress, 1993.

Vansina, Jan. *Oral Tradition: A Study in Historical Methodology*. Translated by H.M. Wright. Chicago: Aldine, 1965.

Villard, Oswald Garrison. *John Brown: A Biography Fifty Years After*. Boston: Houghton Mifflin, 1911.

"Uncle John's Burying Place." Paul Cuffe Manuscript Collection. New Bedford Free Public Library, New Bedford, Massachusetts.

Walker, Alice. *The Color Purple*. 1982. Reprint, New York: Pocket, 1985.

———. "Diary of an African Nun." In *In Love and Trouble*, by Alice Walker. San Diego: Harcourt Brace Jovanovich, 1973.

———. "Everyday Use." In *In Love and Trouble*, by Alice Walker. San Diego: Harcourt Brace Jovanovich, 1973.

———. *Once*. 1968. Reprint, New York: Harcourt Brace Jovanovich, 1976.

———. "The Only Reason You Want to Go to Heaven Is That You Have Been Driven Out of Your Mind (Off Your Land and Out of Your Lover's Arms): Clear Seeing Inherited Religion and Reclaiming The Pagan Self." In *Any-

thing We Love Can Be Saved: A Writer's Activism. New York: Random House, 1996.

———. *Possessing the Secret of Joy.* 1992. Reprint, New York: Pocket, 1993.

———. *The Same River Twice: Honoring the Difficult.* New York: Scribner, 1996.

———. *The Temple of My Familiar.* San Diego: Harcourt Brace Jovanovich, 1989.

———. "Writing *The Color Purple.*" In *In Search of Our Mothers' Gardens: Womanist Prose.* San Diego: Harcourt Brace Jovanovich, 1983.

Walker, Alice, and Pratibha Parmar. *Warrior Marks: Female Genital Mutilation and the Sexual Blinding of Women.* New York: Harcourt Brace Jovanovich, 1993.

Walters, Alexander. *My Life and Work.* New York: Fleming H. Revell, 1917.

Wardlaw, Alvia J. "A Spiritual Libation: Promoting an African Heritage in the Black College." In *Black Art: Ancestral Legacy: The African Impulse in African-American Art,* edited by Robert V. Rozelle, Alvia Wardlaw, and Maureen A. McKenna. New York: Dallas Museum of Art/Harry N. Abrams, 1989.

Was Cleopatra Black?" *Newsweek,* 23 Sept. 1991, 42–50.

Washington, Booker T. *Up from Slavery.* 1901. In *Three Negro Classics,* edited by John Hope Franklin. New York: Avon, 1969.

Washington, Johnny. *Alain Locke and Philosophy: A Quest for Cultural Pluralism.* New York: Greenwood Press, 1986.

Watt, Ian. *Conrad in the Nineteenth Century.* Berkeley: Univ. of California Press, 1979.

Weisbord, Robert G. "Black America and the Italian-Ethiopian Crisis: An Episode in Pan-Negroism." *Historian* (Feb. 1972), 230–41.

West, Norine. "Vibrant 'Tom Tom,' First Negro Opera, Discussed by Author." *Pittsburgh Courier* 16 July 1932, Sec. 2, 1+.

White, Landeg. "Like What Our Peasants Still Are." Review of *Afrocentrism: Mythical Pasts and Imagined Homes,* by Stephen Howe. *London Review of Books,* 13 May 1999, 7–8.

Wilford, John Noble. "Nubian Treasures Reflect Black Influence on Egypt." *New York Times,* 11 February 1992, C1, C10.

Williams, Bruce. "The Lost Pharaohs of Nubia." *Archaeology* 33.5 (Sept./Oct. 1980): 12–21.

———. "Forbears of Menes in Nubia: Myth or Reality?" *Journal of Near Eastern Studies* 46 (1987): 15–26.

Williams, John A. Foreword to *Black Empire,* by George S. Schuyler. Boston: Northeastern Univ. Press, 1991.

———. *Jacob's Ladder.* New York: Thunder's Mouth, 1987.

———. *The Man Who Cried I Am.* New York: NAL, 1967.

Williams, George W. *History of the Negro Race in America 1619–1880.* 2 vols. 1883. Reprint, New York: Arno Press, 1968.

Williams, Walter L. *Black Americans and the Evangelization of Africa.* Madison: Univ. of Wisconsin Press, 1982.

Wilson, Charles Marrow. *Liberia*. New York: Sloane, 1947.

Woodson, Carter G. Introduction to *Negro History in Thirteen Plays*. Edited by Willis Richardson and May Miller. Washington: Associated Publishers, 1935.

Wright, Richard. *Black Power*. New York: Harper and Brothers, 1954.

———. *The Color Curtain*. Cleveland: World, 1956.

———. *Pagan Spain*. New York: Harper and Brothers, 1957.

Yerby, Frank. *The Dahomean*. New York: Dial, 1971.

Index